THE ALBA HOUSE NEW TESTAMENT
The Accounts of Matthew, Mark, Luke and John.

D1565331

A Version of the New Testament in Modern English

alba house • DIVISION OF THE SOCIETY OF ST. PAUL
STATEN ISLAND, N.Y. 10314

THE
ALBA HOUSE
NEW
TESTAMENT

The Accounts of Matthew, Mark, Luke and John.

Prepared by Kevin Condon

The idea of this book came from a German original: *Das Neue Testament für Menschen Unserer Zeit* (Quell-Verlag, Stuttgart 1964), the aim of which was to present the New Testament in the down-to-earth colloquial language of the people. The text of the German original could not be used in the preparation of this book, nor was any of the standard versions quite suited to the purpose envisaged here. A fresh translation from the Greek has been prepared, in plain, simple, modern language, and in a free-flowing style. The aim of the book is to show up the contrast between the ideal of the New Testament and the reality of the world around us. Therefore this is not meant to compete with the well-known standard English versions; if it leads to a greater use and appreciation of these its purpose will have been fulfilled.

Each photograph is related to a text on the opposite page printed in bold. The headings are for the most part lines of poetry, ancient and modern, a circumstance that limits their appositeness. They are not résumés, of the content of each passage but parallel evocations from the poets of a similar line of thought. So, too, the division of the text envisages the human situation rather than the mind of the evangelists.

Original publication: *Das Neue Testament für Menschen Unserer Zeit,* Quell Verlag, Stuttgart 1964

Nihil Obstat: Jeremiah J. O'Sullivan, Censor deputatus, November 23, 1968

Imprimatur: Cornelius, Ep. Corcag & Ross, January 30, 1970

Library of Congress Catalog Card Number: 79-140281

SBN: 8189-0210-8

Printed and bound in the U.S.A. by the Priests and Brothers of the Society of St. Paul, 2187 Victory Blvd., Staten Island, New York 10314 as part of their communications apostolate.

First Printing - December, 1970
Second Printing - June, 1971

MATTHEW'S
ACCOUNT

From everlasting to everlasting

This book tells the story of Jesus Christ.   1, 1
By his family-tree Jesus was descended from King David, who
was himself descended from the patriarch Abraham.

God is working his purpose out

After Abraham came his son Isaac, the father of Jacob.   2
Jacob's sons were Juda and his brothers. Juda was followed by   3
Perez and Zerah, their mother being Thamar, and Perez was the
father of Hezron. Then came Ram, Amminidab, Nahshon,   4
Salma, Boaz (whose mother was Rahab) and Obed, the son of
Ruth.
There followed Jesse and his son, King David.   6
David was the father of Solomon (his mother having been the
wife of Uriah) and then came Rehoboam, Abia, Asa, Jeho-
shaphat, Joram, Uzia, Jotham, Ahaz, Hiskia, Manasse, Amon,
Josia.
Josia had several sons: Joiakin and his brothers, at the time   11
of the deportation to Babylon.
After the Babylonian deportation Shealtiel followed on Joiakin.   12
Then came Zerubbabel, Abiud, Eliakim, Azor, Zadok, Achim,
Eliud, Eleazar, Matthan, Jacob.
Jacob was the father of Joseph, the husband of Mary; and Mary   16
became the mother of Jesus who was known as the Christ.

Thus there were fourteen generations between Abraham and   17
David, and fourteen generations between David and the
Babylonian deportation, and fourteen generations between the
Babylonian deportation and the coming of the Messiah.

The silent God of time

18 Jesus Christ was born in this way.
When his mother Mary was engaged to Joseph and the couple
had not yet begun to live together she was found to be expecting a
child which was of the Holy Spirit.

19 Her husband Joseph, being a decent man, did not want to
expose her and decided to divorce her in secret.

20 And while he was thinking on these lines an angel of the Lord
appeared to him in a dream and said to him, "Joseph son of
David do not be afraid to take Mary home as your wife, for

21 the child she is expecting is of the Holy Spirit. It will be a boy.
You shall name him Jesus, because he will save his people
from their sins."

22 All this took place to fulfil what God had said by the Prophet:

23 'A virgin will become a mother and will have a son,
and his name will be called Emmanuel'
—a name which means 'God is with us'.

24 On waking from his sleep Joseph did what the angel had told
him; he took his wife home, but had no relations with her until
her son was born. And he named the boy Jesus.

For each age is a dream that is dying
Or one that is coming to birth

2, 1 Jesus was born at Bethlehem in Judaea, during the reign of King
Herod. Now who should arrive in Jerusalem at this time but

2 wise men from the East, and they wanted to know, "Where is
this boy who has been born King of the Jews? We have seen his
star in the East and have come to pay him homage."

Here's God down on us! What are you about?

3 King Herod was very upset by this news, and the whole of
Jerusalem as well.

4 So having assembled the priests and the doctors of the law,
he asked them, "Where is the Messiah to be born?"

And they told him, "At Bethlehem of Judaea. For that is what 5
stands written by the Prophet:
'You, Bethlehem, in the land of Juda, 6
are by no means least among the chiefs of Juda;
from you will emerge a leader,
who will rule my people Israel.' "

Herod therefore summoned the wise men to a secret meeting 7
and questioned them in detail about the time when the star
appeared to them. Then he sped them on their way to Bethlehem 8
and told them, "Go and find out all you can about this child.
And when you have found him, send word back to me; I will
come myself and pay him homage."

The vision splendid

With these instructions from the king, the wise men began their 9
journey. And what happened! The same star they had seen in
the East led their way, until it came to a halt over the place
where the child lay, bringing them indescribable joy from the
moment they saw it. So they entered the house and found the 11
child with his mother Mary; and they fell on their knees and
worshipped him. They opened their treasures and offered him
gifts: gold, incense and precious salve.

And having been warned in a dream that they must not go back 12
to Herod, they went home to their own country by a different
road.

Father and Mother and Child

As soon as they had gone, the angel of the Lord appeared in a 13
dream to Joseph and said, "Prepare at once to take the child and
his mother and fly to Egypt; and stay there until I tell you. For
Herod is determined to find the child and kill him."
So when he awoke Joseph took the child and his mother and left 14
that night for Egypt. He remained there until Herod's death. 15
Thus the word of the Lord spoken by the Prophet would come
to pass: 'Out of Egypt I have called my son.'

Out of the mouth of very babes, O God

16 Presently Herod found that he had been tricked by the wise men and was very angry. He ordered the massacre of all the baby-boys in Bethlehem and the surrounding country, up to the age of two, calculating from the details given him by the wise men.

17 And so came to pass what had been said by the prophet Jeremia:
18 'A cry was heard in Rama, of lamentation and loud keening:
Rachel weeping for her children, because they are no more;
nor would she be consoled.'

Here at the quiet limit of the world

19 Then Herod died and the angel of the Lord again appeared in a
20 dream to Joseph down in Egypt, and said to him, "Prepare at once to take the child and his mother and go to the land of Israel; for the people who wanted to kill him are dead."
21 So Joseph, on waking, took the child and his mother back to the
22 land of Israel. But when he learned that Archelaus was reigning in Judaea on the throne of his father Herod, he was afraid to
23 go there. Being warned in a dream, he went to the country of Galilee and settled in a town called Nazareth. And this was to bring about what the prophets had foretold, that Jesus would be called a Nazarene.

All ye, whose hopes rely
On God, with me amidst these deserts mourn

3, 1 At that time John the Baptist appeared, and began to preach in the desert country of Judaea. "Begin a new life," he said, "for the kingdom of God is upon you."
3 It was of John that the prophet Isaia had said,
'Listen! A voice calls in the desert:
Make ready the way of the Lord,
make straight the path for his coming.'
4 And here was John himself; he wore a shirt of camel hair, tied at the waist with a leather belt, and lived on locusts and wild

5 honey. All the people of Jerusalem and the whole of Judaea and the Jordan region went out to him.

6 They confessed their sins and were baptized by him in the river Jordan.

Against revolted multitudes the cause of truth

7 John saw many of the Pharisees and the Sadducees (the leading parties of the time) coming to be baptized and said to them, "You brood of vipers! Who ever gave you to think that you will escape the coming anger of God?

8 Show by your deeds the conversion of your hearts, and do not
9 have the presumption to think: 'We can boast Abraham as father!' For I tell you that God can raise up children to Abraham
10 from these stones. Already the axe is about to touch the root of the trees; any tree that does not produce good fruit will be cut down and thrown in the fire.

11 I baptize you with water, as a token of repentance. But after me there comes one who is stronger than I, one whose shoes I am not worthy to carry; he will baptize you with the holy Spirit
12 and with fire. His winnowing shovel is ready in his hand to purge out the chaff from his threshing-floor. The wheat he will gather into the barn; the chaff he will burn with unquenching fire."

In the roll of the book it is written of me

13 At this time Jesus moved from Galilee to the Jordan and came
14 to John to be baptized. But John wanted to prevent him: "Why do you come to me?" he asked. "It is I who need to be baptized by you."

15 And Jesus replied, "Let be. It is only fitting that we should do whatever God's will demands."
So John yielded.

For God of his gifts pour'd on him a full measure

16 Jesus therefore was baptized; and the moment he came up from

the water the heavens were opened, and he saw the Spirit of God descending like a dove and coming upon him. Then a voice from 17 heaven said, "This is my beloved Son, whom I have chosen."

Because he is at my right hand, I shall not be moved

After this Jesus was led out to the desert by the Spirit, to be 4, 1 tempted by the devil. He had fasted for forty days and nights 2 and was hungry. And the tempter approached him and said, 3 "If you are God's Son, command these stones to become bread." Jesus replied, "It is written in Scripture: 'Not by bread alone 4 shall a man find life, but by every word that God speaks.'"

Then the devil brought him to the holy city and set him on the 5 parapet of the temple. He said to him, "If you are God's Son, 6 throw yourself down; for it is written in Scripture:
'He will command his angels
to bear you in their arms,
lest you strike your foot against a stone.'"
And Jesus replied, "It is also written in Scripture: 'You shall 7 not put the Lord your God to the test.'"

Once again the devil led him away, this time to a very high 8 mountain, and showed him all the kingdoms of the world and all their splendour. "I will give you the lot," he said, "if you 9 bow down and worship me."
But Jesus replied: "Away from me, Satan! It is written in Scrip- 10 ture: 'The Lord your God you shall worship; him alone you shall serve.'"
Then the devil left him and angels came to serve him. 11

Light breaks where no sun shines

Having heard that John had been imprisoned, Jesus returned 12 to his own country of Galilee. But instead of staying at Nazareth 13 he came to live at Capharnaum, a town by the lake-side in the territory of Zabulon and Naphthali. And so the prophecy of 14 Isaia would come true:

15 'Land of Zabulon, land of Naphthali,
on the road by the sea and over the Jordan,
Galilee of the gentiles.

16 The people who sat in darkness have seen a great light;
for those who lived in a land of darkness and death, a light has
risen.'

I receive! I have been received!

17 From then on Jesus began to proclaim his message in these
words, **"Begin a new life, for the kingdom of God is upon you."**

18 One day he was walking by the lake of Galilee when he saw two
men, Simon who was surnamed Peter and his brother Andrew,
as they were working with a net on the lake; they were fishermen.

19 Jesus said to them, "Be followers of mine and I will make you
fishers of men."

20 And they immediately abandoned their nets and followed him.

21 Passing on from there he saw two others, James the son of
Zebedee and his brother John, as they were fixing their nets in
the boat with their father Zebedee. He called them.

22 And they left the boat and their father on the spot, and followed
him.

Lord look down
On this thy world, defaced by usage vile

23 Then Jesus began travelling round all Galilee. He taught in their
synagogues, proclaimed the gospel of God's kingdom, and healed
all kinds of disease and infirmity among the people.

24 His name became known throughout the whole of Syria. People
brought to him all who were sick or infirm; and whatever diseases
or infirmities they suffered, whether disorders of the mind or
crippling ailments of the body, Jesus healed them.

25 People came from everywhere to follow him, from Galilee and
the Ten Cities, from Jerusalem and Judaea, and from across the
Jordan.

All changed, changed utterly

5, 1 So when he saw the crowds he went up the mountain. Then he
sat down, his disciples gathered round, and he began to teach
them.

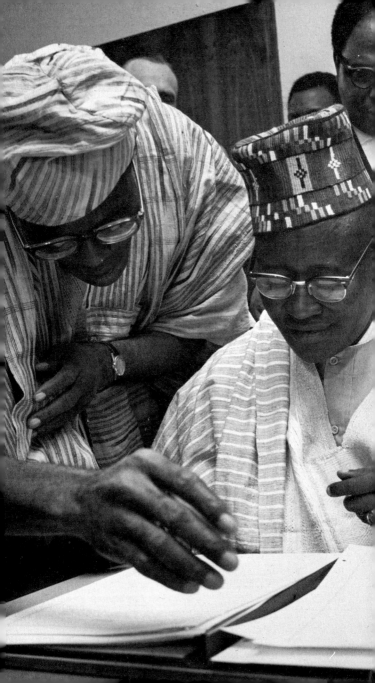

This is what he said:

"Blessed are those who know they are needy; for theirs is the 3 kingdom of God.

Blessed are those who suffer grief; for they shall be comforted. 4

Blessed are the gentle; for they shall inherit the land. 5

Blessed are those who hunger and thirst to do what is right; for 6 they shall be filled.

Blessed are the merciful; for they shall obtain mercy. 7

Blessed are the pure of heart; for they shall see God. 8

Blessed are those who work for peace; for they shall be called 9 God's children.

Blessed are those who suffer for doing what is right; for theirs is 10 the kingdom of God.

And blessed are you, if ever people insult you or persecute you 11 or slander you on my account. Be glad and rejoice, for a great 12 reward awaits you from God. That too was how they treated the Prophets before you.

That Voice is round me like a bursting sea

You are the salt of the earth. If salt becomes insipid, is there any 13 way of restoring its taste? It is good for nothing, except to be thrown out and trodden underfoot.

You are the light of the world. 14

A city built on a hill cannot be hid.

Nor do they light a lamp and place it under a bin; they set it 15 on a stand to shine for all in the house.

Therefore let your light shine before men; let them see your 16 good works and give honour to your Father in heaven.

New-risen into life and liberty

Do not think that I have come to abolish the law of Moses or the 17 writings of the Prophets. Not to abolish have I come, but to bring to completion. In God's name I tell you, heaven and earth 18 will pass away sooner than the smallest letter or stroke of the law will lose its force. Everything shall be brought to completion.

Therefore any man who sets aside even the least of these precepts 19 or teaches others to do so, will count for little in God's kingdom; but any man who observes them and teaches them will count a great deal in God's kingdom.

20 And I tell you this, if your obedience to God does not surpass that of the doctors of the law and the Pharisees, you shall not enter God's kingdom.

Because the Spring is come into our land

21 You know that it was given as a law to your ancestors, **'Do not kill;** anyone who commits murder shall be liable to judgement'.

22 But this is what I say: anyone who is angry with his fellow shall be liable to judgement; if he insults him he shall be liable to a greater judgement; and if he despises him, he shall be liable to everlasting rejection by God.

23 If you are bringing an offering to God's altar and recall a griev-
24 ance that your fellow-Christian has against you, leave your offering there on the spot, and go first to be reconciled with him. After that, you may come and offer your gift to God.

25 Better always to make peace in a hurry with your accuser, while you are on the way to court; otherwise, your accuser will hand you over to the judge, and the judge will hand you over to the
26 police, and the police will throw you in prison. In God's name I tell you, not till you have paid the last penny will you get out.

27 You know that it was laid down, 'Do not commit adultery.'
28 But this is what I say: If a man looks at another's wife, desiring her for himself, he has already committed adultery in his heart.

29 Therefore, if your right eye is a danger to you, pluck it out and throw it away; better to lose one member than to be lost forever yourself.

30 Or if your right hand is a danger to you, cut if off and throw it away; better to lose one member, than to be completely and for-ever rejected.

31 The law was as follows, 'Any man who divorces his wife must certify her dismissal in writing.'
32 But this is what I say: Any man who divorces his wife, apart from a matter of unchastity, causes her to commit adultery; and anyone who marries a divorced wife commits adultery.

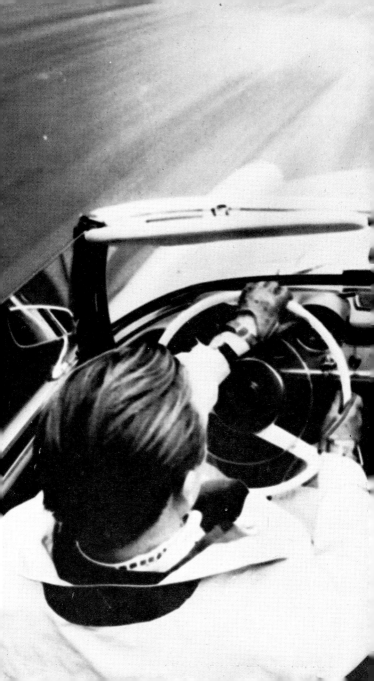

You also know that it was formerly laid down, 'Do not swear 33 falsely; fulfil the oaths you have sworn before God.'

But this is what I say: Do not swear at all. Do not swear by 34 heaven, for it is God's throne; nor by earth, for it is his footstool; 35 nor by Jerusalem, for it is the city of the great King. And do not 36 swear by your head, since you have no power to make one hair white or black.

Speak the truth: 'yes' for 'yes', 'no' for 'no'. Anything beyond 37 this is evil.

You know that it was the law: 'an eye for an eye and a tooth for 38 a tooth'.

But this is what I say: do not set yourself against the man who 39 wrongs you.

If a person strikes you on the right cheek, turn him the other as well.

If a person sues you for a coat, give him your overcoat as well. 40

If a person forces you to do a mile, do another as well. 41

Give to the one who asks of you, and do not turn away from the 42 one who needs your help.

That we may learn to bear the beams of love

You know that it was the law: 'You shall love your neighbour 43 and hate your enemy.'

But this is what I say: You shall love your enemies and pray for 44 your persecutors, that you may be children of your Father in heaven. **For he makes his sun to rise on the bad as well as the** 45 **good,** and gives his rain to the sinners as well as the saints.

If you love only those who love you, what reward do you deserve? 46 Even criminals do the same.

If you greet only your brothers, what is special about it? 47 Even sinners do as much.

Therefore be perfect, as your Father in heaven is perfect. 48

And all for love and nothing for reward

When you do works of charity, take care not to do them in public 6, 1 so as be seen by men; otherwise no reward awaits you from your Father in heaven.

2 Sound no trumpets, therefore, when you are about to give charity, as the hypocrites do in the temples and the streets, so as to be lauded by men. Believe me, they have received their reward.

3 But when you give charity, your left hand must not know what
4 your right hand is doing; let your charity be hidden, and your Father who sees what is hidden will repay you.

God's breath in man returning to his birth

5 And when you pray, take care not to act like those hypocrites who stand around praying in the temples and at the corners of the streets, so as to be seen by men.
Believe me, they have received their reward.

6 Whenever you pray, go into your room, and close the door, and **pray to your Father in secret;** for your Father sees what is secret, and he will reward you.

7 And do not babble at length when you pray, like the pagans, who think that to be heard they have to speak many words.

8 With you it is different; for your Father knows what you need, even before you ask for it.

The soul in paraphrase, heart in pilgrimage

9 This is how you should pray:
Our Father in heaven,
let your holy name be known,
10 let your kingdom come,
and your will be done,
on earth as in heaven.
11 Give us today the bread that we need,
12 and forgive us our wrongs,
as we forgive those
who have done wrong to us.
13 Do not lead us into trial,
but save us from evil.

14 If you forgive others the wrongs they have done, your Father in heaven will forgive you.

But if you do not forgive others, neither will your Father forgive 15
you.

Dead perfection—no more?

When you fast, do not act like the hypocrites who put on gloomy 16
looks and downcast faces, to let others see that they are fasting.
Believe me, they have received their reward.
Whenever you fast, freshen yourself up and put on a cheerful 17
face. Others may not see that you are fasting, but your Father 18
who is hidden will; for he sees what is hidden, and he will reward
you.

Getting and spending we lay waste our powers

Gather no riches on earth, where moth and rust destroy, and 19
thieves break in and steal. Gather riches with God, where moth 20
and rust do not destroy, nor thieves break in and steal.
Wherever your riches are, there your heart will be. 21

The eye gives light to the body. If the eye is clear, the whole 22
body is lighted; but if the eye is evil, the whole body is in dark- 23
ness. And if this light within you is in darkness, how dark is
your night!
No man can serve two masters; he will either hate the one and 24
like the other, or take to the one and detest the other.
You cannot serve God and money.

Love God! Begin to repose yourself on Him

I tell you, therefore, do not burden your life with anxiety over 25
food, or drink, or clothing.
Is not life more important than nourishment, and the body more
important than clothing?
Take a lesson from the birds of the sky. They neither sow nor reap 26
nor gather a store; and yet, your Father in heaven takes care of
them.
Are you not much more important than the birds?
Can any one of you extend the span of his life, no matter how 27
much he worries about it?

28 Or why **worry** about clothing? Learn from the lilies of the field, how they grow, without having to toil or make themselves clothes.

29 And yet, I tell you, **not even Solomon in all his glory was dressed like one of them.**

30 If this is how God looks after the grass of the field, which is here today and gone tomorrow, how much more will he look after you—for all your want of faith!

31 Do not worry therefore: what are we to eat? what are we to drink? where are we to get clothes? These are the worries of pagan people.

32 But your Father in heaven knows that you need all these things.

33 Set your hearts first of all on the kingdom, and whatever he demands.

The rest will all be looked after by God.

34 Have no worry then about tomorrow; tomorrow will look after itself.

Each day has enough trouble of its own.

That my heart may be greater within me

7, 1 Do not judge others, if you do not want to be judged yourselves.

2 As you judge others, so you will be judged; the measure you give will be the measure you will receive.

3 How can you see the speck in your neighbour's eye, if you do
4 not see the spot in your own? Or how can you say to your brother: let me take that speck out of your eye, when there's a blind spot in your own?

5 Do not deceive yourself. First remove the spot from your own eye, and then you'll be in a position to remove the speck from your brother's eye.

6 Holy things are not to be thrown to dogs, nor pearls to swine, lest they trample them in the mud, and then turn and tear you to pieces.

Where ask is have, where seek is find,
Where knock is open wide

7 Ask and God will give to you.

Seek and you will find.
Knock and you will be given entry.
8 The one who asks receives.
The one who seeks finds.
The one who knocks is given entry.
9 Suppose one of your children asks for bread, do you give him a
11 stone? Or if he asks for a fish, do you give him a snake? And if
you, although you're not saints, can give good things to your
children, how much more will your Father in heaven give good
things to those who ask him.

The golden rule

12 Therefore, let this be your rule: Treat others as you would like
others to treat you.
For the whole of the law and the Prophets is summed up in this
rule.

This is the gate of the Lord, the righteous
shall enter through it

13 Enter by the narrow gate; for the gate is wide and the road is
broad that leads to perdition.
There are many who take it.
14 But narrow is the gate and difficult the road that leads to life.
And few find it.

Surviving man betrays with deeds and words

15 Watch out for false prophets; they come with the gentleness of
16 sheep, but with the mind of ravenous wolves. You will know
them by their fruits.
Are grapes picked from hawthorns? Or figs from brambles?
17 A good tree always produces good fruit, and a bad tree bad
18 fruit; for a good tree cannot produce bad fruit, nor a bad tree
19 good fruit. And any tree that does not yield a good crop will be
cut down and burnt.
20 Therefore you will know them by their fruits.

O Lord, who shall sojourn in thy tent?

21 It is not the man who says to me, 'Lord, Lord', that will enter

the kingdom of God, but the man who does the will of my Father in heaven.

On that last day many will say, 'Lord have we not spoken pro- 22 phecy in your name? Have we not driven out demons, and worked many miracles in your name?'

And I will tell them to their faces, 'I have never known you. Go 23 away from me, you doers of evil!'

A forted residence 'gainst the tooth of time

Anyone therefore who hears my words, and acts on them, will be 24 like a thoughtful man who built his house on rock; when the 25 clouds burst and the floods came and the winds blew and beat upon that house, it did not fall, because it had a foundation of rock.

But anyone who hears my words, and does not act on them, will 26 be like a foolish man who built his house on sand; when the 27 clouds burst and the floods came and the winds blew and beat upon that house, it fell and crumbled in a great crash."

But eies, and eares, and ev'ry thought,
Were with his sweete perfection caught

When Jesus had finished this sermon the people were amazed 28 at his teaching. Unlike their own doctors of the law, he taught 29 them as one with authority.

God's finger touched him

Jesus then came down from the mountain and was followed by 8, 1 a large crowd of people. And a leper came to him and said, as 2 he fell at his feet, "Sir, if only you will, you can cleanse me of my disease."

Jesus reached out his hand and touched him. "Yes, I will," he 3 said. "Be cleansed." And the man was immediately cleansed of his leprosy.

Jesus warned him not to tell anyone. "But go," he said, "and 4 show yourself to the priest. Bring the offering prescribed by Moses, so that your cure may be certified."

Lord I am not worthy, but speak the word only

5 As soon as he had arrived in Capharnaum an army officer
6 approached him and said, "Sir, my servant is lying crippled in
bed at home and in great pain."
7 Jesus replied, "I will come and heal him."
8 And the officer said, "I am not worthy, sir, to have you enter
my house. But you need only to say the word and my servant
9 will be healed. I myself belong to the service and have soldiers
under me; if I tell one to go, he goes; if I tell one to come, he
comes; and if I say to my servant 'do this', he does it."
10 Jesus was amazed, and said to the people with him, "Believe me,
such faith I have not found from anyone in Israel.
11 I assure you, **many will come from the east and west,** and
will sit at table with Abraham and Isaac and Jacob in the kingdom
12 of God. But the people of the kingdom will be banished to the
darkness outside; and there, I tell you, will be the wailing and
anguish of remorse!"
13 He turned to the army officer and said, "Go home. As your faith
has been, so let it be done."
And at the same moment his servant was healed.

Christ of his gentleness

14 Jesus went to Peter's house and found Peter's mother-in-law in
15 bed with fever. He took hold of her hand and the fever left her;
and she got up and began to serve him.
16 In the cool of the evening many were brought to him suffering
from possession; he drove out the demons with a word, and
healed all the sick.
17 And so the saying of Isaia the Prophet came true: 'He took away
our sicknesses and bore our infirmities.'

Life's business being just the terrible choice

18 Finding himself surrounded by a large crowd, Jesus gave command to cross over to the other shore.
19 And a doctor of the law came up and said, "Master, I will follow
you wherever you go."

Jesus replied, "The foxes have dens and the birds of the sky have 20 nests, but the Son of Man has nowhere to lay his head."

Another who belonged to the disciples said to him, "Sir, allow 21 me first to go and bury my father."
And Jesus replied, "Follow me. Let the dead bury their dead." 22

O Saviour of those who seek refuge

After he had embarked in the boat along with his disciples a 23 great storm suddenly came down on the lake, so that the boat was almost swallowed by the waves. But Jesus was asleep.
The disciples came to waken him and said, "Lord, save us! We're 25 going down!"
And he replied, "Why this fear? Have you so little faith?" 26
Then he got up, commanded the winds and the waters, and there came a great calm.
And the men were astounded and asked themselves, "What kind 27 of man is this? Even the winds and the waves obey him!"

Thy God, thy life, thy cure

When he arrived at the opposite shore, in the country of the 28 Gadarenes, two possessed men came out from the tombs to meet him; they were bad cases, so violent that nobody could travel that road in peace.
They called out to him, "Son of God, what do you want from 29 us? Have you come to torment us before the time?"
At some distance from them a large herd of pigs was feeding; and 30 the demons begged of Jesus, "If you drive us out, send us into the herd of pigs."
"Go out!" he replied. 32
So the demons came out from the two men and took possession of the pigs; and the whole herd rushed down the slope into the lake and perished in the water.
The herdsmen took to their heels and went off into the town, 33 where they reported the whole story about the possessed men.
And the whole town then came out to meet Jesus; when they 34 saw him they asked him to leave their country.

That the man I am may cease to be

9, 1 Jesus therefore got into a boat and having crossed over came to
  2 his own town, Capharnaum. Here they brought him a cripple,
who lay helpless on a stretcher. And Jesus, struck by their faith,
said to the cripple, "Courage, son, your sins are forgiven."
  3 Now there happened to be some doctors of the law in the company, who said to themselves, "This man is talking blasphemy!"
  4 But Jesus knew their minds and asked, "Why do you have these
  5 wicked thoughts? Do you think it is easier to say, 'your sins are
  6 forgiven' than to say, 'stand up and walk'? But I will let you
see that the Son of Man has power on earth to forgive sins."
So he turned to the cripple and said, "Stand up, take your bed,
and go home."
  7 And the cripple got up and went home to his house.
  8 The people who saw it all felt a strange fear and praised God for
giving such power to men.

The lost days of my life until today

  9 Jesus passed on from there and saw a man sitting at the tax-office
whose name was Matthew.
"Come with me," he said to him.
And Matthew at once packed up and went with him.
 10 Later on he was at dinner in the house and many tax-collectors
and outcast people came and sat down to the meal with Jesus
and his disciples.
 11 The Pharisees saw this and said to his disciples, "Why does
your Master dine with these tax-collectors and other riff-raff?"
 12 But Jesus was listening and said, "It is not the healthy who need
 13 the doctor, but the sick. Go and learn what is meant by the
Scripture where it says, 'I desire mercy, and not sacrificial
offerings.'
I have not come to call the pious but men who are estranged
from God."

A new knowledge of reality

 14 At this time some of John's disciples came to him and asked,
"How is it that we and the Pharisees fast, but not your disciples?"

And he replied, "Do you think that wedding-guests can go 15 mourning while the bridegroom is with them? But days will come when the bridegroom will be taken from them; and that will be the time for them to fast.

Our little systems have their day

No one sews a patch of unshrunk cloth on an old coat, or the 16 patch will shrink and tear the coat, so that a bigger hole is made. And no one pours new wine into old wine-skins, or the skins 17 will burst, so that both wine and skins are lost; **new wine is poured into new skins,** so that both wine and skins are saved."

Everything that lives
Lives not alone, nor for itself

As Jesus was speaking to them, a magistrate came up and bowed 18 to him respectfully. "My daughter has just died," he said. "Please came and lay a hand upon her, and she will live again." Jesus got up and went with him, accompanied by his disciples. 19 Now there was also a woman who for twelve years had suffered 20 from bleeding; she came up behind and touched the fringe of his cloak, saying to herself, "If I only touch his cloak I shall be 21 healed."
But Jesus turned round and saw her. "Courage, daughter," he 22 said, "your faith has saved you." And from that moment the woman was healed.

Can I see another's woe
And not be in sorrow too?

When he came to the magistrate's house he found flute-players 23 there and a large crowd waking the dead girl.
"Go home," he said to them. "The girl is not dead but asleep." 24 And they laughed at him.
Then the crowd was put out from the house. Jesus entered the 25 room, took the girl by the hand, and she was restored to life.
And the news of it spread all over the country. 26

27 As he moved on from there two blind men followed him, crying out, "Son of David, have pity on us".

28 When he entered the house the two came to him; and he asked them, "Do you believe that I can do what you want?"
"Yes, sir," they replied.

29 Then he touched their eyes and said, "In so far as you have faith, so let it be done."

30 And the blind men received their sight.
He gave them a strict warning: "Be sure not to tell anyone about it."

31 But they went off and spread news of him all over the country.

32 Just as they were going away a dumb man afflicted by an evil
33 spirit was brought to him; the spirit was driven out and the dumb man began to speak.
And the crowds exclaimed in astonishment, "Never has the like been seen in Israel!"

34 But the Pharisees said, "It's from the prince of demons that he gets power to drive out demons."

—All ye that labour, come to Me, and rest—

35 Jesus travelled round all their towns and villages, taught in their meeting-houses, proclaimed the gospel of the kingdom, and healed every disease and infirmity.

36 The sight of the multitudes moved him to pity; they were harassed and helpless, like sheep without a shepherd.

37 And he said to his disciples, "How great is the harvest to be
38 reaped, and how few the workers. You must pray the Lord of the harvest to send workers to reap his crop."

World-losers and world-forsakers

10, 1 He summoned his twelve disciples and gave them power to drive out evil spirits and to heal all diseases and infirmities.

2 And the names of the twelve apostles are as follows:
Simon first, who was called Peter, and his brother Andrew;
then James the son of Zebedee, and his brother John;

3 then Philip and Bartholomew;

Thomas and Matthew, who had been a tax-collector;
James, the son of Alphaeus, and Thaddaeus;
Simon the Zealot, and Judas Iscariot who later betrayed him. 4

Yet we are the movers and shakers

He sent these twelve out on a mission and instructed them as 5
follows: "You are not to go to the foreign peoples, nor to any 6
town of Samaria, but to the lost sheep of the house of Israel. And 7
as you go your way let this be your message: 'God's kingdom
has drawn near'. Heal the sick, raise the dead, cure the lepers, 8
drive out the demons. Having received at no cost, you must give 9
service without charge; therefore earn no gold, nor silver, nor
copper, to put in your belts. And carry no knapsack for the 10
journey, nor more than one shirt, nor sandals, nor a walking-
stick; for any man who works deserves his keep.
On coming to a town or a village, look for a citizen who is worthy, 11
and stay with him until you leave again. And when you enter a 12
house bring a greeting with you. If the people are worthy, let 13
your peace be with them; if they are not worthy, let it return
to you. And if anyone refuses to receive you or to listen to you, 14
depart from that house or that town and shake the dust of it
from your feet.
Believe me, on the day of judgement Sodom and Gomorrah will 15
get off more lightly than that town.

How very hard it is to be a Christian!

I send you now as sheep among wolves. 16
Therefore be wary as serpents, and be innocent as doves.
You must also guard against men; for they will hand you over 17
to courts and have you flogged in their synagogues. You will be 18
brought before governors and kings on my account, as witnesses
before them and the foreign peoples.
When you are led away, do not be anxious about what you will 19
say in your speech. For when the moment comes, you will be 20
inspired what to say; it will not be you who will be speaking,
but the Spirit of your Father who will be speaking through you.
Brother will surrender brother to death, and a father his child; 21

even children will rise against their parents and send them to death.

22 You will be hated by all men on my account; but the man who holds out to the end will be saved.

23 If they hunt you down in one town, take refuge in another; for I tell you this: you will not have completed the towns of Irsael before the Son of Man comes.

24 A disciple does not stand above his master, nor a servant above
25 his lord; the disciple must be satisfied to go the way of his master, and the servant the way of his lord.
If they have deemed the householder an agent of Satan, how much more will they malign his household!

Speak no evil of the soul,
Nor think that body is the whole.

26 Do not fear them therefore.
Nothing is covered up, that will not be disclosed; or hidden
27 away, that will not be revealed. What I say to you under cover, tell it in the open day; what is whispered in your ear, proclaim it aloud from the house-tops.
28 Have no fear of those who may kill the body, but cannot kill the spirit; fear rather the one who can destroy in hell both body and spirit.
29 Are not a couple of sparrows sold for a few pence? And yet not a single one of them falls to the ground without your Father's leave.
30 As for you, even the hairs of your head are all numbered. **Have no fear therefore; you count more than all the sparrows.**

32 If anyone declares for me before men, I will declare for him
33 before my Father in heaven; if anyone disowns me before men, I will disown him before my Father in heaven.

The Christian paradox, bringing its great reward
By loss

34 Do not think that I have come to bring peace on earth. No, not

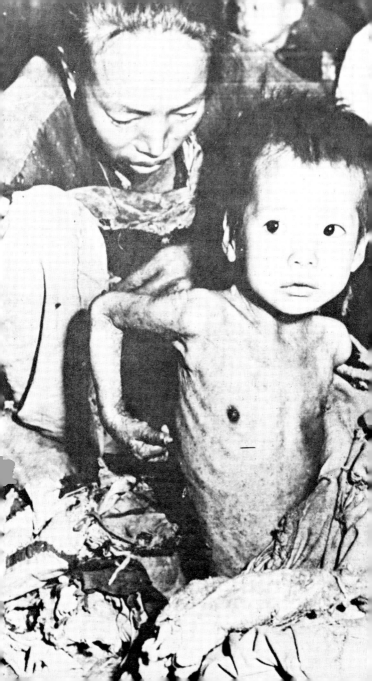

35 peace but the sword. I have come to separate a man from his father, a daughter from her mother, a daughter-in-law from her
36 mother-in-law; and a man's enemies will be the people of his own house.
37 Whoever loves father or mother more than me is not worthy of me; whoever loves son or daughter more than me is not worthy
38 of me; whoever does not take up his cross and follow me is not worthy of me.
39 Whoever has found his life will lose it; whoever loses his life for my sake will find it.

Familiar acts are beautiful through love

40 Whoever receives you receives me; and whoever receives me receives the one who sent me.
41 Whoever receives a prophet, on the ground that he is a prophet, will get the reward of a prophet.
Whoever receives a good man, on the ground that he is a good man, will get the reward of a good man.
42 And whoever gives a cup of fresh water to one of these little ones, on the ground that he is a disciple of mine—in God's name I tell you, he shall not go unrewarded."

11, 1 When he had finished instructing his twelve disciples Jesus departed from there to teach and proclaim the gospel in their towns.

A vision lit
With mighty prophecies

2 Now John the Baptist got news in prison of what Christ was
3 doing; so he sent some of his disciples to ask him, "Are you the one who is to come, or must we wait for someone else?"
4 Jesus replied, "Go back and tell John what you hear and see:
5 how the blind get their sight, and the lame walk, and the lepers are cleansed, and the deaf hear, and the dead are raised to life, and the poor have the gospel preached to them.
6 And well for the man who does not go wrong because of me."

42

The last and greatest herald of Heaven's King

While they were on their way, Jesus began to speak to the crowds 7
about John:
"What brought you out to the desert? To see a reed shaken by
the wind? Was that it?
Or what brought you out? To see someone dressed in soft 8
garments?
But the people who dress in soft garments belong to royal
palaces.
Why then did you go out? To see a prophet?
Yes, I tell you, and more than a prophet. John is the one of 9
whom Scripture says: 'I am sending my messenger ahead of you,
to prepare the way before you.'
Believe me, among all men born of woman no one greater has 11
arisen than John the Baptist; and yet, the least person in God's
kingdom is greater than he.
From the days of John the Baptist until now the kingdom of 12
God has been storming in, and men of violence carry it away.
The prophets and the law all prophesied until John; he is the 13
Elia whose coming was promised, if you are prepared to accept it.
And any man who has ears should use them. 15

We are the hollow men
We are the stuffed men

What example can I give of the present generation? The people 16
of today are like children sitting in the streets and calling out to 17
their playmates: 'We played you a hornpipe and you wouldn't
dance; we keened the dead and you wouldn't mourn.'
John came, neither eating nor drinking, and they say, 'he is mad'. 18
The Son of Man comes, an eater and a drinker, and they say, 19
'here's a glutton, a tippler, a friend of tax-collectors and their
ilk.'
And God's wisdom has been proved right by what she has
accomplished."

Look at it well. This was the good town once

After that Jesus began to reproach the towns where most of his 20 miracles had taken place, because they had not been converted:

21 "Woe to you Chorazin," he said, "and woe to you Bethsaida! If the miracles worked among you had been worked in Tyre and Sidon, they would have long ago mourned for their sins and repented.

22 I tell you this: On the day of judgement Tyre and Sidon will get off more lightly than you.

23 And you Capharnaum? Will you be lifted up to heaven? You shall be brought down to hell! If the same miracles had been worked for the people of Sodom as have been worked for you, Sodom would be there to this day.

24 I tell you this: On the day of judgement the land of Sodom will get off more lightly than you."

Lead, Kindly Light, amid the encircling gloom

25 On that occasion Jesus confessed to his Father, "I thank you, Father, Lord of heaven and earth; you have hidden these things from the wise and the learned, and have revealed them to simple

26 folk. Yes, Father, such was your pleasure.

27 All things have been committed to me by my Father. No one knows the Son except the Father; no one knows the Father except the Son, and those to whom the Son chooses to reveal him.

28 **Come to me, all you people wearied by your heavy burden,** and

29 I will give you rest. Bow yourselves to my yoke and learn of me, for I am kind and humble; and you will find peace in your lives.

30 My yoke is gentle, my burden light."

Christ with his lamp of truth

12, 1 At this time Jesus once passed through wheat-fields on a sabbath-day; and the disciples, being hungry, began to pluck ears of wheat and eat them.

2 But the Pharisees saw it and said to him, "Look, your disciples are doing what is forbidden on the sabbath."

3 And he replied, "Are you not forgetting what David did when

4 he and his companions were hungry? How he entered the temple

of God and ate the holy bread laid out there which neither he nor his companions had any right to eat, but only the priests.

5 Or again, have you not read in the Scripture that the priests in the temple have a right to profane the sabbath, without being blamed for it?

6 I tell you, here stands one that is greater than the temple.

7 If you knew the meaning of the words, 'I desire mercy, and not sacrificial offerings', you would not be so quick to condemn innocent people.

8 For the Son of Man is Lord of the sabbath."

His pity gave ere charity began

9 Moving on from there, he came to their synagogue, where there happened to be a man with a shrivelled hand.

10 And they asked him straight, "Is it permitted to heal on the sabbath?" For they wanted to bring a charge against him.

11 Jesus replied, "Suppose one of you has a sheep and it falls into a pit on the sabbath, will he not get hold of it and pull it out?

12 But how much more does a man count than a sheep! So it follows that a good deed is allowed on the sabbath."

13 He then said to the man, "Put out your hand."
And the moment he put it out, his hand became as sound as the other.

14 But the Pharisees went out and held a meeting to see how they would destroy him.

God's silent servant

15 On hearing of this, Jesus went away from that place and was
16 followed by many people; he healed them all, but gave them strict warning not to make him known.

17 And so the words of Isaia the Prophet were to come true:

18 'Here is my Servant, whom I have chosen,
my beloved, on whom my favour rests.
I will put my Spirit upon him,
and he will proclaim right to the nations.

19 He will not contend or shout;
his voice will not be heard in the streets.

The broken reed he will not crush,   20
the smouldering wick he will not quench,
until he makes right triumphant,
and the nations pin their hopes in him.'   21

We see Him come, and know Him ours

A possessed man was brought to him who was blind and dumb. 22
And Jesus healed the dumb man, so that he could again speak
and see.

The crowds were beside themselves with excitement. "Surely 23
this must be the Son of David," they said.

But the Pharisees, hearing it, remarked, "This man has no power 24
over demons, or if he has, it's from the prince of demons himself."

Jesus however knew their minds and said to them, "A kingdom 25
divided against itself loses its strength; and a city or a house
divided against itself has no future.

If it is Satan who drives out Satan, then Satan is divided; and 26
what future has his kingdom?

And if my power over demons is from the prince of demons, 27
from whom do your own people get their power? Therefore they
shall be your judges.

But if I drive out demons by the power of God's Spirit, then the 28
kingdom of God has already come upon you.

Or is it possible to enter a strong man's house and plunder his 29
property, without first tying up the strong man? Only then can
one plunder his house.

The man who is not with me is against me; the man who does 30
not gather with me scatters.

And for this sin there is no remedy

I tell you this: there is no sin, no slander, for which men will 31
not be forgiven, except slander against the Spirit.

One who speaks against the Son of Man may yet be forgiven; 32 but the person who speaks against the Holy Spirit will never be forgiven—neither in this world nor in the world to come.

Hatred and cark and care, what place have they?

33 Either take the tree to be sound, and the fruit also will be sound; or take it to be bad, and the fruit also will be bad. It is the fruit that shows the tree.

34 You brood of vipers! How can you speak good words, when you are evil yourselves? For the mouth only speaks the thoughts that fill the heart.

35 A good man produces what is good from his store of goodness; and an evil man what is evil from his store of evil.

But if we let our tongues lose self-possession

36 Believe me, on the day of judgement men shall answer for every thoughtless word they shall speak.

37 **By your words you will be acquitted; or by your words you will be condemned."**

No Light, but rather darkness visible

38 Some doctors of the law and Pharisees said to him on that occasion, "Master, we want to see some sign from you as a proof."

39 And he replied, "So this evil and unfaithful generation wants a sign! But no sign will be given it, except the sign of the prophet Jona.

40 As Jona spent three days and three nights in the belly of the monster, so too the Son of Man will spend three days and three nights in the heart of the earth.

41 On the day of judgement the people of Niniveh will rise with the people of this generation, and will speak judgement against them; for they were converted at the preaching of Jona.
And here stands one that is greater than Jona.

42 On the day of judgement the Queen of the south will rise with the people of this generation, and will speak judgement against them;

for she came from the ends of the earth to hear the wisdom of Solomon.
And here stands one that is greater than Solomon.

Passing from deception to deception
From grandeur to grandeur to final illusion

When an unclean spirit goes out from a person it scours the 43
waterless desert looking for a place to rest, and does not find it.
So it says, 'I will go back to my house which I left.' And on going 44
back it finds it still vacant, and everything swept and tidy.
Then it sets out and picks up seven other spirits more evil than 45
itself, and they all enter and take up residence there, so that the
man's plight is worse at the end than it was at the start.
That, too, is how it will be for the people of this generation."

With the eyes of God

While he was speaking to the people it happened that his mother 46
and brothers came and stood outside, wanting to have a word
with him.
Somebody brought him the message: "Look, your mother and 47
your brothers are outside and want to have a word with you."
And he replied, "Who is my mother? And who are my brothers?" 48
He pointed a hand towards his disciples, and said, "Here are 49
my mother and my brothers! Anyone who obeys the will of my 50
Father in heaven is my brother, my sister, my mother."

Soft words of grace he spoke

On the same day Jesus left the house and sat by the shore of 13, 1
the lake. A very large crowd of people gathered round him; so
he got into a boat and sat in it, while all the people stood along 2
the lake-side.
And he spoke to them at length in parables. 3

O be swift, my soul, to answer him!

He said, "**A farmer once went out to sow seed.** And as he 4 scattered the seed, some fell on the path; and the birds came and ate it up.

5 Some seed fell on stony ground where it did not have much soil;
6 and not being very deep it sprouted quickly. Then the sun came up and it was scorched; and because it had no roots it withered.
7 Some seed fell among briars; but the briars shot up and choked the seed.
8 And some seed fell on good soil and produced a crop, increasing up to a hundred or sixty or thirty times.
9 If anyone has ears, let him use them."

Refuse to listen and you will no longer hear

10 Afterwards the disciples came to Jesus and wanted to know, "Why do you speak to them in parables?"
11 And he replied, "Because you have been given to know the secrets of the kingdom of God; but the others have not been given this grace.
12 When a man already has something, he will be given more, and plenty of it.
   When a man has nothing, even the little he has will be taken from him.

13 If I speak to them in parables, it is because they look but do not
14 see, and hear but do not understand. For them, therefore, the prophecy of Isaia has come true:
   'You shall hear and listen, but not understand;
   You shall look and see, but not perceive.
15 For the mind of this people has been blunted;
   their ears have been made deaf,
   and their eyes have been made dim;
   they shall not see with their eyes,
   or hear with their ears,
   or understand with their minds;
   they shall not be converted,
   and I shall not heal them.'

16 **But blessed are your eyes, in that they see;** and blessed are your
17 ears, in that they hear. Believe me, many prophets and many

saints have longed to see what you see, but have not seen it; and have wanted to hear what you hear, but have not heard it.

God comes down in the rain
And the crop grows tall

18 Let you, therefore, listen to what is meant by the parable of the
19 sower: Some people hear the word of God's kingdom but do not take it to heart, because the devil comes and snatches away what has been sown in them; these are the type represented by the seed that falls on the path.
20 The seed that falls on the stony ground stands for others, who
21 hear the word and immediately receive it with joy. With these, however, the seed takes no root and is short-lived; when trouble comes, or any kind of trial on account of the word, this type immediately falls away.
22 Others again are represented by the seed that falls among the briars; these listen to the word, but worldly interests and the lure of wealth choke the word so that it produces no fruit.
23 Then there is the seed that falls on the good soil; it stands for those who hear the word and take it to heart, and go on to produce a rich harvest indeed."

At the end a reckoning

24 He told them another story:
   "God's kingdom may be compared to a farmer who sowed good
25 seed in his field. But while the people were asleep an enemy came who sowed weeds all through the wheat and went off.
26 When the braird grew up and sprouted, then the weeds appeared as well.
27 So the farmer's men came and said to him, 'Sir, didn't you sow good seed in your field? Where have the weeds come from?'
28 'Some enemy has done this,' replied the farmer.
   And the men asked him, 'Do you want us to go and gather up the weeds?'
29 But he said, 'No. If you gather the weeds you run the risk of
30 plucking up the wheat as well. Let both grow together until harvest-time; I'll see that the reapers gather the weeds first,

54

and tie them in bundles for burning, and afterwards gather the wheat into my barn.' "

And new horizons calling

Jesus went on to tell another story: 31
"The kingdom of God is like a mustard-seed which a man sowed in his field. This is the smallest of all the seeds, but when it has 32 grown is bigger than any plant of the garden; it even becomes a tree, so that the birds of the sky can come and roost in its branches."
And another story: 33
"The kingdom of God is like a fermenting yeast which a woman has mixed into three large measures of flour, until the whole cake becomes fermented."

Human kind cannot bear very much reality

All these things Jesus told the people by means of stories or 34 parables; apart from this, he gave them no instruction.
And the word of God spoken by the prophet thus came true: 35
'I will speak in parables;
I will utter age-old secrets.'

O great, just, good God! Miserable me!

Jesus then dismissed the crowds and went home. And the 36 disciples came to him and said, "Explain for us the story of the weeds in the tillage."
He replied, "The sower of the good seed is the Son of Man. 37 The field in which it is sowed is the world. The good seed stands 38 for the men of the kingdom, the weeds for the agents of evil. The enemy who sowed the weeds stands for the devil, the 39 harvest for the end of the world, and the reapers for the angels. Just as weeds are gathered up and burnt, so shall it be at the end 40 of the world. The Son of Man will send out his angels. They 41 will gather out of his kingdom all the agents of corruption and evil and cast them into hell; and there, I tell you, will be the 42 wailing and anguish of remorse!

43 After that the saints will shine like the sun in their Father's kingdom.
Whoever has ears, let him listen.

I have no good apart from thee

44 The kingdom of God is like a man finding a treasure buried in a field; he hides it away himself, and then—so great is his joy—he goes and sells all his property in order to buy that field.

45 Or again, the kingdom of God is like a dealer who is looking for
46 pearls of quality; when he discovers a really valuable one, he goes and sells all his property in order to buy that pearl.

He will judge the world with righteousness

47 Again, God's kingdom is like a great drag-net cast into the sea,
48 which catches all kinds of fish. When it is full it is hauled ashore; and the men sit down to pick out the good fish into a vessel, **and throw away the bad.**

49 That is how it will be at the end of the world. The angels will go
50 out and separate the wicked from the good and will cast them into hell; and there, I tell you, will be the wailing and anguish of remorse!

51 Have you understood all this?"
"Yes," they replied.

52 And Jesus said to them, "It follows that any man who is schooled in God's word and well instructed about the kingdom is like a householder who can draw on his store of wisdom for new stuff or old."

It takes life to love life

53 Having finished his parables Jesus departed from there.
54 He came to his own town and taught his townsmen in their synagogue.
But they were completely baffled. "Where does he get all the
55 learning?" they began to ask. "And these miracles? Isn't he the son of the carpenter? Don't we know his mother Mary and his
56 brothers, James and Joseph, Simon and Jude? His sisters too—

aren't they all neighbours of ours? Where can he have picked up all this?"

57 So they took offence at him.

And Jesus said to them, "Nowhere is a prophet more despised than in his own town, and among his own people."

58 He worked only a few miracles there, because they had no faith.

In this land of unbelief and fear

14, 1 At this time rumours about Jesus came to Herod, the ruler of
2 the province. He said to his men, "This is John the Baptist; the man has been brought to life! That is why these miraculous powers are working in him."

With dark deliberate intent

3 Herod had previously arrested John and thrown him in prison in chains, on account of Herodias, his brother Philip's wife.
4 For John used say to Herod, "It's wrong for you to keep her."
5 And Herod would have liked to kill him; but he feared the people, because they looked on John as a prophet.
6 However, when Herod's birthday was being celebrated, the daughter of Herodias danced before all the guests and pleased
7 the king so much that he swore a solemn oath to give her any-
8 thing she asked. And the girl, prompted by her mother, said to him, "Give me here on a dish the head of John the Baptist."
9 At this the king was saddened; but he had sworn an oath in the presence of his guests, so he ordered that her request should be granted.
10 He sent to have John beheaded in prison. The head was brought in on a dish and given to the girl; and the girl brought it to her mother.

12 Then his disciples came and took away his body for burial; and they brought the news to Jesus.

O cut for me life's bread, for me pour wine

13 When Jesus heard this, he went away in a boat by himself to a deserted place.

But news of his departure got around among the people; they went out from the towns and followed him on foot round the shore of the lake.

So when he got out of the boat he found a large crowd of people. 14 He felt pity for them, and healed their sick.

Towards evening his disciples came to him and said, "This 15 place is a desert and it's past the time. You should send the people away; let them go to the villages and buy themselves food."

Jesus replied, "They don't have to go away. Let you give them 16 food."

"But we have nothing with us," they said, "except five loaves 17 and a couple of fish."

"Bring them here to me," he said. And he told the people to sit 18 on the grass.

He took in his hands the five loaves and the two fish. And raising 19 his eyes to heaven, as he said the grace, he broke the loaves and gave them to the disciples; and they distributed them to the people.

Everybody had a full meal. 20
Then they gathered up what was left over, twelve basketfuls.

And the number of those who had eaten was about five thousand 21 men, without counting women and children.

Jesus then made the disciples embark in the boat and go ahead 22 to the other side while he was dismissing the people.

And having sent them away, he went up into the hills to pray 23 by himself.

Oft he seems to hide his face

Before long the boat was many furlongs out from the shore, 24 being now buffeted by heavy waves, for a head-wind had blown up.

And as night was ending Jesus came towards them, walking on 25 the water. When the disciples saw the figure walking on the 26 water, they were terrified and cried out for fear, "It's a ghost!"

But Jesus spoke to them and said, "Courage! It is I. Have no 27 fear."

And half-made men believe and fear

28 Peter called out to him, "Lord, if it is you, **bid me** come to you over the water."

29 And Jesus said, "Come!"
So Peter got out of the boat and walked on the water till he came to Jesus.

30 When he felt the wind, however, he got afraid; and as he began to sink he cried out, "Lord, save me!"

31 Jesus immediately reached out a hand and said, as he took hold of him, "You man of little faith, why did you doubt?"

32 And when they climbed into the boat, the wind died.

33 The men in the boat fell at his feet and said to him, "You are indeed the Son of God."

The poor and naked come

34 Having crossed over they landed at Gennesareth.

35 And when the people of the place saw who it was, they immediately sent word round the whole area. They brought all

36 their sick to him, asking him only to let them touch the fringe of his cloak; and as many as touched him were healed.

Our learned carelessness

15, 1 At this time some Pharisees and doctors of the law from
2 Jerusalem came up to Jesus and said to him, "Why do your disciples not observe the traditions handed down from the ancient rabbis? They do not wash their hands before meals."

3 Jesus replied, "And why do you break God's commandment
4 because of your traditions? Thus, God commanded, 'Honour your father and your mother; whoever curses his father or mother must die.'

5 But you hold that whenever a man informs his father or mother, 'the support I owe to you has been made an offering to God,' he is no longer allowed to honour his father or mother.

6 So you set aside God's commandment, for the sake of your traditions.

7 Hypocrites! Well did Isaia prophesy concerning you:

'This people honours me with their lips,   8
but their hearts are far from me.
In vain do they worship me,   9
making dogmas of human enactments.' "

Then he called the people to him and said, "Listen to this and 10
understand it: it is not what goes into the mouth that causes 11
defilement, but what comes out of the mouth."

Give us thy light, forgive us what we are

The disciples then came to him and said, "Do you realize that the 12
Pharisees were shocked by your words?"
And he replied, "Any plant that has not been planted by my 13
heavenly Father will be rooted up. Pay no attention to them;
they are blind guides of the blind. When a blind man tries to 14
guide another who is blind, both end up in the ditch."

Deafened and blind, with senses yet unfound

Then Peter said to him, "Please explain the parable for us." 15
And Jesus replied, "Can it be that even you do not understand? 16
Surely you know that whatever food goes into the mouth passes 17
into the stomach and is then discharged. But what comes out of 18
the mouth has its origin in the heart, and it is this that defiles a
person.
From the heart come evil thoughts and sins of murder, adultery, 19
immorality, theft, false evidence, slander. These are what 20
defile a person; but to eat with unwashed hands does not cause
defilement."

Deep in anonymous humility

From there Jesus withdrew to the country of Tyre and Sidon. 21
And even in these remote parts there was a Canaanite woman 22
who came out to him and cried in a loud voice, "Have pity on
me, Lord, Son of David! My daughter is tormented by a demon."
But Jesus gave her no answer at all.   23
His disciples came up and began to advise him: "Send her away;
she keeps on shouting after us."

24 So Jesus said to her, "I have been sent only to the lost children of the house of Israel."

25 But she came up, flung herself at his feet, and begged him, **"Lord, help me!"**

26 And he replied, "It is not right to take the children's bread and throw it to the little puppies."

27 "True, sir," she answered, "but even the little puppies eat the scraps that fall from their masters' table."

28 At that, Jesus gave in, and said to her, "Woman, your faith is very great; what you desire shall be done."

And from that moment her daughter was cured.

'Tis stricken Man in Men that pleads with Thee

29 Jesus then left that country and came to the lake of Galilee.

30 There he climbed a hill and seated himself, while the people flocked to him and brought with them the lame, the crippled, the blind, the deaf and many other suffering people; these they laid at his feet and he healed them.

31 And the wonder of the people knew no bounds, as they saw the dumb speaking, the crippled restored, the lame walking about and the blind able to see again.

They praised the God of Israel.

Hunger and love in their variations

32 He therefore summoned his disciples and said to them, "I feel sorry for these people; they have been with me now for three days and have nothing to eat. I will not send them away hungry; they might well get weak on the way."

33 The disciples said to him, "This is a desert; how can we get enough bread here to feed such a number?"

34 "How many loaves have you?" he asked.

And they said, "Seven, and a few small fish."

35 Then he told the people to sit on the ground. Having taken the seven loaves and the fish he gave thanks; and as he broke them he passed them to the disciples, who gave them to the people.

37 When all had eaten their fill they gathered up what was left

38 and filled seven hampers. And the number of those who had eaten was four thousand, without counting women and children.

39 Having then dismissed the crowd, Jesus got into the boat and crossed to the district of Magadan.

There is not room on earth for what ye seek

16, 1 To put him to the test, the Pharisees and the Sadducees approached Jesus and asked him to call down a sign from heaven
2 as a proof to them. And he replied, "In the evening you say,
3 'We're going to have fine weather. Look at that red sky!' And in the morning, 'There'll be rain today; the sky is all red and fiery.' So you know how to interpret the signs of the weather—but not the signs of God's times!
4 An evil and unfaithful generation of men asks for a sign, but no sign will be given it, except the sign of Jona."
And he left them there and went away.

Oh send out thy light and thy truth; let them lead me

5 When the disciples had crossed to the other side they found that they had forgotten to bring bread.
6 And Jesus said to them: "Keep your eyes open, and guard against the leaven of the Pharisees and the Sadducees."
7 Thinking over this among themselves, they came to the conclusion, "It's because we brought no bread."
8 But Jesus knew their minds and said, "Why have you these misgivings in your hearts about not having bread? Have you so
9 little faith? Or do you still not understand? Can you not remember the five loaves among the five thousand, and the number of
10 baskets you took up? And the seven loaves among the four thousand, and the number of hampers you took up?
11 Why is it that you cannot see? It was not bread that I meant when I said, 'Guard against the leaven of the Pharisees and the Sadducees.' "
12 And in the end they realized that the leaven he was warning them against was not that of bread, but that of the Pharisees' and the Sadducees' teaching.

One burning hour throws light a thousand ways

13 When Jesus came to the region of Caesarea Philippi he asked his disciples, "Who do people say that the Son of Man is?"

They replied, "Some say John the Baptist; others Elia; others 14
again Jeremia or one of the Prophets."

"And what about you?" he asked. "Who do you say that I am?" 15
Simon Peter replied, "You are the Messiah, the Son of the living 16
God."

For fear she might be wilder'd in her way
Because she wanted an unerring guide

In answer Jesus said to him, "Simon, son of John, how blessed 17
you are! Human powers have not revealed it to you, but my
Father in heaven.
To you, therefore, I say: You are Peter, the Rock, and on this 18
Rock I will build my Church, and no powers of death will ever
overcome it.
I will give you the keys of the kingdom of God: whatever you 19
forbid on earth will be forbidden in heaven; whatever you allow
on earth will be allowed in heaven."

He then strictly forbade the disciples to let anyone know that he 20
was the Christ.

The eternal burden

From then on Jesus Christ began to make it clear to his disciples 21
that his divine mission would bring him to Jerusalem; that he
would have to go through great suffering at the hands of the lay
rulers, the chief priests, and the doctors of the law; that he would
be put to death, and on the third day would be raised again.

Servant of God has chance of greater sin

But Peter took him aside and began to rebuke him, "May God 22
forgive you, Lord. To think that you should suffer this—never!"
And turning to Peter Jesus said, "Get behind me, you tempter! 23
You are a pitfall to me. What you desire is not the will of God but
of men."

Set all your mind upon the steep ascent

On this occasion Jesus said to his disciples, "Any man who wants 24 to follow me must renounce himself and take up his cross and come with me.

25 The man who would save his life shall lose it; the man who loses his life for my sake shall save it.

26 For even if a person gains the whole world, **what is the advantage,** if it means losing one's true life? Or is there any price one can pay for one's life?

27 For the Son of Man will one day come with his angels in the glory of his Father, and will reward each one according to his life's work.

28 And believe me, there are some standing here who will not have died before they see the Son of Man coming in his kingdom."

The veils of Time are riven apart

17, 1 Six days after this Jesus took with him Peter, James, and his brother John, and brought them up a high mountain by them-
2 selves. He was transfigured before their eyes; his face shone like
3 the sun and his clothes became like light. And suddenly they saw Moses and Elia, talking with him.

4 Peter spoke up and said to him, "Lord, how good it is that we are here! If you please, I will set up three tents, one for you, one for Moses and one for Elia."

5 As he was speaking a bright cloud overshadowed them; and from the cloud a voice said, "This is my beloved Son, whom I have chosen; listen to him."

6 And the disciples, hearing it, fell prostrate on the ground, and
7 were in great fear. But Jesus came up and touched them: "Stand up," he said. "Do not be afraid."

8 And when they looked up they saw that he was alone.

9 As they were coming down from the mountain, he warned them, "Tell no one of what you have seen until the Son of Man has been raised from the dead."

Mark, the mark is of man's make
And the word of it Sacrificed

10 The disciples asked him, "Why is it, then, that according to the doctors of the law Elia must come first?"

11 And Jesus replied, "Yes, it is written that Elia is to come and
12 restore all things; but I tell you that Elia has already come.
They, however, did not accept him, but did to him whatever
they wanted. So too, even the Son of Man is going to suffer at
their hands."
13 Then the disciples realized that he had spoken to them about
John the Baptist.

Thou mastering me
God, giver of breath and bread

14 When they got back to the people a man came up and knelt at
15 his feet. **"Have pity on my son, sir,"** he said; "he's a bad case of
16 lunacy and often stumbles into the fire or into water. I brought
him to your disciples, but they could do nothing for him."
17 And Jesus answered, "O people of this faithless and misguided
generation, how long shall I be with you? How long shall I bear
with you?
Bring him here to me."
18 Then Jesus reprimanded him, and the evil spirit came out;
and from that moment the boy was healed.

19 Afterwards the disciples came to him and asked, "Why couldn't
we drive out the spirit?"
20 And he replied, "Because you have so little faith. I tell you, if
you had faith no greater than a tiny mustard-seed, you could
say to this mountain, 'Move away there,' and it would move.
Nothing would be impossible to you."

Doomed to go in company with pain

22 After they had been going about with him for some time in
Galilee Jesus said to his disciples, "The Son of Man will be
surrendered to human authorities; they will put him to death;
23 and on the third day he will be raised again." And his words
distressed them very much.

Love virtue, she alone is free

24 Then they came to Capharnaum and the collectors of the temple-

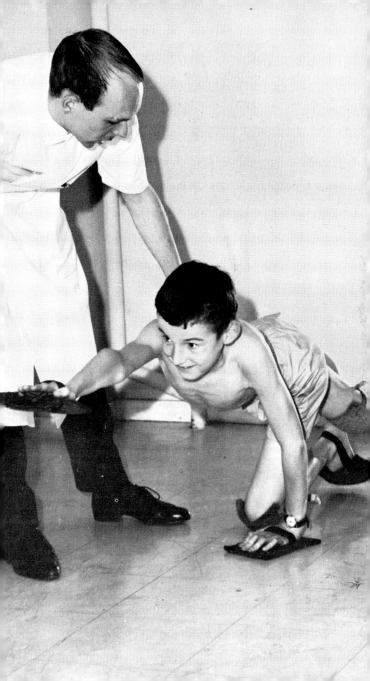

tax approached Peter and said, "Does your master not pay the temple-tax?"

Peter replied, "Yes, he does."

Later, when Peter arrived home, Jesus forestalled him and asked, 25 "What do you think, Simon? From whom do the rulers of the world get tolls and taxes—from their own citizens or from foreigners?"

"From foreigners, I should think," said Peter. 26

And Jesus said, "So the citizens are exempt. At the same time, 27 we must not give them cause for offence. Therefore go down to the lake and cast a line. If you take the first fish that comes up and open its mouth, you will find a coin in it. Bring this, and pay the tax for both of us."

Childhood is health

At this time the disciples came to Jesus and asked him, "Which 18, 1 of us is the greatest in God's kingdom?"

And Jesus, calling over a child, set him in front of them, and 2 said, "In God's name I tell you, **if you are not converted so as to become like little children** you shall not enter God's kingdom. The one who humbles himself, like this little child here, is the 4 greatest in God's kingdom; and whoever receives one such child 5 in my name, receives me.

Elegy of innocence and youth

Better that a man should have a mill-stone tied about his neck 6 and be drowned in the depths of the sea than that he cause the fall of one of these little ones who have faith in me.

Woe upon the world because of scandal and corruption! Scandals 7 there must be, but woe to any man who causes scandal.

If your hand or your foot is a danger to you, cut it off and throw 8 it away; better for you to enter life disabled or lame than to keep both hands or feet and to be thrown into eternal fire.

If your eye is a danger to you, pluck it out and throw it away; 9 better for you to enter life with one eye than to keep both eyes and to be thrown to everlasting perdition.

Whoever degrades another degrades me

10 See that you never despise one of these little ones; for I tell you, their angels in heaven have unceasing vision of my heavenly Father.

12 Suppose a man has a hundred sheep and one of them goes astray, what do you think he will do? Will he not leave the ninety-nine on the mountain-side and go after the one that strayed?

13 And if he is lucky enough to find it, believe me, he rejoices more over it than over the ninety-nine that did not stray.

14 The same too is the mind of your Father in heaven; he does not want a single one of these little ones to be lost.

There is no life that is not in community

15 If your fellow-Christian does wrong, go first and speak straight words to him in private. If he listens to you, you will have won
16 back your fellow-Christian. But if he will not listen, bring one or two others as well, so that every word may be vouched for
17 by two or three witnesses; if he pays no heed to these, bring the matter to the Church; and if he will not heed the Church treat him as a non-Christian or a public sinner.

18 Believe me, anything you forbid on earth will be forbidden in heaven; and anything you allow on earth, will be allowed in heaven.

And no community not lived in praise of GOD

19 Again, I assure you of this, that whenever two of you on earth pray together with one voice for something they need, they will
20 receive it from my heavenly Father. For wherever two or three are gathered in my name, I am there with them."

Of supernatural sympathy
Universal love and hope

21 Peter then came up and asked him, "Lord, how often shall a brother wrong me that I should still forgive him? Up to seven times?"

Jesus replied, "Not so, I tell you. Not only seven times but 22
seventy times seven—always.

God's kingdom therefore is like this: There was once a king who 23
decided to settle accounts with his servants; the bills were sent 24
out, and a debtor was brought in who owed him a hundred
millions. His employer, finding him unable to pay, ordered him 25
to be sold into slavery, with his wife, children and all his property,
so as to meet the debt. But the servant flung himself at his 26
feet and implored him, 'Be patient with me, and I will pay you
all.' And the employer had pity on that servant; he let him off, 27
and even cancelled his debt.
The same man, however, went off and discovered a workmate 28
who owed him a trifling sum of money. He caught him by the
throat and demanded, 'Pay what you owe me!' And the work- 29
mate flung himself at his feet and implored him, 'Be patient
with me and I will pay you.' But he refused and had him thrown 30
in jail, until he paid his debt.
Now when this man's colleagues saw what had happened they 31
were very incensed about it; so they went to their employer and
told him the whole story. And the employer summoned the 32
man and said to him, 'You scoundrel! I cancelled all your debt,
because you implored me. Surely you should have let off your 33
workmate, as I let you off?'
The employer therefore was very angry and gave the man over 34
to the torturers, till he would pay back all his debt.

And that is how my heavenly Father will deal with you, if you 35
do not all forgive your fellow-Christians from your heart."

Two souls with a single thought
Two hearts that beat as one

After concluding his sermon Jesus left Galilee for the borders of 19, 1
Judaea on the other side of the Jordan. Large crowds of people 2
followed him and he healed their sicknesses.
Some Pharisees came up to test him with a question: "Is it 3
lawful for a man to divorce his wife on any and every ground?"
And Jesus replied to them, "You have read in Scripture, have 4

you not, that the Creator from the very beginning made them
5 male and female, and thereby added, 'for this reason a man shall
leave his father and mother, and be so united to his wife that the
two are but one'?
6 No longer therefore are they two persons, but a single being;
and the bond that God has created may not be loosed by man."
7 "In that case," they replied, "why did Moses lay it down that
if a man divorces his wife he should certify her dismissal in
writing?"
8 Jesus replied, "If Moses allowed you to divorce your wives it
was only because of your gross disobedience; the option was not
there from the beginning.
This is what I say: Any man who divorces his wife—except
for unchastity—and marries another, commits adultery."

Grace is given of God

10 His disciples said to him, "If that is how things are between
a man and his wife, there is no sense in marrying."
11 And Jesus answered, "Not all accept this precept—only those
12 to whom the grace has been given. There are people who
cannot marry, because they are born that way; there are people
who cannot marry, because marriage has been made impossible
for them by men; and there are people who cannot marry
because **such is the choice they have made for the kingdom of
God.** Whoever can accept it, let him do so."

A friend for little children

13 On that occasion people brought him children to have him lay
his hands on them in prayer, but the disciples scolded them for it.
14 And Jesus said, "Let the children alone, and do not stop them
from coming to me; for the kingdom of God belongs to their
kind."
15 Then he laid his hands on them.
And afterwards he went away from there.

How do I love thee? Let me count the ways

16 A man came up and said to him, "Master, what good must I do
to enter eternal life?"

And Jesus said, "Why ask me 'what good'? There is only One 17
who is Goodness itself. If you desire to enter eternal life, keep the
commandments."

"Which ones?" asked the man.   18

And Jesus replied, "Do not murder, do not commit adultery,
do not steal, do not give false witness, honour your father and 19
mother, love your fellow-man as yourself."

The young man answered, "All these I have kept. What else 20
must I do?"

And Jesus said to him, "If you want to be perfect, go and sell 21
everything you own. Give the money to the poor, and you will
have riches in heaven; then come and follow me."

And on hearing these words the young man went away in 22
sorrow, for he was very wealthy.

And offers, for short life, eternal liberty

Jesus said to his disciples, "Believe me, it is extremely difficult 23
for a wealthy person to enter the kingdom of God. Again I say, 24
it is easier for a camel to pass through the eye of a needle than for
a wealthy person to enter the kingdom of God."

The disciples were utterly astonished at his reply. "Who then 25
can be saved?" they asked.

But Jesus looked at them and said, "For mere men such is 26
impossible; but for God all things are possible."

The Lord is my chosen portion and my cup

Peter then spoke up and said to him, "See now, we have given up 27
all things in order to follow you; what return shall we get?"

And Jesus replied, "In God's name I tell you, in the coming age 28
of renewal, when the Son of Man sits on his throne as supreme
Judge, you who have followed me will sit on thrones as judges
of the twelve tribes of Israel.

Everyone who for my sake has given up home, or brothers, or 29
sisters, or father, or mother, or children, or lands, will be
richly rewarded, and will inherit eternal life.

Many of the first will be last and the last first.   30

For us there is only the trying.   The rest is not our business

20, 1 For this is how it is with God's kingdom: There was once a farmer who went out early one morning to hire workers for his vineyard.

2 And having agreed with the workers on the wage for the day he sent them into his vineyard.

3 Then, at about nine o'clock, he went out and saw others standing

4 around idle in the square. He said to them, 'Go into the vineyard, you too. I will give you a fair wage.'

5 So they went in.
At about twelve o'clock he went out and did the same again, and also at three o'clock.

6 And on going out about five o'clock he still found some standing around. 'Why are you standing here idle all the day?' he said to them.

7 And they replied, 'Because nobody hired us.'
So he said to them, 'Go in there, you too, to the vineyard.'

8 At the end of the day the farmer said to his foreman, 'Call in the workers and give them their pay, starting with the last and finishing with the first.'

9 So those who had been hired at five o'clock came along, and each of them received a full day's wage.

10 And when it came to the turn of those who had been hired in the morning, they thought they would receive more. But no! They too got what the others had got.

11 So they felt a grievance against the farmer, and began to complain, 'These last have only worked an hour, and yet you put

12 them on the same footing as us. And we have sweated the whole day long, even during the hottest sun.'

13 But he replied, 'Friend, I'm doing you no wrong. Did you not agree with me for what you got? So take your pay and go! If I give the last the same that I gave you, it's because I want it

15 that way. Am I not entitled to do what I like with my own money? Or is it because I am good that your mind is evil?'

16 So the last will be first and the first last.''

A path of suffering decreed

17 In view of the fact that he was going up to Jerusalem, Jesus took

78

the Twelve aside and told them privately, as they were travelling, "We are now going up to Jerusalem, where the Son of Man will 18 be surrendered to the chief priests and doctors of the law; they will sentence him to death and hand him over to the pagans to 19 be mocked, cruelly beaten, and crucified; and on the third day he will be raised to life."

Ranks, conditions, and degrees

At this time the mother of Zebedee's sons came up to him, and 20 brought her sons with her. She knelt at his feet to ask a favour. "What do you desire?" Jesus asked. 21 And she replied, "Say that these two sons of mine shall sit with you in your kingdom, the one on your right, the other on your left."

Jesus answered, "You do not know what you are asking. Can 22 you drink the cup that I am to drink?"

"We can," they replied.

And he said, "My cup of suffering you shall indeed drink. But 23 the favour of sitting at my right or my left is not mine to give; it is for those alone for whom it has been reserved by my Father." When the other ten disciples heard about this, they were very 24 angry with the two brothers.

Small to myself, to others milde

So Jesus called them to him and said, "You know that the rulers 25 of the foreign peoples govern them with an iron hand, and their overlords treat them harshly. But with you it is different. Who- 26 ever wants to be great among you must be the servant of all; whoever wants to be the first among you must be the slave of 27 all.

For the Son of Man too has not come to be served, but to serve 28 and to give his life in sacrifice for all."

I have been blind, and now my eyes can see

As they left Jericho a large crowd was following with him. 29 Two blind men were sitting by the roadside; and when they 30

79

learned that Jesus was passing by, they shouted out, "Lord, Son of David, have pity on us!"

31 The people warned them to hold their tongues.
But they shouted all the more, "Lord, Son of David, have pity on us!"

32 So Jesus stopped and called out to them, "What do you want me to do for you?"

33 And they replied, "Please, Lord, that we may get our sight back."

34 Moved to pity, Jesus touched their eyes and immediately they could see again.
And they followed with him.

Peace above all earthly dignities

21, 1 By now they were approaching Jerusalem. When they reached Bethphage on the Mount of Olives, Jesus sent ahead two of his

2 disciples and said to them, "Go into the village there in front of you and as you enter it you will find a donkey tethered, along

3 with her foal. Untie them and bring them to me. If anyone questions you about it, tell him the Lord needs them and he will let them go at once."

4 This took place to bring about what the prophet had foretold:

5 'Tell the daughter of Sion:
See, your King is coming to you,
humbly riding on a donkey,
and on the foal of a beast of burden.'

6 The disciples went off and followed his instructions; they brought the donkey and her foal and flung their coats on them; and Jesus mounted.

O barefoot King held nothing worth

8 There was a large crowd. Many of them spread their coats on the road; others cut branches from the trees and laid them along it.

9 And all the people—those who led in front of Jesus and those who followed behind—shouted out:
"Greeting to the Son of David!

A blessing on him who comes in the name of the Lord!
Greeting from heaven above!"
As he rode into Jerusalem the whole city was in a ferment. 10
Everyone was asking, "Who is this?"
And the people replied, "This is the prophet, Jesus, from 11
Nazareth in Galilee."

An unweeded garden that grows to seed

On entering the temple-area Jesus drove out the traders who 12
were buying and selling in the holy place; he overturned the
tables of the money-changers and the seats of the pigeon-sellers.
And he said to them:
"It is written in Scripture, 'My house shall be called a house of 13
prayer.' But you make it a hide-out for thieves."

And I cried, once, to God, as a child cries

Blind and lame people also came to him in the temple and he 14
healed them. When the chief priests and doctors of the law saw 15
the extraordinary things he did and heard the children crying
out in the temple, "Greeting to the Son of David!" they became
indignant. "You hear what they are saying?" they said to him.
And Jesus replied, "Yes. Have you not read the words of 16
Scripture: 'Children and infants at the breast you have taught
to sing your praises'?"
Then he left them and went out from the city to Bethany, 17
where he spent the night.

Now I know what was wanting in my youth

On his way back to the city early next morning he felt hungry. 18
So when he saw a fig-tree by the road-side he went over to it, 19
but he found nothing on it except leaves. He said to it, "Let there
never be fruit from you again."
And the fig-tree withered on the spot.
The disciples were astonished and said to him, "How is it that 20
the fig-tree withered on the spot?"
And Jesus replied, "Believe me, if you have faith—unwavering 21

81

faith—not only will you do as I have done to the fig-tree; even if you say to this mountain, 'be lifted and thrown into the sea', it shall be done.

22 Whatever you ask for in prayer, you shall receive—if you have faith."

Our dishonest mood of denial

23 When he entered the temple some of the chief priests and elders of the people approached him as he was teaching and asked, "What authority have you to do these things? Who gave you this authority?"

24 Jesus replied, "I too have a question for you, and if you answer me I will let you know by what authority I act as I do: Was the baptism of John from God or from men?"

25 So they began to talk it over among themselves, "Shall we say it was from God? But he will ask, 'Why did you not put faith

26 in him?' Or shall we say it was from men? But then we must fear the people; for the people all hold John to have been a prophet."

27 They replied therefore, "We do not know."
And he said, "Neither will I let you know by what authority I do these things."

The readiness is all

"But what do you think of this?" he asked.

28 "A man had two sons. He went first to the elder and said, 'Son, go out and work today in my vineyard.'

29 And the son replied, 'Certainly, sir!'—but he did not go.
Then he turned to the other and asked the same of him.

30 And he said, 'I won't go!'
But he was sorry afterwards, and went.

31 Now which of the two sons obeyed his father's will?"
"The second," they replied.
And Jesus said, "Believe me, public sinners and fallen women

32 will get to the kingdom of God before you. When John came to you preaching the will of God, it was not you who put faith in him, but the public sinners and the fallen women. And yet, even with their example, you did not later change heart and put faith in him.

Love and Pity both are dead

Listen to another parable: A landlord once planted a vineyard. 33
He fenced it with a wall, and dug a wine-press in it, and built a
watch-tower, and then leased his vineyard to tenants and went
abroad.

When harvest-time came round he sent his servants to the tenants 34
to collect his share of the harvest.

But the tenants laid hold of the servants; one they whipped, 35
another they murdered, another they stoned.

Next time the landlord sent an even greater number of servants; 36
but the tenants treated them all in the same way.

So at the end he sent them his own son; he said to himself, 37
'They will respect my son.'

But the tenants, when they saw the son coming, decided on their 38
plan: 'This is the heir! Here's our chance to kill him, and the
property will be ours.'

So they seized him, threw him out of the vineyard and killed him. 39
Now what do you think? When the owner of the vineyard 40
comes, how will he deal with those tenants?"

Except the Lord build the house

They said to him, "He will destroy those scoundrels and give his 41
vineyard to other tenants, who will pay him his rent when it is
due."

And Jesus said to them, "Have you not read in Scripture: 42
'The stone rejected by the builders,
has itself become the foundation-stone.
This is the Lord's doing;
our eyes can hardly believe it.'?

Therefore, I tell you, God's kingdom will be taken from you and 43
given to a people who produce the fruits demanded by it.

Anyone who falls on this stone will be broken; and anyone on 44
whom it falls will be crushed."

The timeless end, you never knew,
The peace that lay, the light that shone

And the chief priests and Pharisees, hearing his parables, knew 45
that he was referring to themselves.

46 But, while they would have liked to arrest him, they were afraid of the people; for the people looked on him as a prophet.

Thou preparest a table before me

22, 1 Speaking once again in a parable, Jesus said to them:

2 "The kingdom of God is like a king who gave a banquet for his
3 son's wedding and sent out his servants to summon all who had been invited to the feast.

But they refused to come.

4 So he sent out more servants, and told them to tell the invited guests, 'Look, I have everything prepared for this dinner; my steers and fatted animals have all been slaughtered and everything is ready. So come to the wedding.'

And a time comes when a man is afraid to grow

5 But they were not interested. They went their various ways:
6 one to his farm, another to his business, while others seized his servants, outraged them, and even killed them.

7 And the king was furious; he sent his troops, destroyed those murderers, and burnt their city.

To have known him, to have loved him
After loneness long

8 Then he said to his servants, 'Here we are with a dinner ready,
9 and the invited guests have all been discredited. Therefore go out to the road-crossings and invite to my banquet any people you may find.'

10 So the servants went out on the roads and brought in all they could find, bad as well as good.

And the dining-hall was filled with guests.

The undone years

11 Afterwards the king went into his dining-hall to have a look at the guests and saw there a man who was not properly dressed for a wedding.

84

'Friend,' he said to him, 'how dare you come in here without 12 being dressed for a wedding?'

But the man had nothing to say.

So the king gave orders to the attendants, 'Bind him hand and 13 foot, and throw him out in the dark; there, I tell you, will be the wailing and anguish of remorse!'

For that is how it is: many are called; few are chosen." 14

All is Caesar's; and what odds
So long as Caesar's self is God's

The Pharisees then went off and decided on a plan by which 15 they hoped to snare him.

They sent a delegation of their disciples and some followers of 16 Herod who said to him, "Master, we know that you are an honest man and teach God's way as it really is; you do not bow to public opinion, since you are not the kind who plays up to important folk.

What do you think? Is it right to pay tax to the Roman emperor 17 or not?"

But Jesus knew what was behind it. "How clever!" he said. 18 "So you would trap me? May I see the coin of the tax?" 19 And they brought him a coin.

"Whose is this image?" he asked, "and whose is the name 20 inscribed?"

They replied, "Caesar's." 21

"Give then to Caesar what is Caesar's," he said, "and to God what is God's."

And they were so dumbfounded by his answer that they left 22 him and went away.

All losses are restored and sorrows end

That same day a party of Sadducees—the people who hold there 23 is no resurrection—came to him with this question: "Master, 24 Moses laid it down that if a man dies without children his brother should marry the widow and raise up a family to the dead man. Now we once had seven brothers among us. The first of them 25 married and died, and having no children left the wife for his

26 brother; and the same happened in the case of the second and
27 third and the rest of the seven. Last of all the wife died.
28 Now in your opinion which of the seven will have her as wife
in the life after resurrection, since they had all married her?"
29 Jesus replied, "You are in error, knowing neither the Scriptures
30 nor the power of God. In the life after resurrection men and
women do not marry; they are like angels in heaven.
31 As for the resurrection from the dead, have you not read the word
32 that God spoke to you: 'I am the God of Abraham, the God of
Isaac, and the God of Jacob'? Therefore, he is not a God of the
dead but of the living."
33 And the people who heard all this were astounded at his teaching.

The sum of all law

34 On learning that he had silenced the Sadducees the Pharisees
gathered round again.
35 And one of them, a doctor of the law, put him a leading ques-
36 tion: "Master," he asked, "which is the greatest commandment
of the law?"
37 Jesus replied: "You shall love the Lord your God with all your
heart, and all your soul, and all your mind.
38 This is the greatest and most important commandment of all.
39 And the second is similar: **You shall love your fellow-man as
yourself.**
40 On these two commandments, as on two hinges, hangs the whole
of the law and the Prophets."

I will be his Father, and he shall be my son

41 Then, as the Pharisees were still assembled, Jesus put this ques-
42 tion to them: "What is your view concerning the Messiah?
Whose son is he to be?"
They replied, "David's."
43 "How is it, then," he asked, "that the inspired David calls him
Lord? For David says,
44 'The Lord said to my Lord:
Sit at my right hand,
Until I lay your enemies under your feet.'

45 How can the Messiah be David's son if David calls him 'Lord'?"
46 And not one of them could answer him.

From that day on none of them dared to ask him any more questions.

Their purpose is ambition,
their practice onely hate

23, 1 Speaking then to the people and to his disciples Jesus said, "The doctors of the law and the Pharisees occupy the chair of
3 Moses; therefore you must carry out everything they teach you. But you are not to follow the example of their deeds; for the
4 Pharisees do not practise what they preach. They pile up heavy burdens and place them on men's shoulders, but will not lift a finger to move these burdens themselves.
5 All their actions are for the admiration of the public: they enlarge their prayer-lockets and wear their fringes extra wide;
6 they like to have the top places at the banquets and first seats in
7 the synagogues; they like to be greeted respectfully in the streets and to be hailed with the title 'Master'.

Stamped with the image of the King

8 But you must not be called 'Master'; for One alone is your Master, and you are all brothers.
9 And you must not call any one of yours on earth 'Father'; for One alone is your Father—the One in heaven.
10 And you must not be called 'Guide'; for your Guide is Christ.
11 The greatest among you shall be your servant.
12 Whoever exalts himself shall be humbled; whoever humbles himself shall be exalted.

Self-school'd, self-scann'd

13 Woe to you, doctors of the law and Pharisees, hypocrites! You shut men out from the kingdom of God; you do not enter yourselves and those who are on the way to entering you prevent.
15 Woe to you, doctors of the law and Pharisees, hypocrites! You go round land and sea in your quest for a single convert; and when he has taken the step you put him on the road to perdition even more surely than yourselves.

Woe to you, blind guides! You hold that to swear by the temple 16
does not count, but to swear by the gold in the temple carries
obligation.

Blind fools! Which is the more important: the gold or the temple 17
that consecrates the gold?

You hold that to swear by the altar does not count, but to swear 18
by the offering on the altar carries obligation.

What blindness! For which is the more important, the offering, 19
or the altar that consecrates the offering?

Therefore, to swear by the altar is to invoke not only the altar 20
but the offering laid upon it.

To swear by the temple is to invoke not only the temple but the 21
One who dwells in it.

To swear by heaven is to invoke not only God's throne but God 22
himself.

Woe to you, doctors of the law and Pharisees, hypocrites! You 23
pay tithes of garden herbs and vegetables, but neglect the
weighty obligations of the law: right and mercy and faith. These
it was your duty to observe, whatever about the rest.

Blind guides! You strain out the flies, but swallow the camel. 24

Woe to you, doctors of the law and Pharisees, hypocrites! You 25
polish clean the outside of cup and dish, while the inside reeks
of robbery and insatiable greed.

O blind Pharisee! Cleanse first the inside of the cup, and then 26
the outside will be clean as well.

Woe to you, doctors of the law and Pharisees, hypocrites! You 27
resemble white-washed tombs: outside they look spick-and-span;
inside they are full of dead bones and rottenness.

The same with you: outside you appear to be holy men; inside 28
you are full of deceit and rebelliousness.

Woe to you, doctors of the law and Pharisees, hypocrites! You 29
build the monuments to the prophets and adorn the tombs of
the saints. You say, 'If we were living at the time of our ancestors 30
we wouldn't have taken part in the killing of the prophets.'

And you give yourselves away as the sons of those who murdered 31
the prophets.

32 Go on then to complete the work of your ancestors! You serpents! You brood of vipers! How can you escape the judgement of damnation?

Have I not reason to lament
What man has made of man?

34 Yes, I even send you prophets, wise men, and teachers, and to what effect? Some of them you will murder and crucify; others you will have flogged in your synagogues and hunted from town
35 to town. So that all the innocent blood shed on earth from the days of the righteous Abel to the days of Zacharia, the son of Barachia, whom you murdered between the temple and the altar of sacrifice—all of it will come upon you.
36 In God's name I tell you, all of it will come upon the men of this generation.

The pangs of despised love

37 Jerusalem, O city of Jerusalem, who kill the prophets and stone the men whom God sends to you, how often have I longed to gather your children, as a hen gathers her chickens under her wings; but you refused.
38 And therefore, 'your house will be abandoned.' For I tell you, after this you will not see me again, until you exclaim, 'Blessed he who comes in the name of the Lord!' "

When the earth totters and all its inhabitants

24, 1 Jesus then left the temple. And as he was going along his disciples gathered round to draw his attention to the temple buildings.
2 He said in reply: "You see all these? Believe me, not a stone will be left upon a stone. All will be torn asunder."

And the nations do but murmur, snarling at each other's heels

3 He was sitting at the summit of the Mount of Olives when his disciples came to him alone and asked him, "Tell us when is all

this to happen? And what will be the sign of your coming and of the end of the world?"

Jesus replied, "Take care that you are not led astray; for many 4 will come claiming my name and saying, 'I am the Messiah', and will lead many astray. A time will come when you will hear 6 noises of war, and rumours of war; but do not panic. All this must inevitably happen; it does not mean that the end has come. Nation will rise against nation, kingdom against kingdom; there 7 will be famines and earthquakes in many places. But so far the 8 birth-pangs of the new era are only beginning.

Hurrying with the modern crowd, as eager and fickle as any

Then they will abandon you to the worst, and put you to death; 9 and you will be hated by all peoples, because of my name. Then 10 too large numbers will fall away from God, and will betray one another, and hate one another. False prophets will appear in 11 plenty and will lead many astray.

And with the spread of rebellion against God, the love of many 12 will grow cold; but the man who holds out to the end will be 13 saved. This gospel of the kingdom will by then have been 14 preached throughout the whole world, so that all the peoples will bear responsibility. And then the end will come.

Freedom, free to slay herself, and dying while they shout her name

When therefore you see what the prophet Daniel predicted as 15 the 'desecrating horror' standing in the holy place (if the reader but mark it well!), the day will have come for the people of 16 Judaea to escape to the mountains. Any man who is on the roof 17 of his house, let him not come down looking for anything inside; any man who is working outside on his farm, let him not turn 18 back to pick up his coat.

And alas for women with child, or with infants at the breast, 19 when those days come!

You must therefore pray that your flight will not be in winter- 20 time or on the sabbath. For this will be a time of great affliction, 21 the like of which has never been before, since the world began, and never will be again. Indeed, if those days had not been cut 22 short, no man would be saved; but for the sake of God's chosen ones, those days will be cut short.

23 If people come running to tell you then, 'the Messiah is here!'
24 or 'the Messiah is there!' do not believe them. For false Messiahs will appear and false prophets; and they will work signs and portents, so as to deceive—if that were possible—even God's chosen ones.
25 Remember! I have forewarned you. So if they say to you, 'he is out there in the desert', do not go; or if they say to you, 'he is hidden inside', do not believe it.
27 For as the lightning-flash shines from the east to the west, so it will be at the coming of the Son of Man.
28 Wherever the corpse lies, there gather the vultures.

Chaos, Cosmos! Cosmos, Chaos! who can tell how all will end?

29 Immediately after the affliction of those days the sun will be darkened, the moon will lose its light, the stars will fall from heaven, and the heavenly bodies will be shaken.
30 Then the sign of the Son of Man will appear in the sky; and all the tribes of the earth will wail in remorse, when they see the Son of Man coming in the clouds of heaven, in power and great splendour.
31 At the sound of a mighty trumpet he will send out his angels, and they will assemble his chosen ones from the four corners of the world, from one end of heaven to the other.

Swayed by vaster ebbs and flows than can be known to you or me

32 Learn a lesson from the fig-tree: When its branches grow tender and its leaves begin to sprout, you know that the summer is near.
33 So too, when you see all these things happen, let it be known to you that the judge is already at the gates.
34 Believe me, the present generation will not have passed away
35 before all these things come to pass. Heaven and earth shall pass away; my words shall not pass away. Nevertheless, no one knows
36 of that day or the hour—not even the angels in heaven, not even the Son, but only the Father.

For the coming of the Son of Man will be like the time of Noah. 37
In the days before the deluge people were eating and drinking, 38
marrying and being married, until the moment that Noah
entered the ark; and no one gave heed, until the deluge came 39
and swept them all away.
That too is how it will be at the coming of the Son of Man.
Two men will then be working in a field; one will be taken and 40
the other left. Two women will be grinding flour at a mill; one 41
will be taken and the other left.
Therefore stay awake; for the day of your Lord's coming you 42
do not know.
But you know this much, that if the master of the house knew 43
the hour of the night when the thief was coming, he would stay
awake and would not allow his house to be robbed.
Therefore you too must stand ready, because the Son of Man 44
will come at a time when you least expect him.

This is the next moment. This is the beginning

Who do you think is a reliable and careful servant? Whom does 45
the master put in charge of his household to distribute food at
the right time? Happy that servant if his master finds him doing 46
his duty when he comes!
Believe me, he will put him in charge of all his property. 47
But if that servant thinks to himself, 'My master won't be back 48
for a while yet!' If he starts striking his fellow-servants, or having 49
a good time with drunkards, then his master will come on a day, 50
and at an hour, when he is not expected. He will have him flogged 51
and will throw him out with the hypocrites; and there, I tell
you, will be the wailing and anguish of remorse!

We do not pass twice through the same door

On that day God's kingdom will be like the ten bridesmaids who 25, 1
went out with their lamps to meet the bridegroom; five of them 2
were foolish and five prudent. Whereas the five foolish, in bring- 3
ing their lamps, did not take oil with them, the five prudent 4
brought containers of oil along with their lamps.
Then the bridegroom was delayed and the bridesmaids all got 5
tired and fell asleep.

6 But in the middle of the night there was a cry, 'Here comes the bridegroom! Go out and meet him.'

7 So all the bridesmaids got up and prepared their lamps; and the foolish ones said to the others: 'Give us some of your oil; our lamps are going out.'

9 But they replied 'We cannot; there won't be enough for all of us. Better go to the shops and buy some for yourselves.'

10 So they went off to buy oil. And while they were gone the bridegroom arrived. Those who were ready went in with him to the wedding feast, and the door was closed.

11 When the others arrived it was too late, and they called out, 'Please, Lord, please open to us.'

12 But he replied, 'Why, I don't even know you!'

13 Stay awake, therefore, because you have no idea of the day or the hour.

So in this perilous grace of God
With all my sins go I

14 Or again: A man who was going abroad summoned his servants in order to give over his money to them. Dividing it according

15 to the ability of each, he gave fifty thousand to one, twenty thousand to another, and five thousand to another. Then he left the country.

16 And the man who got fifty thousand immediately started working on it and made another fifty thousand in profit.

17 So too, the man with twenty thousand made another twenty.

18 But the one who got five thousand went out and dug a hole in the ground and hid away his master's money.

19 Then after a long time the master of those servants came back and wanted to know how they had got on.

20 The one who had got the fifty thousand brought along fifty thousand more. 'Sir,' he said, 'you gave me fifty thousand; here now are fifty thousand more which I have made in profit.'

21 And his master said to him, 'Well done! Here's a man who does a good and honest job. You have proved yourself in these little things, so I will place you over many. Go in there and share in your Lord's feast.'

Then came the man with the twenty thousand. 'Sir,' he said, 22 'you gave me twenty thousand; here now are twenty thousand more which I have made in profit.'

And his master said to him, 'Well done! Here's another who 23 does a good and honest job. You have proved yourself in these little things, so I will place you over many. Go in there and share in your Lord's feast.'

Then came the man who had received the five thousand. 'Sir,' 24 he said, 'I knew you to be a hard man. You reap without having planted, and you gather without having scattered. So I was 25 afraid, and I went and hid your five thousand in a hole in the ground. Here now—you have what is yours.'

His master replied, 'You are a useless, lazy fellow. You knew 26 that I reap without having planted, and gather without having scattered. Why, then, your duty was to invest my money in the 27 banks; and on my return I should have got it back with interest. Take that five thousand away from him and give it to the man 28 with the fifty thousand!'

For the more one has, the more one will be given—and plenty 29 of it; whoever has next-to-nothing will lose even the little he has. As for that useless servant, throw him out in the dark; and there, 30 I tell you, will be the wailing and anguish of remorse!

Naught shelters thee, who wilt not shelter Me

When the Son of Man comes in his glory, and all the angels with 31 him, he will sit on his throne as Judge. All the peoples will be 32 assembled before him and he will sort them out, as a shepherd divides the sheep from the goats; the sheep he will put on his 33 right and the goats on his left.

Then the king will say to those on his right, 'Come you chosen 34 of my Father and possess the kingdom prepared for you since the creation of the world. For I was hungry and you gave me to eat; 35 I was thirsty and you gave me to drink; I was a stranger and you welcomed me, naked and you clothed me, sick and you looked 36 after me; I was in prison and you visited me.'

And these good and holy people will ask in reply, 'Lord, when 37 did we see you hungry that we gave you to eat, or thirsty that we gave you to drink? When did we see you a stranger that we wel- 38

39 comed you, or naked that we clothed you? When did we see you sick or in prison, that we visited you?'

40 And the king will reply, **'Believe me, since you did it for one of these brothers of mine—even the least—you did it for me.'**

41 Then he will turn to those on his left and say, 'Go away from me, you reprobate people, to the everlasting fire prepared for the
42 devil and his angels. For you did not give me to eat when I was
43 hungry; you did not give me to drink when I was thirsty; you did not welcome me when I was a stranger; you did not clothe me when I was naked; you did not visit me when I was sick or in prison.'

44 They will ask him, 'Lord, when did we see you hungry, or thirsty, or a stranger, or naked, or sick, or in prison, that we did not come to your help?'

45 And he will say, 'Believe me, since you refused it to one of these —even the least—you refused it to me.'

46 So these will go to everlasting punishment, and the righteous to everlasting life.''

A certain convocation

26, 1 When Jesus had finished this sermon he said to his disciples,
2 "You know that the paschal feast begins in two days time and the Son of Man will be given over to enemies and crucified.''
3 The chief priests and the elders of the people held a meeting in
4 the palace of the high priest, whose name was Caiphas. They
5 discussed a scheme to have Jesus arrested and killed, but decided: "Not during the festival, lest the people start a riot.''

A woman like that is misunderstood.
I have been her kind

6 Now while Jesus was dining at Bethany in the house of Simon,
7 a former leper, a woman came up with an alabaster flask of very expensive perfume and poured it on his head.
8 On seeing this the disciples were indignant. "Why this waste?''
9 they said. "This perfume could have been sold at a high price and the money given to the poor.''

10 But Jesus noticed it and said to them, "Do you have to be unkind
11 to her? This is a fine thing she has done for me. The poor you
12 have with you always, but not me. Her pouring this perfume on
my body was intended for my burial.
13 I tell you, therefore, wherever the gospel is preached in the whole
world, what she has done will also be told in remembrance of her."

Flawed priest

14 At this point one of the Twelve called Judas Iscariot went to the
15 chief priests and asked them, "How much will you give me, and
I will betray him to you?"
They settled with him for thirty pieces of silver.
16 And from then on Judas was on the look-out for a suitable
occasion to betray him.

Through the days that He wrought, till the day that He stayed

17 On the first day of the feast of the unleavened bread the disciples
came to Jesus and asked, "Where do you wish us to prepare for
you to eat the paschal lamb?"
18 And he replied, "Go to our friend in the city and say to him,
'The Master sends this message: My time is drawing near; I
am going to celebrate the pasch with my disciples in your
house.' "
19 The disciples followed his instructions and prepared the paschal
meal.

Am I the man?

20 Late in the evening he sat at table with the Twelve. And during
the meal he said to them, "In God's name I tell you, one of you
is going to betray me."
22 They were very distressed and began to say, every one of them,
'Surely not I, Lord?'
23 He replied, "My betrayer is one who puts his hand with mine
24 in the common dish. The Son of Man must go his way, so that
everything about him in Scripture may come to pass. But woe
to the man by whom he is betrayed! It would have been better
for that man not to have been born."

Then Judas, the traitor, asked, "Am I the one, Master?"   25
And Jesus replied, "You say it."

Still do I love, still shed my blood for thee

During the meal, after he had taken bread in his hands and 26
spoken the blessing, Jesus broke it and gave it to his disciples:
"Take and eat it," he said, "this is my body."
He took the cup, gave thanks, and passed it to them with these 27
words: "Let all of you drink from it; for this is my blood of the 28
covenant, to be shed for all men for the forgiveness of sins.
I tell you, never again shall I drink this wine of the grape, until 29
that day when I drink it with you new in the kingdom of my
Father."

Back to where he started from, alone

Afterwards they sang the hymn and went out to the Mount of 30
Olives.
And Jesus said to them, "Tonight all of you will fall away 31
because of me. For Scripture says, 'I will strike the shepherd and
the sheep of the flock will be scattered.'
But after my resurrection I will go on before you to Galilee." 32
Peter replied, "The others may fall away because of you—but 33
not I. I shall never fall."
And Jesus said to him, "Believe me, before the cock crows 34
to-night, you will deny me three times."
Peter replied to him, "Even if I have to die with you, I will not 35
deny you." And the other disciples were equally confident.

The chalice of the grapes of God

Then Jesus came with them to a place called Gethsemane and 36
said to his disciples, "Sit here, while I go over there and pray."
He took Peter and the two sons of Zebedee along with him; and 37
he began to suffer an agony of grief and anguish. "My heart is 38
breaking with grief," he said to them. "Stay here and keep watch
with me."
Then he went forward a little and fell prostrate on the ground. 39

99

And he prayed in these words, "My Father, if it is possible, spare me this cup of suffering; but let your will be done, not mine."

40 Returning to the disciples he found them asleep and said to
41 Peter, "Could you not stay awake for one hour? Stay awake and pray that you escape trial; the spirit is willing, but the flesh is weak."

42 Then he went back and prayed a second time. "My Father," he said, "if I cannot be spared this cup of suffering, but must drink it, let your will be done."

43 And on his return he again found them asleep, for their eyes had closed from weariness.

44 So he left them and went back again to pray for a third time as he had done before.

45 At the end he came to his disciples and said, "So you still sleep and take your rest? But now the time has come. The Son of Man
46 is to be surrendered to evil men. Rise! We must go. My betrayer is already here."

Judas dost thou betray me with a kiss?

47 As he was speaking Judas arrived, one of the Twelve, and with him a large band of men, armed with swords and clubs; they had been sent by the chief priests and the elders of the people.
48 The traitor had arranged a signal: "The man whom I shall kiss is the one. Arrest him."
49 So without delay he came up to Jesus to say, "Greeting, Master!" and he kissed him.
50 Jesus replied, "Friend, do what you are here for."

We would rather die in our dread
Than climb the cross of the moment

The others then came forward, arrested Jesus, and held him.
51 At that one of those in the company of Jesus reached for his sword and drew it; he struck the high priest's servant and cut off his ear.
52 But Jesus said to him, "Put your sword back where it was. Those

who take to the sword perish by the sword. Do you suppose that 53 I am helpless? Or that if I asked my Father he would not send me more than a dozen armies of angels? But how then could the 54 Scriptures come to pass, which ordain these things?"

As darker grows the night

Jesus said to the crowd, "Am I a common criminal that you 55 come with swords and clubs to arrest me?
Every day I sat teaching in the temple, and you did not arrest me. 56 But all this has taken place that the Scriptures may be fulfilled."
Then the disciples all left him and ran away.

Mine own deare people cry, Away! Away!

Having arrested Jesus they brought him to the high priest 57 Caiphas, with whom the doctors of the law and the elders of the people sat in council.
Peter followed him, at some distance behind. On reaching the 58 high priest's palace he went inside and sat there with the servants to see how things would go.
Meanwhile, the chief priests and the whole council were looking 59 for some kind of evidence against Jesus to warrant a death-sentence; but they found none, although many witnesses came 60 forward.
Finally, two came forward and said, "This man once affirmed, 'I 61 can destroy the temple of God and in three days build it again.' "
The high priest stood up and asked him, "Have you nothing to 62 say? What is this charge they bring against you?"
But Jesus did not answer.
Then the high priest said to him, "I put you under oath by the 63 ever-living God that you tell us whether you are the Messiah, the Son of God."
Jesus replied, "You have said the words. And I tell you, here- 64 after you will see the Son of Man sitting at the right hand of God and coming in the clouds of heaven."
At that, the high priest tore his robes and said, "He has blas- 65 phemed! Do we need any more witnesses? You have just heard blasphemy. What do you think?"
And the judges replied, "He deserves to die." 66

67 Then they spat in his face and hit him with their fists. Others
68 struck him with a stick and called out to him, "Prophesy to us,
Messiah, who it was that struck you!"

This is the porcelain clay of humankind

69 Meanwhile Peter was sitting outside in the courtyard when a
young servant-girl came up and said, "You too were a friend of
Jesus the Galilean."
70 But Peter denied it before them all, "I don't know what you are
talking about."
71 Then he went out to the entrance where another girl saw him
and said to the bystanders, "Here's one who was a friend of
Jesus the Nazarene."
72 But Peter denied it again, and swore that he never knew the man.
73 And a little later those who were standing around came up to
Peter and said, "Of course you belong to them! Your very accent
gives you away."
74 But Peter began to curse and swear, "I tell you, I don't know
the man."
75 The cock crew at that very moment; and Peter recalled the
words spoken by Jesus: "Before the cock crows you will deny
me three times."
He went outside and wept bitter tears.

All who hate me whisper together about me

27, 1 Early next morning the chief priests and elders of the people
2 decided their plan for the execution of Jesus. They led him away
bound and handed him over to Pilate, the Roman governor.

Then Judas cried out and fled
Forth into the night

3 His betrayer Judas, when he saw that he had been condemned,
was seized with remorse and brought back the thirty pieces of
4 silver to the chief priests and the elders. "I have sinned," he
said, "in betraying an innocent man."
But they replied, "It's not our concern. Look to it yourself."
5 Then, flinging the silver pieces on the floor of the temple, he
went off out and hanged himself.

6 And the priests, taking up the silver, said to one another, "This is blood-money; it cannot be given into the sacred treasury."

For thirty pence he did my death devise

7 They decided therefore on a plan; they bought with the silver a plot called the 'potter's field', to be a burial place for strangers.
8 And that is why the place is called 'Blood-acre' to this day.
9 Thus the prophecy of Jeremia came true: 'They took the thirty pieces of silver, the price set on the man as it was estimated by
10 the Israelites, and used them to buy the potter's field, as the Lord directed me.'

I have become like a broken vessel

11 Jesus was then brought before the governor; and Pilate asked him, "Are you the king of the Jews?"
He replied, "As you say."
12 But to all the charges brought against him by the chief priests and the elders he gave no answer.
13 Then Pilate said to him, "Do you appreciate how grave are the charges they bring against you?"
14 But Jesus gave no reply to anything he said.
And this made the governor wonder very much indeed.

Some from fear of weakness
Some from fear of censure

15 During the festival it was the governor's custom to release a
16 prisoner whom the populace requested. A notorious prisoner called Barabbas was in custody at the time.
17 So Pilate asked the assembled people, "Which of the two do you want me to release to you: Barabbas, or Jesus, the so-called Christ?"
18 For he knew that he had been handed over out of spite.

I have suffered in a dream because of him

19 Meanwhile, as Pilate was sitting in court, his wife sent this message to him: "Have nothing to do with that innocent man. Last night he troubled me very much in a dream."

I will content the people as I can
And give up these to them : Behold the man!

However, the chief priests and the elders persuaded the people 20
to ask for the release of Barabbas and the execution of Jesus.
So when the governor addressed them and said: "Which of the 21
two do you want me to release to you?" they replied:
"Barabbas!"
Pilate asked, "What am I to do with Jesus, the so-called Christ?" 22
And they all cried out, "Have him crucified!"
"What wrong has he done?" asked Pilate. 23
But they shouted all the more, "Have him crucified!"

Men wash their hands in blood, as best they can
I find no fault in this just man

Pilate saw that he was getting nowhere, that rabble-law was in 24
fact prevailing. So he got water and washed his hands before the
whole crowd: "To let you see," he said, "that I have no part in
the shedding of this man's blood; it's your concern."
And the whole populace answered back, "His blood be on us 25
and on our children."
After that Pilate released Barabbas to them and handed Jesus 26
over to be crucified, having had him flogged.

I was wounded in the house of my friends

The governor's soldiers then took Jesus into the barracks and 27
gathered up the whole troop. They took off his clothes and 28
dressed him in a scarlet robe; and they plaited a crown of briars 29
and fixed it on his head, and put a cane in his right hand. Then
they knelt before him in mockery and called out, "Greeting to
the King of the Jews!" They spat on him; and they would take 30
the cane from his hand and strike him on the head.
When they had finished their mockery they took off the robe and 31
dressed him in his own clothes. And they led him out to crucify
him.

My pilgrimage's last mile

As they were going out they met a man from Cyrene called Simon 32
and they forced him to carry the cross of Jesus.

I am the man, I suffer'd, I was there

33 They came to a place called 'Golgotha', that is, the place of the
34 'skull', and they offered him a drink of wine seasoned with bitter
juice. He tasted it, but would not drink it.

35 Then they crucified him, and divided his garments by drawing
36 lots; and they sat down to keep guard.
37 Above his head they fixed a notice, proclaiming the cause for
which he died: "This is Jesus, the king of the Jews".

38 And along with him they crucified two criminals, one on his right
and one on his left.

39 As they passed by the cross people hurled abuse at him. Wagging
40 their heads they would say, "Look at him—the one who was to
destroy the temple and build it in three days! Why not save yourself? If you are the Son of God, come down from the cross."
41 And the chief priests also mocked him, with the doctors of the
42 law and the elders: "The man who saved others cannot save
himself," they said. "So this is the king of Israel! Let him come
43 down now from the cross and we'll believe in him. Did he trust
in God? Well, let God save him now, if he favours him. For he
44 claimed to be the Son of God." Even the criminals who were
crucified with him taunted him in the same way.

In darkest night

45 From about midday until three o'clock darkness came over the
46 whole land. And about three o'clock Jesus called out in a loud
voice, *Eli, Eli, lema sabachthani*; **"My God, my God, why have
47 you forsaken me?"** On hearing it, some of those standing around
48 thought he was calling on Elia. One of them came running up,
got a sponge and filled it with vinegar, fixed it on a cane and
gave him a drink.
49 The others said, "Leave him! Let's see whether Elia comes to
save him."
50 But Jesus shouted again in a loud voice and breathed his last.

Our cold mechanic world awhile was still

51
52 Then the curtain of the temple was torn in two, from top to bottom. The earth shook, the rocks split, the graves opened up, and many of the dead saints were awakened.

53 After the resurrection of Jesus they left their graves and came into the holy city, where they appeared to many.

54 The officer and his men who were keeping guard on Jesus, when they saw the earthquake and all the rest, were seized with great fear and confessed, "This was indeed the Son of God."

Their name liveth for evermore

55
56 Several women were also present, looking on from a distance; they had accompanied Jesus from Galilee and had worked in his service. Among them were Mary of Magdala and Mary the mother of James and Joseph, and the mother of the sons of Zebedee.

57 In the evening there came a man called Joseph, a prosperous citizen of Arimathaea who had himself become a disciple of Jesus.

58
59
60 He approached Pilate to ask for the body of Jesus; and Pilate ordered it to be given to him. So Joseph took the body, wrapped it in a clean linen sheet, and laid it in a new tomb of his own which he had excavated from rock. He rolled a heavy stone against the tomb entrance and went away.

61 Mary of Magdala and the other Mary were also present, sitting opposite the tomb.

Weavings of plot and plan

62
63 The following day, after the so-called 'day of preparation', the chief priests and the Pharisees had a meeting with Pilate. They said, "We remember, sir, that while this impostor was alive he

64 said, 'After three days I will rise again.' We pray you to order a guard on the tomb until the third day; otherwise his disciples may come and steal the body and tell the people, 'he has risen

from the dead'. The final deception would then be worse than
the first."

Pilate answered them, "You have a guard. Go and make secure 65
as you know best."

So they went and made the tomb secure, sealing the entrance 66
in the presence of the guard.

He is not here. He is risen

After the sabbath rest, when dawn broke on Sunday, Mary of 28, 1
Magdala and the other Mary came to see the grave.

Suddenly there was a violent earthquake; an angel of the Lord 2
had descended from heaven, had come and rolled away the stone
and sat on it.

His face shone like lightning and his garments were white as 3
snow.

The guards had been struck down with panic at the sight, and 4
lay as if dead.

And the angel said to the women, "Have no fear! You are look- 5
ing, I know, for the one who was crucified, Jesus. But he is not 6
here; he has been raised to life, as he foretold. See here the place
where he was laid! So go quickly and tell his disciples that he 7
has been raised from the dead and is going on before them to
Galilee; there they will see him.

Remember, I have told you!"

His presence is the stillness. He
Fills the earth with wonder and mystery

Then, as they hurried away from the tomb in fear and great joy 8
and ran to tell the news to his disciples, the women were actually
met by Jesus himself. He greeted them.

And they, approaching, fell before him in homage, clasping his 9
feet. Jesus then said to them, "Do not be afraid. Go and tell my 10
brothers to leave for Galilee, where they will see me."

The oldest sins in the newest kind of ways

While the women were on their way, some of the guards went 11
ịnto the city and reported to the chief priests all that had

12 happened. These then conferred with the elders and decided
what they would do. They offered a handsome bribe to the sold-
13 iers and suggested, "Say that his disciples came at night and
14 stole the body while you were sleeping. If the rumour comes
to the governor's ears, we will have a word with him; we shall
15 see to it that you are not blamed." The soldiers accepted the
money and followed their instructions.

And the same story has been current among the Jews to this day.

And I drank life through God's own death

16 The eleven disciples made the journey to Galilee, to the moun-
17 tain appointed by Jesus; there they saw him and did him homage,
although some doubted.
18 And Jesus, coming to them, addressed them in these words:
"Supreme authority has been given me in heaven and on earth.
19 Go out, therefore, and make all the peoples of the world disciples
of mine; baptize them in the name of the Father and of the Son
20 and of the Holy Spirit, and teach them to observe all that I have
commanded you.

Never shall I cease to be with you, until the world ends."

MARK'S
ACCOUNT

This is where you start from

Here begins the gospel of Jesus Christ, the Son of God. 1, 1
In Isaia the prophet the words stand written: 2
'I am sending my messenger ahead of you,
to prepare the road before you.
Listen! A voice calls in the desert: 3
Make ready the way of the Lord;
make straight his paths.'

And make a new beginning

So John the Baptist appeared in the desert proclaiming baptism, 4
calling on men to begin a new life, so as to be freed from their
sins.
The whole country of Judaea and all the people of Jerusalem 5
went out to him; they confessed their sins and were baptized
by him in the river Jordan.

John wore a shirt of camel hair, tied at the waist with a leather 6
belt, and lived on locusts and wild honey.
And this was the message he proclaimed: "After me comes a 7
man who is stronger than I, the straps of whose shoes I am not
worthy to loose. I have baptized you with water; he will baptize 8
you with the Holy Spirit."

*His Spirit still doth move
On a new way of love*

At this time Jesus came from Nazareth in Galilee and was 9

10 baptized by John in the Jordan. As he was coming up from the water he saw the heavens torn open and the Spirit coming down
11 upon him, like a dove. And a voice from heaven said, "You are my beloved Son; you have I chosen."

'Tis well an old age is out

12 Immediately afterwards God's Spirit drove him out to the
13 desert. There he remained for forty days, being tempted by Satan and living among the wild beasts. And afterwards angels came to serve him.

And time to begin a new

14 When John had been arrested, Jesus came to Galilee and began
15 to preach the gospel of God: "The awaited time has come and the kingdom of God has drawn near; therefore begin a new life and have faith in the gospel."

With the drawing of this Love and the voice of this Calling

16 As he was walking along the lake of Galilee, he saw Simon and his brother Andrew at work with a casting-net; they were fishermen.
17 "Come with me," Jesus said to them, **"and I will make you fishers of men."**
18 And they left their nets and followed him.

19 A little further on he saw the sons of Zebedee, James and his
20 brother John, who were also in a boat fixing nets. He called them at once.
And they left their father Zebedee with the hired workers in the boat and followed him.

For I greet him the days I meet him, and bless when I understand

21 They came to the town of Capharnaum; and on the first sabbath
22 Jesus went into the synagogue and began to teach. The people were amazed at his teaching; here was one who taught with authority, unlike the doctors of the law.

There happened to be in their synagogue a man with an evil 23
spirit, who shouted out, "Leave us alone, Jesus of Nazareth! 24
Your coming means destruction for us. Well I know who you
are: God's Holy One!"

Jesus reprimanded him, "Silence! Go out frcm him!" 25

At that the unclean spirit lashed the man into a fit and then 26
came out from him with a loud shriek.

And they were all seized by a strange fear and began to ask one 27
another, "What can this be? This is new teaching. Here is one
who speaks with authority, who even commands evil spirits and
they obey him!"

Soon his name was on everybody's lips, all over the country of 28
Galilee.

These outstretched feverish hands, this restless heart

On leaving the synagogue, they went to the house of Simon and 29
Andrew, accompanied by James and John. Simon's mother-in- 30
law was in bed with a fever, so they told him about her. He 31
went to her, took her by the hand, and raised her up; the fever left
her, and she began to serve them.

In the cool of the evening, when the sun had set, they brought 32
the sick to him and all who suffered from evil spirits; the whole 33
town was gathered at the door of the house. And he healed large 34
numbers who were afflicted with diseases of every kind, and
drove out many demons; but he would not allow the demons
to talk, because they knew who he was.

'Tis not too late to seek a newer world

It was still dark in the morning when Jesus got up and went out 35
to a deserted place. He was praying there. Presently, Simon and 36
his companions went out after him and told him, when they 37
found him, **"The people are all looking for you."** But Jesus 38
replied, "Let us move on to the other villages round about. In
these too I must preach the gospel; for that is why I have come."

39 So he went round all Galilee, preaching the gospel in their synagogues and driving out demons.

The face of some strange thing that once was man

40 **A leper once came to him** and knelt at his feet, imploring his help, "If only you want to, you can heal me of my disease."

41 And Jesus had pity on him. "Yes, I do," he said, as he reached out his hand to touch him—"Be healed."

42 The man's leprosy disappeared at once and he was healed.

43 And Jesus without more ado gave him a strict warning and sent

44 him off. "See that you tell no one about it," he said. "But go at once and show yourself to the priest. Since you have been cleansed of leprosy, bring with you the offering prescribed by Moses, to certify your cure to them."

45 So the man went off. But he could not hold his tongue; everywhere he went, he had to tell the story. The result was that Jesus could not enter a town without causing a scene; he had to stay outside in country places.
And yet, people flocked to him from all over.

New freedom and new hope

2, 1 Some days later he returned to Capharnaum. And when news had got around that he was at home so many people gathered, as he preached the word to them, that there was no room even

3 at the door. A party then arrived with a cripple, who was carried

4 by four of them, and tried to bring the man up beside Jesus, but could not do so because of the crowd. So they removed some of the roof and made a hole over the place where Jesus was; then they lowered the stretcher through the hole, with the cripple lying on it.

5 And Jesus, struck by their faith, said to the cripple, "Friend, your sins are forgiven."

Where do miracles begin—or end?

6 Now there were some doctors of the law sitting around and they

7 began to ask themselves, "How can this man speak such blasphemy? Surely God alone has power to forgive sins?"

But Jesus, knowing immediately what was on their minds, said 8 to them, "Why do you think these thoughts? Which is the easier, 9 to say to the cripple, 'Your sins are forgiven', or to say, 'Stand up, take your stretcher and walk'?

But I will let you see that the Son of Man has power on earth 10 to forgive sins."

So he turned to the cripple and said, "Stand up, I tell you, take 11 your stretcher and go home."

And the man got up, picked up his stretcher immediately, and 12 walked away in the sight of everybody, so that all were utterly astounded and began to praise God, saying to themselves, "Never have we seen the like before!"

But ah for a man to arise in me!

Another time he went out by the lake-side; the people all came 13 to him and he was teaching them.

As he was going along he saw Levi, the son of Alphaeus, sitting 14 at the tax-office.

"Come with me," he said to him.

And Levi packed up and went with him,

Afterwards he was a guest at a meal in his house. And a large 15 number of tax-collectors and other outcasts were sitting at table with Jesus and his disciples. (For there were many of this kind, and they were disciples of his.)

Now when the Pharisee doctors of the law saw that Jesus was 16 eating with the sinners and the tax-collectors, they brought it to the notice of his disciples, "You see! He eats with tax-collectors and sinners."

But Jesus was listening and said, "It's not the strong who need 17 the doctor but the sick. I have not come to call the pious but men who are estranged from God."

New ways—new forms

John's disciples and the Pharisees were keeping a fast. Some 18 people therefore came to him and asked, "Why is it that the disciples of John and the Pharisees keep fasts, while yours do not?"

And Jesus replied, "Is it right for wedding-guests to fast while 19

123

they have the bridegroom with them? Surely they cannot do so while they enjoy his presence?

20 But a time will come when the bridegroom will be taken from them; and that will be the time for them to fast.

21 No one patches a piece of unshrunk cloth on an old coat, or the new patch tears away from the old cloth and a bigger hole is made.

22 No one pours new wine into old wine-skins, or the new wine will burst the skins, so that both wine and skins are lost. New wine must be poured into new skins."

Authentic humanism

23 One sabbath-day Jesus was passing through wheat-fields; and as they went along his disciples began to pluck ears of grain.

24 The Pharisees said to him, "Now look, why are they doing what is forbidden on the sabbath?"

25 And Jesus replied, "Have you never read the story of what David did in a time of need, when he and his companions were

26 hungry? How he went into the temple of God, during the time of the high priest Abiathar, and ate the holy bread laid out there, sharing it even with his companions?"

27 He added, "The sabbath was made for man, not man for the sabbath. Therefore the Son of Man is Lord even of the sabbath."

The world that was ours is a world that is ours no more

3, 1 On another occasion he went into a synagogue where there was
2 a man with a shrivelled hand; and they, in the hope of being able to accuse him, were watching him to see if he would heal him on the sabbath.

3 Jesus said to the man with the shrivelled hand, "Come out here in front."

4 And he said to them, "Which do you think is permitted on the sabbath? To do good or to do wrong? To save life or to kill?" But they would not answer.

5 Jesus looked round angrily on them, pained by their stubbornness, and said to the man, "Put out your hand."
And the moment he did so his hand was restored.

The Pharisees then went straight out and consulted with the 6
followers of Herod to see how they would destroy him.

The still, sad music of humanity

Jesus therefore went back with his disciples to the lake-side. 7
And a huge throng of people from Galilee followed him. Many
others too had heard of his wonderful deeds and came in crowds
from Judaea and Jerusalem, from Idumaea and across the 8
Jordan, and even from the country of Tyre and Sidon.
He told his disciples to have a boat ready for him because of the 9
large crowd and the danger of their crushing him. He had 10
healed so many that all who were afflicted with plagues were
crowding in on him, trying to touch him. And the unclean 11
spirits, whenever they saw him, would fall down before him and
cry out, "You are the Son of God." But Jesus warned them 12
strictly not to make him known.

And the need of a world of men for me

He went up into the hills and called to him the men of his own 13
choice, who then went out to him. And he appointed twelve 14
as his special companions, whom he would also send out to 15
proclaim the gospel and equip with authority to drive out
demons.
So he appointed the Twelve, and gave to Simon the name Peter. 16
Then James and his brother John, the sons of Zebedee, whom 17
he called Boanerges, "sons of thunder";
then Andrew and Philip, 18
Bartholomew and Matthew,
Thomas and James, the son of Alphaeus;
Thaddaeus also, and Simon the Zealot,
and Judas Iscariot, the man who later betrayed him. 19

Such a thing
Has never happened in our family

Then he came home. And the crowd gathered round once again, 20
giving them no chance even for a meal. So his own people, 21

hearing of it, came to take him in charge; for it seemed to them that he was out of his mind.

22 But there were also some doctors of the law who had come down from Jerusalem; and it was their opinion that he was possessed by Beelzebub and was driving out demons by the power of the ruler of demons.

When evil is knotted and demons fight

23 Jesus therefore called them over and gave his answer in the form
24 of parables. "How can Satan drive out Satan?" he asked. "If a
25 kingdom is divided against itself, it cannot survive; if a house is
26 divided against itself, it cannot last. And if Satan has become divided by rebelling against himself, he cannot survive; his end has come.
27 No one can enter a strong man's house and rob his property unless he first ties up the strong man. Only then will he be able to rob his house.

Desolation final

28 Believe me, all things will be forgiven to men, no matter what their sins, or the blasphemies they may utter.
29 But the man who slanders the Holy Spirit will never be forgiven; he is guilty of an everlasting sin."
30 This was because they held that he was being used by an unclean spirit.

I am my own and not my own

31 Then his mother and his brothers came and stood waiting outside while they sent someone to call him.
32 There was a crowd sitting round him, and they said to him, "Listen, your mother and your brothers are looking for you outside."
33 But he replied, "Who is my mother? And who are my brothers?"
34 He looked around on those who were sitting in the circle and said, "See them here—my mother and my brothers! Anyone who does the will of God is my brother, and sister, and mother."

Words of the fragrant portals, dimly starred

Once again Jesus began to teach by the lake-side. There was such 4, 1
a large throng of people gathered round him that he got
into a boat and sat in it on the water, while the people all took
position along the lake.

He taught them a great deal in parables, and said in the course 2
of his teaching:

And of ourselves and of our origins

"Listen! There was this farmer who went out to sow seed. And as 3
he scattered the seed some of it fell by the path and the birds
came and devoured it.

Some seed fell on stony ground where there was little soil, and 5
having so little depth it shot up immediately. But when the sun 6
came up it was scorched; and not being able to take root it
withered.

Some seed fell among briars; but the briars grew up and choked 7
it, so that it produced no fruit.

Then there was the seed that fell on good soil and produced a 8
crop; it sprouted and grew and bore fruit, increasing up to
thirty, sixty and a hundred times."

And Jesus said, "The man who has ears to hear with, let him 9
listen."

I and this mystery here we stand

Afterwards, the people around him with the Twelve asked him 10
privately about the parables.

And he said to them, "To you the secret of God's kingdom has 11
been given; but for the others outside everything is in parables,
so that the words of Scripture may come true:
'for all their seeing they shall not perceive, 12
and for all their hearing they shall not understand,
lest they return and be forgiven.' "

O friend! I think they are truly wise
Who take and take and never analyse

"So you do not understand this parable?" he said. "How then 13
will you grasp all the parables?

14 What the sower sows is the word. Sometimes when the word is sown and certain people hear it, Satan immediately comes and snatches up the word that was sown in them; these are the seed that falls by the path.

16 Then there is the seed scattered on the stony ground. Here we have people who, when they listen to the word, receive it with

17 joy. But they have no roots, and therefore they do not last; at the first onset of trial or persecution on account of the word, these immediately fall away.

18 Other hearers of the word are represented by the seed scattered

19 in the briars; here worldly anxieties and the lure of wealth and all the other desires enter in and choke the word, so that it yields no fruit.

20 Then the seed scattered on the good soil stands for those who hear the word and take it to heart and give a rich yield, increasing up to thirty, sixty or a hundred times."

Make thy way straight before me

21 He also said to them, **"Does a light make appearance just to be set under a flour-bin or a bed?** Surely its purpose is to be set on a lamp-stand?

22 For nothing is hidden, if not in order to be revealed; nothing is put under cover, if not in order to be brought to light.

23 Whoever has ears to hear with, let him listen."

24 And he added, "Pay heed to what you hear. The measure you give will be the measure you will receive—and more besides.

25 The man who starts with reserves will be given more; the man who has no reserves will forfeit even the little he has."

O God, like Love, revealing yourself in absence

26 He also said, "God's kingdom is like a man who scatters seed in

27 his field. While he sleeps every night and gets up every morning, the seed sprouts and grows, and he has no idea what is going on.

28 The earth produces fruit of itself: first the stalk, then the ear,

29 then the full grain in the ear. But the moment the crop is ready, he immediately gets out the reaping hook; for the harvest has come."

This is life, the bud
This is life, the bloom

"How are we to illustrate the kingdom of God?" he asked. 30
"Is there any parable we can use for it?
It is like a mustard-seed. When it is sown in the ground the 31
mustard-seed is the smallest seed on earth. But once it is sown 32
it grows up to become bigger than any plant in the garden and
throws out large branches, so that the birds of the sky can roost
in its shade."

In many other parables like these Jesus spoke the word to them, 33
so far as they were capable of receiving it. But he only spoke 34
parables to them; for his own disciples he used explain everything in private.

And whither is the Maker of it fled?

The same day, when it was evening, he said to them, "Let us 35
cross over to the other side."
The disciples therefore sent the people away and took him in the 36
boat, just as he was; and other boats too accompanied him.
But a great storm suddenly blew up and the waves began to 37
beat into the boat, so that it was soon in distress.
And Jesus? He was up in the prow, sleeping on a cushion. They 38
woke him up. "Master," they said, "how can you just lie there?
We're going down!"
And he, awakened, commanded the wind and said to the waves, 39
"Be silent! Calm down!"
And as the wind died there came a great calm.
"Why this anxiety?" he said to them. "Are you still without 40
faith?"
But they were shaken to the depths. "Who can this be?" they 41
said to themselves. **"Even the winds and the waves obey him!"**

To man of all beasts be not thou a stranger

When they arrived at the other side of the lake, in the country of 5, 1
the Gerasenes, a man from the tombs came to meet Jesus, as he 2

3 was stepping out of the boat. He was possessed by an unclean spirit and made the tombs his dwelling-place. No one could

4 keep him in check—not even with fetters. For he had often been bound hand and foot, but he would break the manacles and wear out the fetters, and nobody had the strength to master him.

5 Night and day he was inside in the tombs or out on the hills, shrieking and cutting himself with stones.

6 When he saw Jesus in the distance he ran up and fell in homage

7 before him, shouting at the top of his voice, "What do you want from me, Jesus Son of the Most-high God? I beg you in God's name not to torment me."

8 For Jesus was commanding the unclean spirit to go out from the man.

9 "What is your name?" he asked.

10 And he replied, "My name is Army, for we are many;" and he began to beg Jesus not to send him outside the district.

11 Now there happened to be a large herd of pigs feeding there at

12 the foot of the hill. So the demons begged him, "Send us into the pigs; let us enter them."

13 And Jesus gave them leave.
Then the unclean spirits came out from the man and took possession of the pigs; and the whole herd of about two thousand rushed headlong down the hill into the lake and was drowned.

14 The men who were tending them ran off and told the news in the villages and on the farms; and all came out to see what had happened.

15 When they came to Jesus and saw the possessed man, the one who had the 'Army', sitting there clothed and in his right mind,

16 they were afraid. The story of what had happened to the possessed man and all about the pigs was given them by those who had seen it.

17 So the people began to request Jesus to leave their district.

In his will is our peace

18 When he was about to embark in the boat, the man who had the

19 demons asked to be allowed to join him. But Jesus refused. "No," he said. "Go home to your own people and tell them what

the Lord has done for you and the mercy he has shown you."

So he went off and began spreading news all over the Ten Cities 20 of what Jesus had done for him.

And all were wondering.

Teach me to feel another's woe

When Jesus had crossed again in the boat to the other side, a 21 large crowd gathered round him, as he was by the lake-side.

A synagogue-ruler called Jairus came to him and, on meeting 22 him, fell at his feet to implore his help. "My daughter is dying," 23 he said. "Come and lay your hands on her that she may be saved and live."

Jesus went with him; and a large crowd followed, pressing round 24 him.

Among them was a woman who for twelve years had been 25 troubled by bleeding; she had been under several doctors and 26 had spent all her savings—but to no avail. She had rather become worse. And now she had heard about Jesus; so she came up 27 from behind among the crowd and touched his cloak.

"If only I touch his clothes," she said to herself, "I shall be 28 healed."

Immediately her bleeding dried up at the source; she could feel 29 in her body that she had been cured of her plague.

And Jesus too was aware at the same moment of a force going 30 out from him. Turning round in the middle of the crowd, he asked, "Who has touched my clothes?"

His disciples replied, "The crowd are pressing all round you, 31 as you can see. What do you mean: 'Who has touched me?'"

Nevertheless Jesus kept looking round for the woman who had 32 done this.

And the woman, trembling with fear because she knew what had 33 happened to her, came forward and fell at his feet and told him the whole truth.

He said to her, "Daughter, your faith has saved you. Go in 34 peace; you are healed from your plague."

He was still speaking when people from the synagogue-ruler's 35 house came to tell him, "Your daughter is dead; why bother the Master any further?"

36 But Jesus overheard the message and said to the synagogue-
37 ruler, **"Have no fear. Only have faith."** And he allowed no one to come with him, except Peter, James, and John the brother of James.

38 On arrival at the house he found mourners making a din,
39 wailing and keening aloud. He went in and said to them, "Why all this keening and wailing? The child is not dead but asleep." And they laughed at him.

40 But he put them all out and went in to where the child was lying, taking with him the child's father and mother and his
41 companions. He took her by the hand and said to her, *Talitha kumi*, which means, "Little girl, I tell you, get up!"

42 And the little girl got up at once and began to walk, for she was twelve years old.

43 They were all beside themselves with utter astonishment. But he gave them strict orders not to let anyone know of it. And he told them to bring her something to eat.

And his own received him not

6, 1 He left the place and came to his native town, accompanied by
2 his disciples; and when the sabbath came round he taught in their synagogue before a large congregation. They were utterly astounded at what they heard. "Where does this fellow get all this?" they began to ask. "This wisdom that has been given
3 him? And all these miracles that have been worked by him? Who is he but the carpenter, the son of Mary, and the brother of James and Joseph, Jude and Simon? Don't his sisters live here in our village?"
So they took offence at him and refused him faith.

4 And Jesus said to them, "A prophet does not go unhonoured except in his native town, among his own relatives and in his own home."

5 And he found it impossible to work any miracle there, apart from a few people whom he healed by laying his hands on them.
6 He was astonished at their refusal of faith.

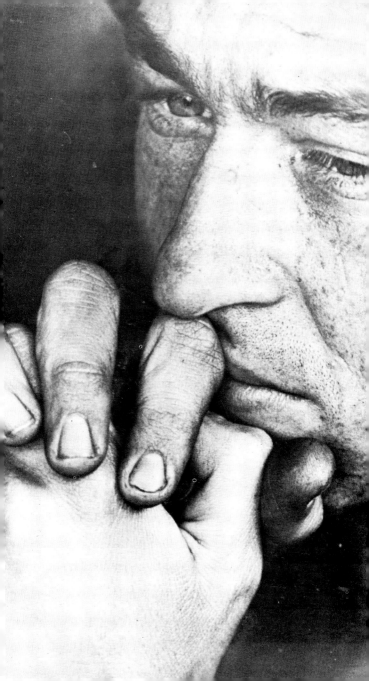

And their eternal dialogue is peace

He then began to go round the villages teaching.
And he also called the Twelve and began to send them out in 7
twos, giving them power over unclean spirits. His instructions 8
were that they should take nothing for the road except a
walking-stick: no bread, no knapsack, no money in their belts.
They could have shoes on their feet, but were not to wear two 9
shirts. This is what he said to them: "When you go to a place 10
and enter a house, remain there until you are going away. If 11
any place refuses you a welcome, or its people refuse to listen to
you, go out from it and shake off the dust from your feet, as
evidence against them in judgement."

The disciples went out and proclaimed the gospel, calling on 12
people to begin a new life. They drove out many demons, and 13
also anointed many of the sick with oil and healed them.

And that unrest which men miscall delight

Now Herod learnt of all this; for the fame of Jesus had spread 14
abroad. People were saying, "John the Baptist has been raised
from the dead; that is why these miracles are being worked by
him."
Others thought that he was Elia; others again that he was a 15
prophet, like one of the great prophets.
But when Herod came to hear of it he said, "This is John whom I 16
beheaded; he has been raised to life."

Herod himself had previously arrested John **and had kept** 17
him chained in prison, because of Herodias, his brother Philip's
wife, whom he had married.
For John used say to Herod, "It is not right for you to have your 18
brother's wife."
Herodias therefore had a grudge against John and wanted to 19
have him killed; but she did not get her way. For Herod had a 20
certain fear of John, knowing him to be a good and holy man.
He even protected him; and whenever he gave him a hearing
he would ask him many questions, and listened to him gladly.

137

21 Nevertheless Herodias got her chance. On his birthday Herod gave a banquet for his chief men and officers and the leading
22 people of Galilee. And the same Herodias had a daughter who went in and danced, giving great pleasure to the king and to his guests. "Ask me anything you like," said the king to the girl, "and I will give it to you."
23 He even swore an oath, "Go ahead! Ask me anything—even a half-share of my kingdom—and I will give it to you."
24 So the girl went and said to her mother, "What shall I ask for?" And Herodias replied, "Ask for the head of John the Baptist."
25 The girl then hurried back to the king and said, "I want you to give me right away the head of John the Baptist on a dish."
26 And the king, although grieved by her request, did not want to refuse her, because of his oath and the guests; he immediately sent an executioner, with orders to bring his head.
27 And the man went and beheaded John in prison. He brought the head on a dish and gave it to the girl; and the girl gave it to her mother.
29 When his disciples heard about it, they came and took away his body for burial in a tomb.

Come apart and rest awhile

30 Then the Apostles rejoined Jesus and reported to him all they had done and taught.
31 He said to them, "Come away by yourselves to a quiet place and rest a while." **For so many people were coming and going** that they hardly got time to eat.

Holy, divine, good, amiable and sweet

32 They rowed away in the boat to a desert place, where they
33 would be alone. But they were seen leaving, and others got to hear of it; so the people hurried out from the towns and arrived at the place before them, on foot.
34 On landing from the boat Jesus found a large crowd, and he felt pity for them since they were like sheep without a shepherd. He began to teach them.

35 Then, when it got late, his disciples came to him and said,

36 "We're in a desert here and it's late in the day. Send them away. Let them go to the farms and villages round about and buy themselves something to eat."

37 "Let you give them food," he replied.
And they said, "Are we to go and spend a lot of money on bread, so as to give them food?"

38 "How many loaves have you?" he asked. "Go and see."
And having found out they told him, "Five loaves and two fish."

39 Then he told them to get the people sitting in groups on the green grass.

40 So they sat down, grouped in parties of fifties and hundreds.

41 Jesus took in his hands the five loaves and the two fish, raised his eyes to heaven, and spoke the grace.
He broke the loaves and gave them to the disciples to lay before them, and he also divided the two fish among all.

42 All had a full meal and were satisfied. They gathered up what
44 was left over, including the fish, and filled twelve baskets; and the number of those who had eaten the loaves was five thousand men.

45 Then Jesus made the disciples embark in the boat and go across to Bethsaida ahead of him, while he himself was sending the people away.

46 And having seen them off he went up into the hills to pray.

For without thee I cannot live

47 As night came down the boat was in the middle of the lake and
48 Jesus was alone on the land. He could see them labouring at the oars—for the wind was against them—so he came towards them about three in the morning, walking on the lake; he intended to pass them by.

49 But when they saw him walking on the lake they thought it was a
50 ghost and gave a loud cry; for they had all seen him and were frightened.
And he immediately called out to them, "Do not worry. It is I. Have no fear."

51 Then he climbed into the boat with them, and the wind died.

52 And they were utterly dumbfounded; they had not learned the lesson of the loaves but still had their minds closed.

Without thee I dare not die

Having made the crossing they landed at Gennesareth and 53
moored there. And when they got out of the boat Jesus was 54
immediately recognized; so the people ran around all that district 55
and began to bring their sick on stretchers, wherever he was
reported to be.

Wherever he went, in all the villages, towns or farms, they laid 56
the sick in the open places and would beg him merely to let
them touch the fringe of his cloak.

And all who touched him were healed.

Rank on rank
The army of unalterable law

Having noticed how some of his disciples ate meals with 7, 2
'common' or unwashed hands, a party of Pharisees gathered 1
round him, along with some doctors of the law who had come
from Jerusalem.

For the Pharisees, and indeed all the Jews, hold fast to the 3
tradition handed down from the rabbis; they will not eat without
rinsing their hands in a handful of water. And when they return 4
from the market they will not have a meal without a thorough
washing. Many other customs too, such as the ritual washing
of cups, pots and bronzes, they hold to by tradition.

The Pharisees and the doctors of the law therefore asked him, 5
"Why do your disciples not conform to the tradition handed
down from the rabbis? They take their meals with unwashed
hands."

And Jesus replied, "How right was Isaia when he prophesied in 6
Scripture concerning you hypocrites:
'This people honours me with their lips,
but their hearts are far from me;
in vain do they worship me,   7
making dogmas of human enactments.'
For you abandon what God has ordained and hold to a tradition 8
established by men."

*Making small things important, so that everything
May be unimportant*

9 He said to them, "How cleverly you set aside God's commandment, in order to observe your tradition!

10 Moses said, 'Honour your father and mother'; and also, 'Whoever curses his father or mother must die.'

11 But according to you, if a man says to his father or mother, 'The support due to you from me has been made *korban*' (in other

12 words, a votive offering), then you no longer allow him to do

13 anything for his father or mother. So you set aside the commandment of God by your tradition, which you have handed on; and you have many similar practices."

Man is what he does

14 He summoned the people to him again and said to them, "Listen to me all of you and understand this: nothing that enters

16 a person from outside can make him unclean. What comes out from a person—this is what makes him unclean."

17 When he had left the people and come home, his disciples asked him the meaning of the parable.

18 "So you too are without understanding?" he said to them. "Surely you see that nothing can enter a person from outside

19 and make him unclean? Foods do not go into the heart but into the stomach, and are then discharged." (Thus Jesus declared all foods to be clean.)

20 "No," he said, **"it is rather what comes out from a person** that

21 makes him unclean. Evil thoughts have their origin inside, in

22 men's hearts—whence immorality, theft, murder, adultery, greed, malice, debauchery, envy, slander, pride, prejudice.

23 All these evils have their origin in man's heart and render him unclean."

The bruised reed he shall not break

24 Jesus set out from there and went away to the territory of Tyre. He entered a house, desiring that no one should know of it, but he could not remain hidden.

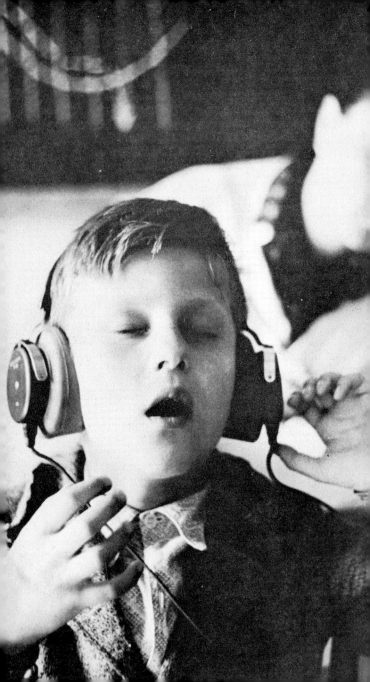

As soon as she had heard about him, a woman whose daughter 25 had an unclean spirit came and flung herself at his feet, begging him to drive out the spirit from her daughter. She was a pagan 26 woman, a native of Syrophoenicia.

Jesus said to her, "The children of the house must get their fill 27 first; it is not right to take the children's bread and throw it to the puppies."

"True, sir," she replied, "but even the puppies under the table 28 can eat the scraps dropped by the children."

And Jesus said to her, "You have spoken well! For this you may 29 go home; the demon has gone out from your daughter."

So she went home to her house and found the child lying in bed 30 and the demon gone out.

The smouldering wick he shall not quench

He again left the region of Tyre and came by Sidon to the lake 31 of Galilee, through the country of the Ten Cities.

And they brought him a deaf man who had an impediment in 32 his speech, imploring him to lay his hands on him. Jesus took 33 him aside, away from the crowd.

He put his fingers into his ears and touched his tongue with spittle. Then he raised his eyes to heaven and sighed, as he said 34 to him, *Ephphatha,* which means 'be opened'.

The man's ears were opened at once, his tongue was freed of its 35 impediment, and he was able to speak perfectly.

Jesus forbade them to make it known; but the more he forbade 36 them, the more they spread the news. Their astonishment knew 37 no bounds, as they exclaimed, "He has done all things well; **he makes the deaf to hear** and the dumb to speak."

Hungrie I was, and had no meat :
I did conceit a most delicious feast

During this period, when a large multitude had again come 8, 1 together and had nothing to eat, Jesus summoned his disciples 2 and said to them, "My heart goes out to these people; they have been with me now for three days and have nothing to eat. If I 3

145

let them go home hungry they will get weak on the way, and there are some who have come a great distance."

4 "But this place is a desert," his disciples replied. "What hope is there of getting bread here to feed these people?"

5 "How many loaves have you?" he asked.
And they said, "Seven."

6 Then he told the people to sit on the ground.
He took the seven loaves and gave thanks; and breaking them, he gave them to the disciples to serve to the people.
This they did.

7 They also had a few small fish; Jesus said grace over them and told them to serve these as well.

8 And when everyone had eaten and was satisfied, they gathered
9 up the scraps that remained, twelve basketfuls; and there were about four thousand people.

10 He then sent them away, embarked in the boat with his disciples, and came to the region of Dalmanutha.

The age demanded an image

11 The Pharisees came out and began to argue with him, asking him, as a test, to procure a miraculous sign from heaven.

12 Jesus sighed deeply to himself and said, "Why does this generation want a sign? In God's name I tell you, no sign will ever be given to this generation."

13 And he left them there, embarked again, and crossed to the other side.

But, rising, open to me for truth's sake

14 The disciples had forgotten to bring bread and had none with them in the boat except a single loaf.

15 So when Jesus began to warn them, "Be on your guard against
16 the leaven of the Pharisees and the leaven of Herod," they began to think among themselves, "it's because we brought no bread!"

17 But Jesus, knowing their minds, said to them, "Why these thoughts about not having bread? Can you still not see or
18 understand? Or do you suffer total blindness? You have eyes,
19 yet you do not see; you have ears, yet you do not hear. Do you

not remember? When I broke the five loaves among the five thousand, how many hampers did you fill with the scraps you took up?"

They said, "Twelve."

"And when I broke the seven loaves among the four thousand, 20 how many baskets did you fill with the pieces you took up?"

They replied, "Seven."

"Well," he said, "do you still not understand?" 21

Beggars of light

When they came to Bethsaida some people came to him with 22 a blind man, begging him to touch him.

So he took the blind man by the hand and led him outside the 23 village. He put spittle on his eyes, laid his hands on him, and asked, "Do you see anything?"

The man gave a look. "Yes," he said, "I see people; I see them 24 like trees walking about."

Once again he laid his hands on his eyes; and when the man 25 looked hard his sight was restored and he saw everything clearly.

Then he sent him home and warned him, "Do not go into the 26 village."

Two worlds meet in him

Jesus went out to the villages of Caesarea Philippi, along with 27 his disciples. And as they were travelling he questioned them, "Who do people say that I am?"

They replied, "Some say John the Baptist; others Elia; others 28 again one of the prophets."

"And what about you?" he said. "Who do you say that I am?" 29

Peter answered, "You are the Messiah."

And he strictly forbade them to reveal this to anyone about him. 30

Nothing in that abyss is alien to you

He then began to teach them as follows: "The Son of Man must 31 go through great suffering; he will be rejected by the elders, the

147

chief priests, and the doctors of the law; he will be put to death, and after three days he will rise again."

32 He said this quite openly.

So Peter took him aside and spoke strong words to him.

33 And Jesus, turning round and looking at his disciples, spoke a sharp rebuke to Peter: "Get away from me, you Satan! What you desire is not the will of God but of men."

The eternal not ourselves that makes for righteousness

34 Calling the people to him along with his disciples, he said, "Any man who wants to be a follower of mine must renounce
35 himself and take up his cross and come with me. The man who would save his life shall lose it; the man who is prepared to lose his life, for my sake and that of the gospel, shall save it.
36 Even if one gains the whole world, what is the advantage, if one loses one's true life?
37 **Or is there any price one can pay for one's life?**
38 If anyone in this faithless and sinful generation is ashamed of me and of my words, the Son of Man also will be ashamed of him, when he comes with the holy angels in the glory of his Father."

That day of wrath

9, 1 He also said, "Believe me, there are some standing here who will not have died before they see the kingdom of God coming in power."

What think you of the Christ?

2 After six days Jesus took with him Peter, James, and John, and brought them up a high mountain where they were alone.
3 He was transfigured before their eyes, his clothes becoming extremely white and dazzling, with a whiteness that no bleacher on earth could match.
4 And they saw Moses and Elia talking with Jesus.
5 Peter said to him, "Master, how good it is that we are here! Let us make three tents: one for you, one for Moses, and one for Elia."

148

6 But Peter really did not know what to say, for they were very
7 frightened. Then a cloud came, overshadowing them; and from
the cloud a voice: "This is my beloved Son; listen to him!"
8 And suddenly, when they looked around, they found Jesus alone
with them again.

O truth and pain immortally bound together

9 As they were coming down from the mountain he warned them
not to tell anyone of what they had seen, until the Son of Man
should have risen from the dead.
10 So the disciples kept the matter to themselves, discussing with
one another what this 'rising from the dead' could mean.
11 They asked him, "Why do the doctors of the law say that Elia
must come first?"
12 And he replied, "Yes, Elia is to come first and 'restore all
things'. But why do the Scriptures say of the Son of Man that
he must go through great suffering and be treated with con-
13 tempt? Because Elia has already come, I tell you, and they did
to him all that they wanted, to fulfil what Scripture had predicted
of him."

There are no tricks in plain and simple faith

14 When they reached the disciples they found them in the middle
of a large crowd, involved in an argument with doctors of the
15 law. All the people were utterly astounded on seeing Jesus and
ran forward to greet him.
16 "What are you discussing with them?" he asked.
17 And a man from the crowd replied, "Master, I have brought
18 you my son, afflicted by a spirit that makes him dumb. Whenever
it seizes him, the spirit tears at him, so that he foams at the mouth
and grinds his teeth and becomes rigid. I asked your disciples to
drive it out, but they couldn't."
19 And Jesus said to them, "O faithless people of this generation!
How long shall I be with you? How long shall I endure you?
Bring the boy to me."
20 They brought him up. And the moment the spirit saw Jesus it
threw the boy into a fit; he fell to the ground and began to roll
about, foaming at the mouth.

Jesus asked the father, "How long has he been like this?" 21
And the father answered, "Since he was a child. Many a time 22
it has tried to throw him into the fire or into water and destroy
him. But if you can do anything, have pity on us and help us."
Jesus replied, "What do you mean: 'if you can do anything'? 23
Nothing is impossible for the man who has faith."
And the boy's father immediately cried out, "I do have faith! 24
Help my want of faith!"
Then, seeing that the crowd was closing in, Jesus commanded 25
the evil spirit, "Dumb and deaf spirit, go out from him and
stay out!"
And the spirit, after convulsing the boy, came out with a shriek. 26
He lay there like a corpse and the people began to think he was
dead.
But Jesus took him by the hand, raised him up, and he stood 27
again.

Later, when he had entered the house, his disciples asked him 28
privately, "Why could not we drive out the spirit?"
And he replied, "Only by prayer can this kind be driven out— 29
nothing else."

Weakness shall bind and pierce My hands
And make a world for me wherein to die

They left that place and travelled through Galilee; and Jesus 30
did not want it to be known, for he was teaching his disciples.
He said to them, "The Son of Man will be given over to human 31
authorities. They will kill him; and three days after his death
he will rise again."
But they did not understand what he was talking about and were 32
afraid to question him.

Leave nothing of myself in me

They came to Capharnaum. And when he arrived home, Jesus 33
asked them, "What were you arguing about on the way?"
But they said nothing, because on the way they had been 34
squabbling as to which of them was the greatest.
Jesus therefore, having sat down, called over the Twelve and 35

said to them, "If anyone wants to be the first, he must be the last of all and the servant of all."

36 He then took a child and set him in front of them; and putting
37 his arm round him, he said, "Whoever receives one of these little children in my name receives me; and whoever receives me receives him who sent me."

The love nothing, the fear all

38 On one occasion John reported to him, "Master, we saw a man who doesn't belong to our group driving out demons in your name; we tried to stop him because he wasn't one of ours."
39 But Jesus said, "You should not stop him; no man can work a miracle in my name and be ready in the same breath to speak
40 evil of me. Whoever is not against us is on our side.

Rightly to be great

41 Believe me, if ever a man gives you a cup of water, because you belong to Christ, he shall not go unrewarded.
42 But if anyone destroys the faith of one of these little ones, it would be better for him to be pitched into the sea with a millstone tied about his neck.

The thorns of death and shame

43 If your hand is a danger to you, cut it off; better for you to enter life maimed than to keep both hands and go to the unquenching fire of hell.
45 **And if your foot is a danger to you,** cut it off; better for you to enter life crippled than to keep both feet and be thrown into hell.
47 And if your eye is a danger to you, pluck it out; better for you with one eye to enter the kingdom of God than with both eyes to be cast into hell, to everlasting pain and anguish.
49 For everyone shall be salted with fire.

Nothing is enough

50 Salt is good. But if salt loses its quality, is there anything you can do to restore it?
Have salt in you. And keep peace with one another."

Which of us two then is the worse off?
And how did this separation come about?

Jesus left there and came to the borders of Judaea and the 10, 1
Transjordan, where crowds flocked to him again and he began as
usual to teach them.

Some Pharisees came up to him and asked if it was lawful for a 2
husband to divorce his wife, wanting to test him.

And in reply he asked them, "What did Moses command you?" 3
They said, "Moses allowed a man to divorce his wife by giving 4
her a written dismissal."

And Jesus said to them, "It was by reason of your stubborn 5
disobedience that Moses wrote you this commandment. But 6
originally, at the creation, God made mankind male and female;
and for this reason a man shall leave his father and mother and 7
become one with his wife. **So they are no longer two persons
but one being;** and therefore the bond created by God may not 9
be loosed by man."

When they were back in the house his disciples asked him about 10
this.

And he said to them, "Any man who divorces his wife and 11
marries another commits adultery against her; any wife who 12
divorces her husband and marries another commits adultery."

What thou lov'st well is thy true heritage

There were some who wanted to bring children to him, to have 13
him touch them, but the disciples warned them off.

Jesus however was angry when he saw it, and said to the disciples, 14
"Let the children come to me, and do not stop them; for God's
kingdom belongs to their kind.

Believe me, if a man does not receive God's kingdom as a child, 15
he shall not go into it."

And he embraced them in his arms, laid his hands on them, and 16
blessed them.

The apprehension of the Good

When he was taking to the road again a man ran up and fell on 17
his knees before him. "Good master," he asked, "what must I
do to enter eternal life?"

18 And Jesus replied, "Why do you call me good? God alone is the
19 Good—no one else. You know the commandments: 'Do not
kill, do not commit adultery, do not steal, do not give false
witness, do not commit fraud, honour your father and mother.' "
20 But the man answered, "Master, all these I have observed from
my youth."
21 And Jesus looked him in the face and liked him. "You lack only
one thing," he said. "Go and sell everything you own. Give
the money to the poor, and you will have riches in heaven. Then
come and follow me."
22 But as soon as he heard this, the man's face fell and he went
away in sorrow. For he was very wealthy.

If thou art rich, thou'rt poor

23 Looking round upon his disciples, Jesus said to them, "How hard
it will be for the wealthy to enter God's kingdom."
24 And they were amazed at his words.
But he said again, "My friends, how hard it is to enter God's
25 kingdom. It is easier for a camel to pass through the eye of a
needle than for a wealthy person to enter God's kingdom."
26 And they were still more amazed and said to one another,
"Can anyone then be saved at all?"
27 But Jesus, fixing his eyes on them, replied, "For men it is
impossible, but not for God. For God everything is possible."

The one remains, the many change and pass

28 Then Peter spoke up: "See now, we have left all things in order
to follow you."
29 And Jesus said, "Believe me, no man gives up home, or brothers,
or sisters, or mother, or father, or children, or lands, for my
30 sake and that of the gospel, who will not receive a rich reward:
now, and in this world, houses and brothers and sisters and
mothers and children and lands—as well as persecution—and in
the world to come eternal life.
31 And many who are first will be last; and the last will be first."

God's creation became my cross

32 They were on the road, heading up to Jerusalem, with Jesus

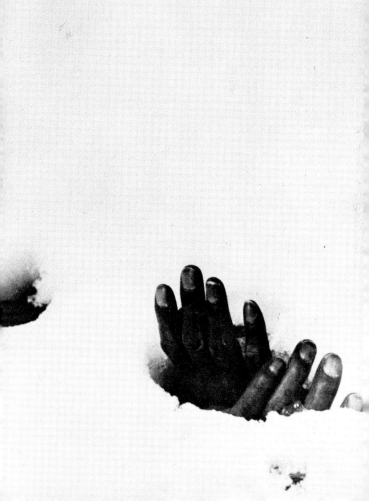

leading the way. A sense of foreboding hung over them; and those who followed behind were afraid. Once again he took the 33 Twelve aside and told them the fate that awaited him. "See, we are now going up to Jerusalem. The Son of Man will be given up to the chief priests and the doctors of the law. They will condemn him to death and hand him over to the pagans. By these he will be mocked, spat upon, cruelly beaten, and put 34 to death. And after three days he will rise to life."

Ill-weaved ambition

James and John, the sons of Zebedee, came to him and said, 35 "Master, we would like you to do something for us."
"What do you want me to do for you?" he asked. 36
And they replied, "Grant that we may sit, the one on your right 37 and the other on your left, when you come to your glory."
But Jesus said to them, "You do not know what you are asking. 38 Can you drink the cup that I drink? Can you suffer the baptism that I suffer?"
They replied, "We can." 39
And Jesus said to them, "The cup that I drink you too will drink; and the baptism that I suffer you too will suffer. But to 40 sit at my right hand or my left is not mine to give; it is for those for whom it has been reserved."

When the other ten heard about this they were angry with James 41 and John.

The mocking taunt, See then whether you shall be master?

So Jesus called them over and said to them, "You know that 42 those who pass as rulers of the pagan peoples trample on their rights and their great men wield absolute power over them. But with you it must be different. Whoever wants to rank high 43 among you **must be your servant;** and whoever wants to be the 44 first among you must be the slave of all. For the Son of Man too 45 did not come to be served but to serve, and to give his life in sacrifice for all."

159

Tears pouring from this face of stone

46 They entered Jericho. And as he was leaving Jericho with his disciples and a large crowd, the son of Timaeus, a blind beggar

47 with the name Bartimaeus, was sitting at the roadside. When he heard that it was Jesus of Nazareth he began to shout out, "Son of David, Jesus, have pity on me!"

48 Several turned on him to make him hold his tongue. But he only shouted the more, "Son of David, Jesus, have pity on me!"

49 Jesus stopped and said, "Call him here."
So they said to the blind man, "Get up! He's calling you. Cheer up!"

50 And he threw off his cloak, sprang to his feet, and came to Jesus.

51 "What do you want me to do for you?" he asked.
And the blind man replied, "*Rabbuni*—Master—**if only I could see again.**"

52 He said to him, "Go! Your faith has saved you."

53 And immediately he could see again and began to follow him along the road.

Blessed with the soft phrase of peace

11, 1 As they approached Jerusalem and came to Bethphage and Bethany at the Mount of Olives, Jesus sent ahead two of his

2 disciples with the following instructions: "Go into the village facing you and as soon as you enter it you will find a donkey tethered on which no man has yet ridden. Untie it and bring it

3 to me. If anyone asks you what you are doing, say to him, 'The Lord has need of it, but will send it back without delay.' "

4 The disciples went off and found a donkey tethered outside a door on the street; they untied it.

5 Some of the people standing around said to them, "What are you doing there, untying the donkey?"

6 So they told them what Jesus had said and were allowed to go ahead.

7 When they had brought the donkey to Jesus they flung their

8 coats on its back, and he sat on it. Many spread their coats on the road. Others cut bundles of green stuff in the fields and

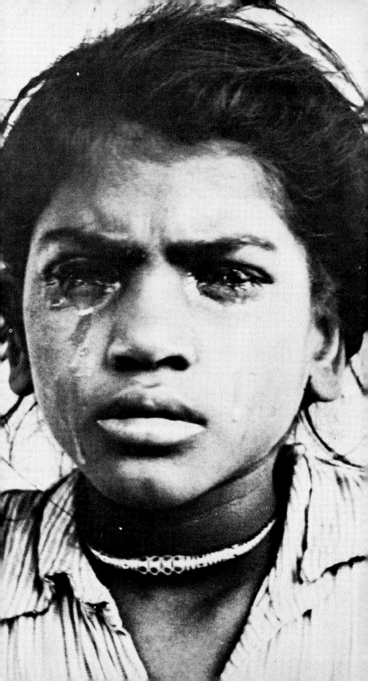

9 scattered them. Some led the way in front of Jesus, others
followed behind, and they shouted:
"Praise to God!
A blessing on him who comes in the name of the Lord.
10 A blessing on the coming kingdom of our father, David.
Praise to God in heaven!"

11 So he entered Jerusalem and went to the temple. And having
looked around at what was going on, he went out to Bethany
with the Twelve; for it was now late.

We call it health when we find no symptom
Of illness

12 Next day, as they were leaving Bethany, Jesus felt hungry. On
seeing in the near distance a fig-tree covered with leaves, he
went over to it to see if he would find anything on it; but when
he came to it he found nothing on it except leaves, for it was
not the fig-season.
14 He said to the tree, "May nobody ever eat fruit from you again."
And the disciples were listening.

Zeal for thy house hath consumed me

15 They arrived in Jerusalem, and Jesus entered the temple and
began to drive out the people who were buying and selling in
the holy place; he overturned the tables of the money-changers
16 and the seats of the pigeon-dealers, and would not allow goods
to be carried through the temple-area.
17 And he explained in his teaching, "Does it not stand written in
Scripture, 'My house shall be called a house of prayer for all the
peoples'?
But you have made it a hide-out for thieves."

18 When they heard about this, the chief priests and the doctors
of the law were most anxious to find a way of doing away with
him; but they had to proceed cautiously, because the people
were very impressed by his teaching.
19 In the evening Jesus left and went outside the city.

How can I dream except beyond this life?

As they were passing by early next morning they saw the fig-tree 20
withered from the roots.

And Peter, remembering, said to Jesus, "Look, Master, the fig- 21
tree you cursed has withered."

Jesus replied, "Have faith in God. Believe me, if one should 22
say to this mountain here, 'Be lifted and thrown into the sea,'
without any doubt in his heart, but with faith that what he prays
for is being done, he shall have it done.

I tell you, therefore, anything you ask for in prayer, believe that 24
you have received it, and it shall be yours.

But whenever you stand in prayer, first forgive the grievances 25
you have against others; only then will your Father in heaven 26
forgive you your own misdeeds."

But there are shadows in my mind

Once again they arrived in Jerusalem. And as Jesus was walking 27
about in the temple, the chief priests, the doctors of the law, and
the elders approached him and asked, "What is your authority 28
for doing these things? Or who gave you authority to act in this
way?"

Jesus said to them, "I too have a question for you, and if you 29
answer me I will let you know by what authority I do these
things: Tell me, was the baptism of John from God or from 30
men?"

So they threshed it out among themselves: "Shall we say it was 31
from God? But he will surely say, 'Why did you not put faith
in him?' Or shall we say it was from men?"—but they were 32
afraid of the people; for everyone held that John was really a
prophet.

So they gave as their reply to Jesus, "We don't know." 33
And he answered, "Neither will I let you know by what authority
I do these things."

Full of one passion, vengeance, rage or fear

He began to speak to them in figures: 12, 1
"There was this man who planted a vineyard. Having fenced it

163

with a wall and dug a wine-press and built a watch-tower, he leased his vineyard to tenants and went abroad.

2 In due course he sent a servant to the tenants to collect from them
3 his share of the harvest; but they gave the servant a threshing and sent him back empty-handed.

4 He sent another servant, but they beat him on the head and affronted him.

5 Yet another he sent, but they killed him; and several others, but these too they either beat up or killed.

6 When only one still remained to him—his own son whom he loved—he sent him last of all, thinking to himself, 'They will respect my son.'

7 But these tenants had other thoughts: 'This is the heir! Let's kill him and the property will be ours.'

8 So they seized and killed him and threw his body out of the vineyard.

9 Now what will the owner of that vineyard do?
He will come and destroy those tenants and give the vineyard to others.

10 Have you not read in Scripture:
'The stone which the builders rejected
has itself become the corner-stone.

11 By the Lord has this been done,
and our eyes can hardly believe it.'?"

12 And they were most anxious to arrest him, knowing that he had spoken this parable against themselves, but they were afraid of the people.
So they left him alone and went off.

Breathing his law and heaven's tranquillity

13 However, they sent a party of Pharisees and followers of Herod to trap him in his speech.

14 So these came up and said to him, "Master, we know that you are an honest man and not worried about what people think; you do not play up to important folk but teach the way of God in all truth.

164

What then? Is it right to pay tax to the Emperor? Shall we pay or shall we not?"

And Jesus, knowing what was behind it, said to them, "So you 15 would trap me! Bring me a coin, please. I would like to see one." They brought him one. 16

Then he asked them, "Whose is this image? And whose is the name inscribed?"

They replied, "Caesar's."

And he said to them, "Give then to Caesar what is Caesar's, 17 and to God what is God's."

And they could not withhold their admiration of him.

Gleams that untravelled world

A party of the Sadducees (the people who hold that there is no 18 resurrection) came up and put a case to him: "Master, Moses 19 laid it down that if there are brothers and one of them dies, leaving a wife but no child, another brother should marry the wife and raise up a family to the dead man.

Now there were once seven brothers. When the first had married 20 a wife and died without leaving children, then the second married 21 her, and he too died without leaving children. In the same way, 22 the third and the rest of the seven all died without leaving children; and in the end the wife died.

Which of them, now, will have her as wife on the day of resurrec- 23 tion, when all rise again? For all seven had married her."

And Jesus replied, "How wrong you are! And for what other 24 reason than that you are ignorant of the Scriptures and of the power of God? When men and women rise from the dead they 25 do not marry; they are like angels in heaven.

As for the dead and their resurrection to life, have you not read 26 in the book of Moses, where he speaks of the burning bush, how God said to him, 'I am the God of Abraham, the God of Isaac, the God of Jacob'?

Therefore he is not a God of the dead, but of the living. You 27 are very wrong indeed!"

Give all to love

A doctor of the law, who had overheard the discussion and 28 observed how ably Jesus had answered, came up and asked him, "Which of all the commandments is the most important?"

29 And Jesus replied, "The most important commandment is this:
30 'Hear, O Israel, the Lord our God is one Lord. You shall love the Lord your God with all your heart and all your soul and all
31 your mind and all your strength.' And the second is this: **'You shall love your neighbour as yourself.'** There is no other commandment greater than these."

32 The doctor of the law said to him, "You are right, Master. What you say is true: 'There is one God, and no other apart from him'; and what you say about 'loving him with all one's heart and all
33 one's mind and all one's strength', and about 'loving one's neighbour as oneself.' This is more important than all holocausts or sacrifices."

34 Jesus observed how intelligently he answered and said to him, "You are not far from the kingdom of God."

And from then on no one dared to put him any more questions.

One small page of Truth's manuscript made clear

35 But Jesus turned to them and asked, as he was teaching in the temple, "On what basis do the doctors of the law hold that the
36 Messiah is David's Son? For the inspired David himself wrote:
'The Lord said to my lord: Sit at my right hand,
until I lay your enemies under your feet.'
37 If David calls him 'Lord', how can the Messiah be David's son?"

And the large crowd of people listened to him with pleasure.

Here's a world of pomp and state

38 He said in the course of his teaching, "Beware of the doctors of the law! They like to parade in long robes and to be greeted
39 respectfully in public; they like to have the first seats in the
40 synagogues and the top places at table; they know how to devour the property of widows, but they can also put on a show of praying long prayers.
For them judgement will be all the more severe."

Gold is worth but gold;
  Love's worth love

He was sitting opposite the temple-treasury, watching the people 41
put their money into it. Several rich people threw in large 42
amounts; and a poor widow also came and threw in a couple of
small coins, equal to a few pence.
Jesus called over his disciples and said to them, "Believe me, 43
this poor widow has given more to the treasury than all the others.
They gave what they all could well afford; but she in her poverty 44
gave everything she had—her whole living."

A time to every purpose under heaven

As he was leaving the temple one of his disciples said to him, 13, 1
"Look, Master! There's stonework for you! Look at those for
buildings!"
And Jesus said to him: "You see these splendid buildings? Not 2
a stone will be left on a stone. All will be torn asunder."

A time to be born and a time to die

When he was sitting on the Mount of Olives, opposite the temple, 3
Peter, James, John and Andrew came by themselves to ask him,
"Tell us when will these things happen? And what sign will there 4
be of this universal consummation?"
Jesus replied, "Watch lest anyone lead you astray. Many will 5
come claiming my authority and saying, **'I am the one',** and will
lead many astray. And when you hear news of wars and rumours 7
of wars, do not be alarmed. For all this must happen; but it does
not signify the end.
Nation will rise against nation, kingdom against kingdom; there 8
will be earthquakes and famines in many places. All this is but
the beginning of the birth-pangs.

A time to plant

Then you must look to yourselves. You will be arraigned in 9
courts, and flogged in synagogues, and brought before governors
and kings, to testify against them on my behalf.

169

10 And the gospel must first have been preached to all the peoples.

11 Whenever you are handed over and led away, do not be anxious about what you are going to say. When the moment comes speak whatever you are inspired to speak; for the Holy Spirit will be speaking—not you.

12 Brother will surrender brother to death, and a father his child; children will rise against their parents and send them to death.

13 You will be hated by all men because of my name; but the man who holds out to the end will be saved.

And a time to pluck up

14 But as soon as you see the 'desecrating horror' standing where he ought not to be—if the reader but take note—then let the people of Judaea make for the mountains.

15 Whoever is up on the roof, let him not come down or re-enter

16 his house looking for something; whoever is out in the fields, let

17 him not return for his coat. And alas for women with child, or

18 with infants at the breast, when those days come! Let your prayer be that it happen not in winter-time.

19 For these will be days of great affliction, such as the world has never seen since the beginning of God's creation, and never will

20 see again. If the Lord had not cut them short, no living being would be saved; but for the sake of the elect whom he has chosen God has cut those days short.

21 If anyone says to you then, 'See the Messiah here!' or 'See him

22 there!' do not believe it; for false Messiahs and false prophets will appear, and will work great miracles and portents, to lead even the chosen astray—if that were possible.

23 Therefore keep your eyes open. I have told you all beforehand.

The great stage-curtain about to drop

24 A time will come however after that great affliction when the sun will be darkened and the moon will no longer give its light,

25 when the stars will fall from the sky and the heavenly bodies

26 will be shaken. And then the Son of Man will be seen coming

27 in the clouds with great power and splendour; he will send out the angels and will gather the chosen from the four winds, from the ends of the earth to the ends of heaven.

Though I tarry, wait for me, trust me, watch and pray

Learn a lesson from the fig-tree: When its shoots are tender and 28
its leaves begin to sprout you know that summer is near.

So too, when you see these things happen, let it be known to you 29
that the end is near—at the very gates.

Believe me, the people of this generation will not have passed 30
away before all these things come to pass. Heaven and earth will 31
pass away; my words will not pass away.

And yet that day or the hour no one knows, not even the angels 32
in heaven, not even the Son, but only the Father.

Therefore keep your eyes open and stay awake; for you do not 33
know when the time will be.

So too, when a man leaves home and goes abroad, he puts his 34
servants in charge, and gives each one his work to do, and tells
the porter to stay awake.

Stay awake, therefore. For you do not know when the master 35
of the house is going to come, whether in the evening or at
midnight, whether at cock-crow or at dawn. If he comes without 36
warning, let him not find you asleep.

And what I say to you I say to all: Stay awake!" 37

All except only Love. Love *had died long ago*

The feast of the pasch and the unleavened bread was in two 14, 1
days time. And the chief priests and the doctors of the law were
trying to devise some scheme to have Jesus arrested and put to
death. But they decided, "Not during the festival, or the people 2
may start a riot."

Love is here, love is not dumb

When Jesus was at dinner in the house of Simon the leper, at 3
Bethany. And a woman came with an alabaster flask of pure and
very expensive perfume, which she poured on his head, having
broken open the flask.

Now some people were indignant over this and said to one 4
another, "Why this waste of expensive perfume? This kind 5

could have been sold at a high price and the money given to the poor."
And they criticized the woman harshly.

6 But Jesus said, "Leave her alone. Must you be unkind to her?

7 What she has done for me is a noble deed. The poor you always have at hand, to attend to as often as you like, but I am not here always.

8 She has done all that she could; she has anointed my body beforehand for burial.

9 And I assure you of this: wherever the gospel will be preached in the whole world, what she has done will also be told in remembrance of her."

One of the Twelve

10 Then Judas Iscariot, who belonged to the Twelve, went to the
11 chief priests to betray Jesus to them. Having heard his plan they were pleased and promised him money.
So Judas was keeping an eye out for a suitable chance to betray him.

This day shall be for you a memorial day

12 On the first day of the festival known as the unleavened bread it was the custom to sacrifice the paschal lamb. His disciples therefore asked Jesus, "Where do you wish us to go and prepare the pasch for you?"

13 And Jesus sent off two of them, with the following instructions, "Go into the city and you will be met by a man carrying a jar

14 of water. Follow him to the house he will enter, and say to the owner, 'The Master has sent us to ask, Where is the dining room reserved for me, in which I am to eat the pasch with my

15 disciples?' He will show you a large room upstairs, with a table set out in readiness. There you shall prepare for us."

16 The disciples went off and on entering the city found everything as he had told them; so they prepared the pasch.

Even my bosom friend in whom I trusted

17 In the evening he came there with the Twelve.

And while they were at table Jesus said in the course of the meal, 18 'I tell you this, one of you—one who shares meals with me—is going to betray me."

The disciples were very distressed and began to ask him, one 19 after another, "Surely not I?"

He replied, "One of the Twelve, one who eats with me from the 20 same dish. For the Son of Man goes his way, as the Scriptures 21 have laid down for him; but woe to the man by whom the Son of Man is betrayed! It would have been better for that man not to have been born."

A memorial of his death

During the meal Jesus took bread and spoke the grace. And as 22 he broke the bread and gave it to them, he said, "Take it; this is my body."

Then he took a cup of wine and spoke the thanksgiving; he gave 23 it to them and they all drank from it.

And he said, "This is my blood of the covenant which is shed 24 for many.

I assure you, never again shall I drink of the fruit of the vine 25 until that day—the day when I shall drink it new in the kingdom of God."

Be thine the glory and be mine the shame

Having sung the hymn, they went out to the Mount of Olives. 26 And Jesus said to them, "All of you will fall away because of me. 27 For it is written, 'I will strike the shepherd and the sheep will 28 be scattered.' But after my resurrection I will go on before you to Galilee."

Peter said to him: "All may fall, but not I." 29

And Jesus answered, "The truth is, I tell you, that you are the 30 one who will deny me three times—this very night before the cock crows twice."

Peter, however, spoke with even greater assurance, "Even if I 31 must die with you I will not deny you!"

And the others were equally confident.

Wheresoever thou art our agony will find thee

32 They came to a place called Gethsemane; and Jesus said to hi
disciples, "Sit here while I pray."

33 He took Peter, James, and John along with him; and an agony
34 of distress and anguish came upon him. He said to them, "My
heart grieves even to breaking point. Wait here and stay awake."

35 He then went forward a little and fell to the ground. And he
prayed God to spare him, if it were possible, the hour of suffering

36 "Abba, Father," he said, "all things are in your power. Take
this cup from me. Nevertheless, let your will be done, not mine."

37 On coming back he found them asleep. And he said to Peter
"Simon, are you sleeping? Have you not been able to stay

38 awake for one hour? Stay awake, all of you, and pray that you
escape trial. The spirit is willing, but the flesh is weak."

39 He went away a second time and prayed as before. And on his
return he again found them asleep, for their eyes were weighed
down. They did not know what to answer him.

41 Returning for a third time he said, "So you still sleep and take
your rest! It is enough. **The hour has come for the Son of Man
to be given over to evil men.**

42 Rise! We must go. See, my betrayer is already here."

They use that power against me which I gave

43 Judas, one of the Twelve, arrived as he was speaking, and with
him a crowd of men armed with swords and clubs, who had
been sent by the chief priests, the doctors of the law and the
elders.

44 His betrayer had agreed with them on a signal: "The one whom
I shall kiss is the man. Arrest him and lead him away under
guard."

45 So when he arrived Judas immediately went up to him and said
46 "Rabbi!" and he kissed him. The others seized Jesus and held
him.

47 One of those who were standing by drew his sword, struck the
high priest's servant, and cut off his ear.

48 And Jesus said to them, "Am I a common criminal that you
49 have come with swords and clubs to arrest me? Every day I wa

with you teaching in the temple, and you did not arrest me; but the Scriptures must be fulfilled."

50 Then all of them ran away and left him. A youth followed him with a sheet wrapped about his naked body, and they caught
52 him; but he let go of the sheet and ran away naked.

The Princes of my people make a head
Against their maker

53 Jesus was led away to the high priest; and all the priests, elders and doctors of the law were gathered in council.
54 Peter followed him at a distance into the high priest's courtyard he was sitting there along with the attendants, warming himsel at the fire.
55 And the chief priests and all the council were trying to find evidence against Jesus to warrant a sentence of death, but they
56 could not find any. Several did come forward with false evidence
57 against him, but their testimonies did not agree. However, there
58 were some who got up and testified falsely as follows: "We heard this man speak these words: 'I will destroy this temple made with hands, and in three days will build another not made with hands.' "
59 But even on this point their testimonies did not agree.
60 So the high priest stood up before the council and asked Jesus "Have you nothing to say? What charge is this that these bring against you?"
61 Jesus remained silent and gave no answer.
The high priest questioned him again and asked, "Are you the Messiah, the Son of God?"
62 And Jesus answered, "I am. You will see the Son of Man seated at the right hand of God and coming in the clouds of heaven."
63 At that the high priest tore his clothes and said, "Do we need any more witnesses? You have heard the blasphemy. What is your verdict?"
64 And they, unanimously, judged him deserving of death.
65 Some began to spit on him. Having blindfolded him they would strike him and call out, "Tell us who struck you!"
And the attendants, as they took him in charge, showered blows on him.

But who can plumb the sinking of that soul?

Meanwhile Peter was below in the courtyard, when one of the 66
servant-girls came by and saw him warming himself. She looked 67
closely at him and said, "You were a friend of this Jesus from
Nazareth."
Peter denied it, "I have no idea what you are talking about." 68
And he went out to the entrance-court. 69
The girl, however, on seeing him there, said again to those
standing around, "This man belongs to them."
But he again denied it. 70
And shortly afterwards the bystanders said to Peter, "Of course
you belong to them! Aren't you from Galilee?"
Peter began to curse and to swear, "I tell you, I don't know this 71
man you are talking about."
The cock then crowed a second time. 72
And Peter remembered how Jesus had said to him, "Before the
cock crows twice you will deny me three times."
He began to weep.

But when I view abroad both Regiments,
The worlds, and thine

First thing in the morning the chief priests, in plenary session 15, 1
with the elders and the doctors of the law, reached a decision.
They had Jesus led away in chains and handed him over to
Pilate.
Pilate asked him, "Are you the king of the Jews?" 2
And Jesus replied, "The words are yours."
The chief priests were bringing grave charges against him. 3
So Pilate again questioned him, "Have you nothing to answer? 4
You realize how serious are the charges they bring?"
But Jesus gave no further answer; and Pilate could not under- 5
stand it.

My silence rather doth augment their crie

During the festival it was Pilate's custom to release a prisoner at 6
the request of the people. A man called Barabbas was being held 7

177

in custody, along with rioters who had committed murder in the uprising.

8 So the people went up to Pilate, and began to ask for his usual
9 concession. Pilate said in reply, "Would you like me to release to
10 you the King of the Jews?" For he knew that the priests had handed him over out of spite.

11 But the chief priests stirred up the people to ask instead for the release of Barabbas.

12 Pilate therefore addressed them again and asked, "What shall I do with the man whom you call the 'King of the Jews'?"

13 They shouted back, "Crucify him!"

14 "What wrong has he done?" asked Pilate.

And they shouted still louder, "Crucify him!"

15 So Pilate, in his desire to satisfy the crowd, released Barabbas to them. Jesus he handed over to be crucified, having had him flogged.

Of sharp thorn I have worn a crown on my head

16 The soldiers led him away inside the palace called the praetorium
17 and gathered up the whole troop. First they dressed him in a purple robe; then they plaited a crown of thorns and fixed it on
18 his head; and they began to salute him, "Greeting to the king
19 of the Jews!" They also struck him on the head with a cane, and spat on him, and bent their knees to him in pretended homage.

20 When they had finished their mockery, they took off the purple robe and dressed him in his own clothes; and they led him out to crucify him.

The decreed burden of each mortall Saint

21 They forced a passer-by who was coming from the country— Simon of Cyrene, the father of Alexander and Rufus—to carry his cross.

For you, for me

22 They bring him to a place called Golgotha (a word which means
23 'the place of the skull'); they offer him wine drugged with myrrh, which he would not take.

And they crucify him. 24
Then they divide his clothes by drawing lots to see what each
would get.
And it was about nine o'clock, as they crucified him. 25

A notice proclaimed the cause for which he died; on it was 26
written, THE KING OF THE JEWS.
And along with him they crucify two criminals, one on his right 27
and one on his left.

As they passed by the cross people took occasion to jeer at him. 29
Wagging their heads, they would say, "Ha! The one who destroys
the temple and in three days builds it again! Save yourself and 30
come down from the cross."
And the chief priests, along with the doctors of the law, also 31
mocked him, saying to one another, "The man who saved others
cannot save himself—this Messiah, this King of Israel! Let him 32
now come down from the cross; when we see it, then we'll
believe!"
Even the two who were crucified with him taunted him.

Death has done all death can

About midday darkness came over the whole land and lasted 33
for some three hours. And at three o'clock Jesus cried in a loud 34
voice, *Eloi, Eloi, lama sabachthani,* which means: "My God, my
God, why have you forsaken me?"
Hearing him, some of those standing around said, "Listen, he 35
is calling Elia."
And one of them ran up, filled a sponge with vinegar, fixed it 36
on a cane and gave him a drink. "Let's see whether Elia comes
to take him down," he said.
But Jesus gave a loud cry and breathed his last. 37

Curtains of rock
And tears of stone

Then the curtain of the temple was torn in two, from top to 38
bottom.

39 And the officer who was standing in front of him saw how he had
   expired and said, "This man was indeed a son of God."

40 There were also some women looking on from a distance—among
   them Mary of Magdala, and Mary the mother of the lesser James
41 and Joseph, and Salome. These had followed him and served
   him while he was in Galilee; and several other women who had
   come up to Jerusalem with him were also there.

What though my bodie runne to dust
Faith cleaves unto it

42 By this time evening had come. It was the day of 'preparation',
43 that is, the day before the sabbath. So when Joseph of Arimathaea
   came, a prominent councillor who was himself expecting the
   kingdom of God, he boldly went up to Pilate and requested the
   body of Jesus.
44 Surprised that Jesus should be dead so soon, Pilate summoned
   the officer in charge and asked him if he had already died.
45 And when he had been assured by the officer, he allowed Joseph
   to take the body.
46 Having bought a linen shroud, Joseph then took the body of
   Jesus down from the cross and wrapped it in the shroud; he
   laid the body in a tomb, which had been excavated from rock,
   and rolled a stone against the entrance.

47 Mary of Magdala and Mary the mother of Joseph were watching
   where the body was laid.

The world's too little for thy tent

16, 1 When the sabbath was over Mary of Magdala, with Mary the
      mother of James, and Salome, bought spices with a view to
      anointing him.
   2 Then, very early after dawn on the Sunday, they came to the
      tomb.
   3 Both were wondering to themselves, "Who will roll away the
      stone for us from the entrance to the tomb?"
   4 But when they looked up they saw that the stone had already
      been rolled away; it was very big.

So they entered the tomb and saw a young man sitting to the 5
right, clothed in a white robe. They were seized with fear and
dread.
But he said to them, "Do not be alarmed. You are looking for 6
Jesus of Nazareth who was crucified? He has risen; he is not here.
Look and see the place where they laid him.
But go and bring this message to his disciples and Peter: 'He is 7
going on before you to Galilee; there you will see him, as he told
you.'"

So the women went out and hurried away from the tomb, over- 8
come by fear and wonder. They said nothing to anyone, for they
were frightened.

Rise heart; thy Lord is risen. Sing his praise
Without delayes

[When he had risen, early on the first day of the week, he appeared 9
first to Mary the Magdalene, from whom he had driven out
seven demons. She went and announced the news to those who 10
had been his companions, who were now mourning and weeping.
But when they were told that he was alive and had been seen by 11
her, they would not believe it.

Afterwards he appeared in another form to two of them as they 12
were travelling on foot to the country; these too went off and 13
brought the news to the others, but they were not believed either.

Finally, he appeared to the eleven as they were at table, and 14
scolded them for their disbelief and prejudiced minds, since
they would not put faith in those who had seen him raised from
the dead.

All knees shall bow to thee; all wits shall rise
And praise him who did make and mend our eies

Then he said to them, "Go out to the whole world and proclaim 15
the gospel to all creatures. All those who have faith and are 16
baptized will be saved; but whoever refuses faith will be condemned.

17 At every step, those who have faith will be attended by miracles
18 such as these. In my name they will drive out demons. They will
speak new tongues. They will handle snakes. Even if they drink
poison they will not suffer harm. They will lay their hands on
the sick and restore them to health."

19 After he had spoken to them the Lord Jesus was raised to heaven
and took his seat at God's right hand.

20 And the disciples went out and proclaimed the gospel everywhere. The Lord worked with them and confirmed the word of
the gospel by the miracles that followed them.]

LUKE'S
ACCOUNT

Approach and read

Already several have set about drawing up a report of the events 1, 1
brought about in our midst, following the tradition handed down 2
to us by the earliest witnesses and servants of God's word.
I have therefore decided, my dear Theophilus, to look carefully 3
into the details from the very beginning and to write you the
story as it happened, to prove for you the soundness of the 4
teaching you have received.

The time draws near the birth of Christ

During the reign of Herod, king of Judaea, there lived a priest 5
called Zachary, who belonged to the priest group of Abia; his
wife was of Aaron's stock and her name was Elizabeth.

They were both good people in the eyes of God, scrupulously 6
exact in the observance of the Lord's commandments and
ordinances. But they had no child, since Elizabeth was barren 7
and the two of them were getting on in years.

Now Zachary's group was assigned to do service before God and 8
it fell to him one day to go into the temple of the Lord and offer
incense according to the priestly custom. During the incensation 10
the whole congregation of the people was praying outside.
And Zachary had a vision of an angel of the Lord, standing to the 11
right of the incense-altar. He was greatly troubled by what he 12
saw, and very apprehensive.
But the angel said to him, "Have no fear, Zachary, for your 13
prayer has been granted; your wife Elizabeth will give you a son, 14

and you shall call his name John. You will have great joy and
15 gladness; and many others too will rejoice at his birth. For this
boy is destined to be great before God: he will drink no wine or
strong drink; he will be filled with the Holy Spirit from the
16 moment of his birth; and he will bring many Israelites back to
17 the Lord their God. With all the divine power of Elia he will go
before God, reconciling fathers and children, restoring the
rebellious to the way of obedience, and preparing for the Lord
a people in readiness."

Say yes, say yes, and doubt not
Bright threads of light

18 "But how can I be sure of this?" Zachary said to the angel. "I
am an old man, and my wife is advanced in years."
19 And the angel replied, "I am Gabriel who stand at the service
of God, and I have been sent to speak to you and to announce
this good news.
20 So you will be dumb, and will have no power to speak until the
day when all these things come to pass; this is your punishment
for refusing to believe my words.
And my words will come true in their own time."

21 Now the people were waiting outside for Zachary and wondering
what was keeping him in the temple.
22 Then, when he came out, he could not speak to them and they
realized he had seen a vision in the temple.
He himself could only make signs and remained dumb.

23 In due course, when he had completed his period of service in
the temple, he returned to his home.
24 And after some time his wife Elizabeth became pregnant, and
25 for five months withdrew from the world. She said to herself:
"This favour the Lord has done for me; now at last he has willed
to end my disgrace among men."

Grace was in all her steps

26 When Elizabeth was in her sixth month, the angel Gabriel was

sent by God to a young girl in a town of Galilee called Nazareth. 27
She was engaged to a man of the house of David called Joseph;
and the girl's name was Mary.

The angel went in to Mary and said, "Greeting to God's favoured 28
one! The Lord is with you."

And Mary was troubled at his words, wondering what was 29
behind this greeting.

But the angel said to her, "Have no fear, Mary. God's favour 30
is with you. You shall become a mother and shall give birth to 31
a son, whose name you shall call Jesus. He will be great, and will 32
have the title 'Son of the Most-high'. The Lord God will give
him the throne of his father, David; he will be king for ever over 33
the house of Jacob, and his reign will never end."

The mother of my Lord

Mary said to the angel, "How can this be? I am a virgin." 34
And the angel replied, "A holy Spirit will come upon you and 35
the power of the Most-high will overshadow you; for this reason
the holy child to be born will be called 'Son of God'.

And not only that! Even your cousin Elizabeth is going to have 36
a son, in spite of her years. Although she was supposed to be
barren she is now in her sixth month; for the word of God 37
never fails."

Mary said, "I am the Lord's servant; let it be done as you say." 38
And the angel left her.

Deliberate speed, majestic instancy

Presently, Mary got ready and set out in haste for a town in the 39
hill country of Judah. She entered Zachary's house and greeted 40
Elizabeth. And when Elizabeth heard Mary's greeting, the infant 41
leaped in her womb. She was filled with a holy Spirit and in 42
animation cried out to Mary, "Of all women you are blessed, 43
and blessed is the infant in your womb! Who am I, that I should
be favoured with a visit from the mother of my Lord? Indeed, 44
the very moment I heard your greeting, the infant in my womb
leaped for joy. How blessed she is who has had faith in what the 45
Lord promised her!"

Millions this night will sing Magnificat

46 **And Mary said:**
"My soul sings the praise of the Lord.
47 My heart rejoices in God my Saviour.
48 For he has looked to the lowliness of his servant.
Yes. All generations will count me blessed.
49 The Almighty has done great things for me;
holy is his name.
50 From age to age his mercy never ends,
for men who fear him.
51 He shows his might in the strength of his arm,
and smites the proud, in their arrogance.
52 He brings down the mighty from their seats,
and raises up the lowly.
53 He fills the hungry with good things,
and sends the rich empty away.
54 Mindful of his promised mercy,
he has come to the aid of Israel, his servant,
55 keeping his pledge to our fathers,
his covenant for ever to Abraham and his posterity."

56 Mary remained with Elizabeth for about three months and then
returned to her home.

And joy is in the throbbing tide

57 In due course the time of Elizabeth's pregnancy came to an end
58 and a son was born to her. And when news got around of the
Lord's great kindness to her, her neighbours and relations all
rejoiced with her.

59 On the eighth day they gathered for the circumcision of the child,
and wanted to name him after his father Zachary.
60 But his mother would not hear of it. "No!" she said, "he shall
be called John."
61 So they pointed out that none of her family was called by this
62 name; and they made signs to the father to see what he wanted
to call the child.

Demanding a writing-block, Zachary wrote, "His name is John." 63
And this set them all wondering.
Then Zachary immediately got back the use of his tongue and 64
began to speak, praising God.

A strange fear came upon all the neighbours. Indeed the whole 65
hill country of Judaea was soon talking about these things.
Pondering them deep in their hearts, all the people had one 66
question: "What is this child to become?"
For the hand of the Lord was surely upon him.

Perpetual benediction

His father Zachary was filled with the holy Spirit, and prophesied 67
in these words:
"Blessed the Lord God of Israel, 68
who has visited his people and brought them salvation,
who has raised up a strong saviour, in the house of David his 69
servant.
Already he had promised it of old, 70
speaking by the lips of his holy prophets,
that he would save us from our enemies, 71
from the hands of those who hate us.
Already he had shown kindness to our ancestors, 72
fidelity to his holy covenant.
He had promised on oath to our father, Abraham, 73
to deliver us from the hand of our enemies, 74
to enable us to serve him without fear, 75
and walk before him in holiness and justice,
all the days of our lives.

And you, child, will be called a prophet of the Most-high; 76
you will go before the Lord to prepare for his coming,
to bring to his people assurance of salvation, 77
through forgiveness of their sins.
By the pity and mercy of our God 78
the morning-star will visit us from on high,
to shine on men who sit in darkness and the shadow of death, 79
to lead our steps in the way of peace."

And all who would save their lives must find the desert—
The lover, the poet, the girl who dreams of Christ

80 The child grew up and became strong in spirit; **and he lived alone in the wilderness** until the day of his manifestation to Israel.

God's most deep decree

2, 1 At that time a decree went out from Augustus Caesar that the
2 whole empire should be registered for taxes, a census that first took place when Quirinius was governor of Syria.
3 So all the people set out to have themselves registered, each to his own town.
4 And Joseph, who belonged to the house and family of David, went from the town of Nazareth in Galilee to the town of David
5 in Judaea, which is called Bethlehem, to be registered there with Mary, his pledged wife, who was expecting a child.
6 And it happened that while they were in Bethlehem the time came for Mary's child to be born.

Adore and draw near

7 She gave birth to a son, her 'first-born'; and she wrapped him up, and cradled him in a manger, because they could not find lodging at the inn.

Harping in loud and solemn quire

8 In the same district there were shepherds, spending the night in the fields and taking turn watching their flocks.
9 And an angel of the Lord came to them, and the splendour of the Lord shone all round them; and great fear came upon them.
10 But the angel said to them, "Have no fear. I bring you good news
11 of a great joy that is to come for all the people: Today a Saviour has been born to you in the town of David; he is the Lord Messiah.
12 This will be a sign for you: you will find the infant all wrapped up, and cradled in a manger."

Suddenly a multitude of the heavenly army was with the angel; 13
and they sang the praise of God:
"Glory to God on high, 14
and on earth peace,
among God's chosen people."

Great things and full of wonder in our ears

When the angels had departed to heaven, the shepherds said to 15
one another, "Why don't we go over to Bethlehem and see what
has happened, according to this word revealed to us by the
Lord?"
So they hurried there and found Mary and Joseph, and the 16
infant cradled in the manger.
Having seen it all, they made known what the word of the Lord 17
had revealed about this child.
And all who heard it were astonished at what the shepherds told 18
them.

The still, small voice

Mary, too, took all these words to heart and pondered them to 19
herself.

Look down on us gently who journey by night

Then the shepherds went back to work, praising God and thank- 20
ing him for all they had heard and seen, as had been promised
them.

That which was our duty to do

A week later, when the child was circumcised, he was given the 21
name Jesus, which the angel had announced before his concep-
tion.
And in due course, when the time of purification laid down by 22
Moses was also completed, his parents brought him to
Jerusalem to offer him to the Lord, in accordance with the law of 23
Scripture: "Every first-born male shall be deemed consecrated

24 to the Lord"; and also to offer the sacrifice prescribed by the law, "a pair of turtle-doves or two young pigeons."

They that wait upon the Lord

25 At Jerusalem there was a man called Simeon, an honest, god-fearing man, who lived for the day when the fortunes of Israel
26 would be restored. The Holy Spirit was with him, and he had been given to know by the Spirit that he would not die before he had seen the Lord's Messiah.

Give thanks and lie down in peace

27 So he came to the temple, under the impulse of the Spirit. And when his parents brought in the child Jesus to do for him what
28 was customary under the law, he took him in his arms and gave thanks to God in these words:
29 "Almighty God,
   now you are letting your servant die,
   in the peace you promised.
30 For my own eyes have seen your Saviour,
31 prepared by you in the sight of all the peoples,
32 as a light of revelation for the nations,
   as a glory for your people Israel."

Death died and Birth was born with one great cry

33 No little wonder was caused to the child's father and mother by
34 all these things. Simeon blessed them, and said to his mother Mary, "This child will decide the future of many in Israel—their rise or their downfall—so that the inmost thoughts of men may stand revealed. A sign he will be, but a sign to be rejected;
35 and you yourself will have your heart pierced by a sword."

But the hope of the poor shall not perish for ever

36 There was also a prophetess, Anna, a daughter of Phanuel of the
37 tribe of Asher, who was now well on in years. At the age of eighty she still remained a widow, having lived after girlhood seven

years of married life with her husband. She spent all her time
in the temple, serving God day and night, fasting and praying.
At this very moment she came on the scene, and gave praise to 38
God. And she used speak about the child to all who were looking
for the liberation of Jerusalem.

Then, when they had carried out everything prescribed by the 39
law of the Lord, the parents returned to Galilee, to their own
town of Nazareth. And the boy grew up to be strong and full of 40
wisdom; God's grace was upon him.

This birth was hard and bitter agony for us

His parents used go up every year to Jerusalem for the paschal 41
feast; so when he reached the age of twelve, they made the 42
pilgrimage as usual. But at the end of the festive week, when 43
they set out for home, Jesus unknown to them stayed behind in
Jerusalem. Thinking all the time that he was with the other 44
pilgrims, they had travelled a whole day's journey before they
began to search for him among the relatives and friends. And 45
having failed to find him, they returned to Jerusalem to look
for him.

Only after three days did they discover him in the temple. There 46
he was, seated among the learned doctors, listening to them and
asking them questions! And all were astounded at his intelligence 47
and his answers.
They could hardly believe their eyes when they saw him. "My 48
son," said his mother to him, "why did you do this on us? Your
father and I have been so worried looking for you."
He replied, "Why were you looking for me? Were you not aware 49
of my duty to be in my Father's house?"
But they did not understand what he meant. 50

He then went home with them to Nazareth and lived in obedience 51
to them. And his mother stored up all these things in her heart.

As he grew up, Jesus was outstanding both for his wisdom and 52
for the favour he enjoyed before God and men.

I heard a herald's note announce the coming of a king

3, 1 It was the fifteenth year of Tiberius Caesar's reign. Pontius
Pilate was the governor of Judaea, Herod the ruler of Galilee,
Philip his brother the ruler of Ituraea and Trachonitis, Lysanias
2 the ruler of Abilene; and the high priests were Annas and
Caiphas.

That was when God's call came to John, the son of Zachary, in
the desert.

3 He went all over the Jordan region, proclaiming baptism and
calling on men to begin a new life, so as to be freed from their
sins.

4 For so it stood written in the book of Isaia the prophet:
'A voice calls in the desert:
Make ready the way for the Lord,
make straight the path for his coming.

5 Every valley shall be filled,
every mountain and hill levelled down.
The crooked shall be made straight,
the rough made smooth.

6 And all mankind shall see the salvation of God.'

7 Crowds of people were flocking to John to be baptized. And he
said to them, "Who has given you to think, brood of vipers, that
8 you shall escape the coming anger of God? Show by your deeds
the conversion of your hearts; and do not have the presumption
to think, 'We have Abraham for father.' For I tell you that God
9 can raise up children to Abraham from these stones! Already the
axe is laid to the roots of the trees; any tree that does not produce
the right fruit will be cut down and thrown in the fire."

A way of life becoming to mankind

10 The people asked him, "What then must we do?"
11 And John answered, **"Whoever has two coats, let him share with
the man who has none;** whoever has food let him do the same.'

12 Even tax-collectors came to John to be baptized.
"What must we do, Master," they asked him.

13 And he answered, "Do not exceed the assessment laid on you."
14 The soldiers came and asked him, "What are we to do?"
And he replied, "No bullying or oppression! And be satisfied with your pay."

All prophecy, all medicine, is mine

15 The people were expecting great things of John, and all were wondering whether perhaps he was the Messiah.
16 John however spoke out openly and said, "I baptize you with water; but another is coming who is stronger than I, the thong of whose sandals I am not worthy to untie. He will baptize you
17 with a Holy Spirit and with fire. His winnowing shovel he has ready in his hand, to cleanse out the chaff from his threshing-floor; the wheat he will gather into his barn, the chaff he will burn with unquenching fire."
18 And many other things, too, John demanded of the people in his preaching of the gospel.

The climbing, the endless turning

19 Even Herod the king was taken to task by John, because of Herodias, his brother Philip's wife, and all the wicked things
20 he did. And to top them all he now put John in prison.

Anointed with the Spirit and with power

21 It was at this time, when all the people were being baptized, that Jesus too was baptized.
22 And as he was praying, heaven opened and the Holy Spirit came down upon him in bodily form, like a dove. And there was a voice from heaven: "You are my beloved Son. You have I chosen."

Noblest scion of the human race

23 When Jesus began his work he was about thirty years old, the son, as it was thought, of Joseph. And the line of his ancestors

went back from Joseph to Heli, Matthat, Levi, Melchi, Jannai, 24
Joseph, Mattathiah, Amos, Nahum, Esli, Naggai, Maath, 25
Mattathiah, Semein, Josech, Joda, Johanan, Rhesa, Zerubbabel, 27
Shealtiel, Neri, Melchi, Addi, Cosam, Elmadam, Er, Joshua, 29
Eliezer, Jorim, Matthat, Levi, Symeon, Juda, Joseph, Jonam, 30
Eliakim, Melea, Menna, Mattatha, Nathan, David, Jesse, Obed, 32
Boaz, Salmon, Nahshon, Amminadab, Admin, Arni, Hezron, 33
Perez, Juda, Jacob, Isaac, Abraham, Terah, Nahor, Serug, Ragu, 34
Phalek, Eber, Sala, Kainam, Arphachsad, Shem, Noah, Lamech, 36
Methuselah, Enoch, Jared, Mahalaleel, Kainam, Enosh, Seth, 38
Adam.
Finally to God.

I have chosen thee in the furnace of affliction

Filled with the Holy Spirit, Jesus then departed from the Jordan 4, 1
valley, and for forty days was led by the Spirit in the desert, 2
while being tempted by the devil.

During all this period he had eaten no food, and was hungry
when it was over. And the devil said to him, "If you are God's 3
Son, say the word and let this stone become bread."
But Jesus replied, "It is written in Scripture: 'Not on bread 4
alone shall man live.' "

Thy word is a lamp unto my feet, and a light unto my path

Then the devil took him up and showed him in a flash all the 5
kingdoms of the world. "I will give you all this," he said, "—all 6
this power and splendour; for it is mine to dispose of, and I can
give it to whom I choose. You have only to pay homage to me, 7
and all will be yours!"
And Jesus replied, "It is written in Scripture: 'You shall worship 8
the Lord your God; him alone you shall serve.' "

He will not suffer thy foot to be moved

Then the devil brought him to Jerusalem and set him high on 9
the parapet of the temple. "Are you not God's Son?" he said.

10 "Well, throw yourself down! For it is written in Scripture, 'God
11 will give his angels charge over you, to protect you.' And also,
'they will bear you in their arms, lest you strike your foot against
a stone.' "

12 And Jesus replied, "God has also commanded, 'You shall not
put the Lord your God to the test.' "

13 Having thus completed the temptation, the devil departed from
him for the time being.

In wisdom bidding aloud
To world-wide brotherhood

14 And Jesus, in fulness of power from the Spirit, returned to
Galilee.
15 Reports about him spread throughout the country; he himself
was teaching in their synagogues and was highly thought of by
all.

16 He came to Nazareth, where he had been brought up, and went
17 to the synagogue on the sabbath, as was his custom. When he
stood up to read the Scripture he was given the book of the
prophet Isaia; so he opened it and found the place where it was
written:
18 'The Spirit of the Lord rests upon me, because he has anointed
me.
He has sent me to announce good news to the lowly,
to proclaim release for the captives,
and sight for the blind,
to let the broken victims go free,
19 and to herald the Lord's year of grace.'

Out of key with his time

20 Then he closed the book, gave it back to the attendant, and sat
down; and all the people in the synagogue had their eyes fixed
21 on him. The theme on which he preached was this: "Today, as
you are listening here, these words of Scripture have come to
pass."

22 And they were all duly impressed, but they could not understand how he should have been gifted with such words. "Isn't this the son of Joseph?" they said.

23 And Jesus replied, "No doubt you will quote me the proverb, 'Physician heal yourself: the miracles we hear you have worked down in Capharnaum, do them here in your own town.'

24 But how true it is that a prophet never gets a welcome in his own town!

25 Indeed, there were many widows in Israel during the time of Elia, when the rains of heaven were stopped for three years and

26 a half and famine came to the whole country; yet to none of these was Elia sent, but to a widow of Sarepta in the land of Sidon.

27 There were many lepers in Israel in the days of Elisha the prophet; and yet not one of these was healed, but Naaman from the land of Syria."

28 And the people in the synagogue became furious at these words.

29 Rising from the meeting, they drove him from the town and brought him to the brow of the hill, where their town was built, intending to hurl him down.

30 But he passed through the crowd and departed.

He is a presence to be felt and known

31 He went down to the town of Capharnaum in Galilee and used
32 teach them there on the sabbath. And they were all astounded at his doctrine and the authority with which he spoke.

33 In the local synagogue there was a man with an unclean spirit,
34 who shouted at the top of his voice, "Ha! Jesus of Nazareth! What do you want from us? Have you come to destroy us? I know who you are—God's Holy One."

35 But Jesus rebuked him, "Silence! Go out from him!" And the demon, dashing the man down before all the people, went out and left him unharmed.

36 A strange fear came upon all of them.
"What can this be at all?" they were saying to one another. "Here is one who commands evil spirits with authority and power, and they go out!"

And the fame of Jesus spread to every corner of the country. 37

On leaving the synagogue he went to Simon's house. Simon's 38
mother-in-law was in the grip of a high fever, so they asked him
to do something for her.
Standing over her bed, he commanded the fever to leave her. 39
And so it did.
Immediately she got up and began to serve them.

At sunset all those who had sick people afflicted with various 40
diseases brought them to him; and he would stand over each
one, lay his hands on them, and heal them.
Evil spirits, too, came out from many; and they used shout out 41
and say, "You are the Son of God."
But Jesus would not allow them to speak, because they knew
that he was the Messiah.

His reign of peace upon the earth began

When morning came he went away out to a lonely place. The 42
people went looking for him and, when they came to him, wanted
to hold him, and not to let him go away from them.
But he said to them, "I must preach to the other towns too the 43
gospel of the kingdom of God; this is why I have been sent."
So he went about preaching the gospel in the Jewish synagogues. 44

And we have come into our heritage

On one occasion, when he was by the lake of Gennesareth and 5, 1
all the people were pressing round to hear him preach the word
of God, he saw two boats by the lake-side; the fishermen had 2
left them and were cleaning their nets. He got into one of them— 3
it was Simon's—and asked Simon to pull out a little from the
shore.
He then sat in the boat and taught the people from it.

When he had stopped speaking he said to Simon, "Push out to 4
the deep water and let out your nets for a catch."

5 And Simon replied, "Master, all the night we have been working hard and have caught nothing; however, seeing it's you that say it, I will let out the nets."

6 So they did this, and made such a huge catch of fish that the nets
7 were bursting. They hailed their workmates in the other boat to come and help them; and when these drew up, the two boats were loaded till they were almost sinking.

8 The sight of this was enough to make Peter fall on his knees before Jesus.

"Lord," he said, "go away from me! I am a sinful man."

9 A strange fear had come upon him, and upon all the others, over
10 the catch of fish they had just made; so too James and John, the Sons of Zebedee, who were Simon's partners.

Jesus, however, said to Simon, "Have no fear. From now on your nets will capture men."

11 Then, having rowed their boats ashore, they left all things and followed him.

Our goal which we compel: Man shall be man

12 Jesus was in one of their towns when a man who was covered with leprosy happened to come along; the moment he saw him he fell prostrate before him and begged his help. "Sir," he said, "if only you want to, you can heal me of my disease."

13 "Yes, I do," said Jesus, as he reached out his hand and touched him. "Be healed!" And his leprosy disappeared at once.

14 Jesus, however, would not allow him to tell anyone, except to go to the priest and let him see that he was cured; having been healed of leprosy he was to bring the offering prescribed by Moses, to have the cure certified.

And mark in every face I meet
Marks of weakness, marks of woe

15 In spite of this, however, news about him was actually spreading; and large crowds of people would gather to hear him and to be cured of their sicknesses.

16 And from time to time he himself used withdraw to lonely places for prayer.

Punished by crimes of which I would be quit

One day, as he was teaching, some Pharisees and doctors of the 17
law were sitting around, having come from Judaea and
Jerusalem as well as the villages of Galilee; and he was favoured
by the Lord with power to heal.
Who should arrive just then but a party of men carrying a cripple 18
on a stretcher. They were trying to bring him in and lay him
down before Jesus, but they could not reach him on account of 19
the crowd; so they climbed up to the roof, made an opening in
the tiles, and let the man down on the stretcher, right in front
of him.
And when he saw their faith he said, "Friend, your sins are 20
forgiven."

With tranquil restoration

A debate then started among the doctors of the law and the 21
Pharisees. "How can he have the nerve?" they said. "This is
blasphemous talk! Who but God alone can forgive sins?"
But Jesus, knowing their minds, said to them, "Why have you 22
these thoughts? Which do you think is the easier, to say, 'Your 23
sins are forgiven', or to say, 'Get up and walk'?
But I will let you see that the Son of Man has power on earth to 24
forgive sins."
So he turned to the cripple and said, "Stand up, I tell you, take
your stretcher and go home."
In a twinkle the man was on his feet before them all; he took the 25
bed on which he had lain and went home, praising God. And 26
they were all utterly dumbfounded. A strange fear came upon
them and they began to praise God, saying to themselves, "What
we have seen today is incredible!"

The Father's will
May we also know and may we fulfil

Afterwards Jesus went out and saw a tax-collector, whose name 27
was Levi, sitting at the tax-office. "Follow me," he said to him.
And Levi packed up, and left all behind to follow him.   28

29 He gave a great party for Jesus at his home; and among the guests were a large number of tax-collectors and their friends.
30 So the Pharisees and their learned doctors began to complain to his disciples, "How is it that you take meals with these tax-collectors and sinners?"

The silver answer rang, . . . 'Not Death but Love!'

31 Jesus replied, "It is not the healthy who need a doctor but the
32 sick. I have not come to call the pious to penance, but men who are remote from God."

And bade the world forget it had been sad

33 They said to him, "Why is it that the disciples of John and of the Pharisees observe fasts and times of special prayer, while yours go in for eating and drinking?"
34 And Jesus answered, "Can you expect the bridegroom's friends
35 to go fasting while the bridegroom is with them? But a time will come when the bridegroom will be taken from them; and when that time comes, **they will have good reason to fast.**"

I make all things new

36 To illustrate his point he went on to say, "Nobody cuts a piece from a new coat to patch an old one. For one thing the new coat will be torn; for another, the new patch will not suit the old material.
37 Nor do people pour new wine into unseasoned skins, or if so, the new wine bursts the wine-skins, so that the wine is lost and the
38 skins are destroyed. New wine is poured into new skins.
39 And no person with a taste for the old will drink new wine; he will say, 'You can't beat the old!' ' "

Glad from a world grown old and cold and weary

6, 1 On one occasion, as he was passing through wheat-fields on a sabbath, his disciples began to pluck ears of wheat, rubbing them in their hands and eating the grains.
2 Some of the Pharisees remarked, "Why are you doing what is not allowed on the sabbath?"

3 And Jesus replied, "Do you not remember the story in the Bible of what David did when he and his companions were hungry?

4 How he entered the house of God and took the sacred loaves laid out there, eating them and sharing them with his companions —although only the priests are allowed to eat them."

5 He added, "The Son of Man is Lord of the sabbath."

6 On another sabbath when he had gone into a synagogue and was teaching, there was a man present whose right hand was shrivelled

7 up. The doctors of the law and the Pharisees were watching him to see if he would heal him on the sabbath, so as to be able to bring a charge against him.

8 But he knew their minds and said to the man with the shrivelled hand, "Stand out here in the middle."
The man did so.

9 And Jesus said to them, "I ask you, is it right to do good on the sabbath, or to do evil; to save life, or to destroy?"

10 Then, looking round on all of them, he said to the man, "Stretch out your hand."

11 And the moment he did so, his hand was restored.
So they were furious and began discussing among themselves what they would do with Jesus.

They love the Good : they worship Truth

12 At this time Jesus once went out to the hills to pray and passed

13 a whole night in prayer before God. When the day broke he summoned his disciples and selected twelve from among them, whom he named Apostles.
Their names were as follows:

14 Simon, whom he named Peter,
and his brother Andrew;
also James and John,
Philip and Bartholomew,

15 Matthew and Thomas,
James, the son of Alphaeus,
and Simon, who was called the 'Zealot';

16 then Jude, the son of James,
and finally, Judas Iscariot, who turned traitor.

For lives that slyly turn in their cramped holes

He then went down with them to a level area; and he stood 17
there, surrounded by a large number of his disciples and a great
multitude of people from all over Judaea and from Jerusalem
and the coast of Tyre and Sidon, who had come to hear him and 18
to be healed of their diseases. Those who were troubled by evil
spirits were cured; and all the people wanted to touch him, 19
because of this extraordinary power that came out from him and
healed them all.

Into a transcendental innocence

And Jesus, with his eyes raised towards his disciples, said to 20
them:
"Well for you poor; for yours is the kingdom of God.
Well for you who are now hungry; for you will be filled. 21
Well for you who now weep; for you will laugh.
Well for you when people hate you, and shun you, and slander 22
you, and disown your name as evil, because of the Son of Man.
Let it be for you a day of joy and gladness, because your reward 23
in heaven will be great; for that was how their ancestors treated
the prophets.

But woe to you rich; for you have had your comfort. 24
Woe to you who are now filled; for you will go hungry. 25
Woe to you who now laugh; for you will mourn and weep.
Woe to you when all men speak well of you; 26
for that was how their ancestors treated the false prophets.

A terrible beauty is born

I say to you who listen: 27
Love your enemies.
Do good to those who hate you.
Bless those who curse you. 28
Pray for those who show you malice.
If a man strikes you on one cheek, turn him the other as well. 29
If a man takes your overcoat, let him have your coat as well.

30 Give to the one who asks.
Do not seek the return of what has been taken from you.

The flower of the Ages
And the first love of the world

31 Treat others as you would like others to treat you.

32 If you love only those who love you, what thanks can you expect? Even sinners return love for love.

33 If you do good only to those who do good to you, what thanks can you expect? Even sinners do as much.

34 If you lend only when you expect a return, what thanks can you expect? Even sinners lend to sinners, when they expect to get their money back.

35 With you it must be different: Love your enemies, and do good, and lend to others, even when you expect no return. Your reward will be very great, and you will be true children of God; for God also is good to thankless people and evildoers.

36 Be merciful, as your Father is merciful.

37 Do not judge others, and you will not be judged.
Do not condemn, and you will not be condemned.
Forgive others, and you will be forgiven.

38 Give to others, and God will give to you.
A good measure, well-shaken, well-packed and flowing over, God will give to you; **for the measure of your giving will be the measure of God's giving to you."**

My heart in unison with all mankind

39 He also gave them a proverb: "Can a blind man be guided by another blind man? Will not both fall into the ditch?

40 A disciple is not above his master, but if he is properly trained he will be like his master.

41 How can you see the speck in your friend's eye, if you cannot
42 see the splinter in your own? How can you say to your friend, 'Friend, let me take that speck out of your eye', if you do not see the splinter in your own? Do not deceive yourself! First take the splinter out of your own eye; then you will be in a position to take the speck out of your friend's eye.

Christen me, therefore, that my acts in the dark may be just

43 A good tree does not yield bad fruit, nor does a bad tree yield
44 good fruit; every tree is known by its fruit.
Figs are not gathered off brambles, nor grapes off briars.
45 A good man yields what is good from the good that is stored in
his heart; an evil man yields what is evil from the evil that is
stored in his heart. Whatever is stored in the heart, that is what
the mouth speaks.

Nothing half-hearted or ambiguous
But the perfected diamond of my will

46 What is the point of appealing to me, 'Lord! Lord!' if you will
not do what I tell you?
47 The one who comes to me, and listens to my words, and acts
48 on them—what is he like? Let me tell you: he is like a man who
builds a house, and digs deep, and sets the foundation on solid
rock; when the waters run high, and the floods come beating
against that house, they cannot shake it, because it is solidly
built.
49 But the one who hears my words, and does not act on them, is
like a man who builds a house on earth, without a foundation;
when the floods come beating against it, it tumbles down.
And great is the crash of that house."

Lord, let this man live

7, 1 Having completed his discourse to the people, Jesus moved on
2 to Capharnaum. And a certain officer had a servant who was
very dear to him, who had now fallen ill and was at death's door.
3 The officer had heard about Jesus, so he sent him a delegation
of senior Jewish citizens, to ask him to come and save his
servant.
4 When they came to Jesus, these people presented their plea with
5 urgency: "This man deserves a good turn from you; he is a
friend of our people and has actually built our synagogue."
6 So Jesus accompanied them.
He had almost reached the house when the officer sent out some

of his friends to say to him, "Sir, don't trouble yourself. I'm not
good enough to receive you in my house—which is why I didn't 7
think fit to approach you myself. Just say the word, and my
servant will be healed. I'm a man under authority, and I have 8
soldiers in my charge. If I tell one to go, he goes; if I tell one to
come, he comes; and if I tell my servant to do something, he
does it."

Hearing all this, Jesus was astounded at the man; he turned to the 9
people who were following him and said, "Not even in Israel, I
tell you, have I found faith like this."

And when the delegates returned to the house, they found the 10
servant fit and well again.

O stricken mother's soul!

Subsequently he came to a town called Nain, accompanied by 11
his disciples and a large crowd.

As he approached the town-gate it so happened that a dead man 12
was being brought to the grave, the only son of a widowed mother.

A large body of people from the town were in the procession
with her.

Seeing her, the Lord was moved to pity for her and said, "Do 13
not weep!"

And as he walked over to the coffin and laid his hand on it, the 14
bearers halted. "Young man," he said, "I command you to rise."

And the dead man sat up and began to talk; Jesus gave him back 15
to his mother.

A strange fear came upon them all and they gave praise to God: 16
"A great prophet has come among us," they said. "God has
looked with kindness to his people."

And this latest report about him spread to the whole of Judaea 17
and all the surrounding country.

The clue of reality

News of these things was also brought to John by his own dis- 18
ciples. So he summoned two of them and sent them to the Lord 19
to ask, "Are you really the one who is to come, or must we wait
for another?"

20 When they came to Jesus the men said, "John the Baptist has sent us to ask, 'Are you the one who is to come, or must we wait for another?' "

The glimpses of his Father's glory shine

21 At that time he had just cured many people of diseases and plagues and evil spirits, and had restored sight to many who were blind.

22 So this is how he answered John's disciples: "Go back and tell John what you have seen and heard: how the blind see, and the lame walk, and the lepers are healed, and the deaf hear, and the dead are raised, and the gospel is being preached to humble folk.

23 And well for the man who does not go wrong because of me!"

—What did you see?
—I saw myself and God

24 When the messengers had left, Jesus began to speak to the people about John: "That time you went out to the desert, what were you looking for? **A reed shaken by the wind? Was that it?**

25 Or what did you go out to see? Perhaps a man dressed in soft garments?
But the people who live and dress in luxury, you find them in the palaces of kings.

26 So what did you go out to see? A prophet?

27 Yes, I tell you, and more than a prophet. John is the one of whom Scripture says:
'I am sending my messenger ahead of you,
to prepare the road before you.'

28 Among all who have ever been born, I tell you, there is none greater than John.
And yet the least person in God's kingdom is greater than he.'

29 All the people who listened to him, tax-collectors included, had acknowledged the will of God by receiving John's baptism.

30 But the Pharisees and the teachers of the law rejected God's will in their regard, and would not have themselves baptized by him

All instincts immature
All purposes unsure

Jesus said, "How can I describe the people of this generation? 31
What are they like?
They are like the children you find sitting in the streets, who 32
call to one another:
We played you pipes, and you would not dance.
We keened the dead, and you would not mourn.'
John the Baptist came, eating no bread and drinking no wine; 33
and you say, 'He is mad!'
The Son of Man came, an eater and a drinker; and you say, 34
Here's a glutton, a drinker of wine, a friend of tax-collectors and
their ilk!'
So wisdom has been proved right by all her children." 35

You know what I was,
You see what I am : change me, change me!

One of the Pharisees invited Jesus to dinner; he went to the 36
Pharisee's house and sat down to table.
And a woman of the town who led a sinful life got to know that 37
Jesus was dining with the Pharisee. So she brought an alabaster
flask of expensive perfume, and finding a place behind at his feet 38
she began to weep; **she wet his feet with her tears,** wiped them
dry with her hair, kissed his feet, and anointed them with the
perfume.
Now the Pharisee who had invited Jesus was looking on and said 39
himself, "Surely if this man were a prophet he should have
known all about this woman who is touching him here, the kind
he is and the life she leads!"
And Jesus said to him, "Simon, I would like to say something 40
to you."
Certainly, Master!" replied Simon.

Love, it is certain, continues till we fail

And Jesus said, "A money-lender once had two debtors, one of 41
whom owed him fifty thousand, and the other five thousand.

42 But since neither could pay, he wrote off the debts of both. Now which of the two will like him the more?"

43 Simon replied, "Presumably the one whom he let off with the greater debt."

And Jesus said, "You are right."

Enough religion to hate but not enough to love

44 Turning then towards the woman he said to Simon, "You see this woman? When I came to your house you gave me no water for my feet; but she has wet them with her tears and dried them

45 with her hair. You gave me no kiss of welcome; but since I

46 came in here she has not ceased to kiss my feet. You did not anoint my head with oil; but she has even anointed my feet with expensive perfume.

That what has been may never be again

47 And therefore, I tell you, her many sins are forgiven her because she has loved much.

If one is forgiven but little, one loves but little."

48 And he said to the woman, "Your sins are forgiven."

49 The other guests at the table began to ask one another, "Who is this man who even forgives sins?"

50 But he said to her, "Your faith has saved you. Go in peace."

Lifting up, friend, upon you
The light of His countenance

8, 1 After this there followed a period when Jesus went from town to town and village to village proclaiming the joyful news of

2 God's kingdom. With him were the Twelve, and also some women who had been healed from evil spirits and other diseases. Mary, who was called the Magdalene, from whom seven demons

3 had been driven out, Johanna, the wife of an official of Herod called Chusa, and Susanna and many others. These women assisted them from their private means.

O Christ who drives the furrow straight

When a large crowd had assembled and people were flocking to 4
him from the towns, Jesus told them this parable:
"A sower went out to scatter his seed. As he scattered it some 5
fell on the path, and it was trampled on and eaten by the birds
of the sky.
Some seed fell on stony ground; and no sooner had it sprouted 6
than it withered, because it had no moisture.
Some fell among briars; but the briars grew up and choked it. 7
The rest of the seed fell on good soil; it grew up and produced 8
a rich harvest."
And Jesus said, "Whoever has ears to hear with, let him listen."

When his disciples asked him what the parable was about, Jesus 9
replied, "To you God has given the grace to know the secrets 10
of his kingdom; but for the others everything is in parables, so
that they may see, yet not perceive, and hear, yet not understand.

This is what the parable means:
The seed represents the word of God.   11
The seed that falls on the path stands for those who hear the 12
word, but the devil then comes and takes the word from their
hearts to prevent them from having faith and being saved.
The seed on the stony ground stands for those who, when they 13
hear the word, receive it with joy; but they have no roots. For
a while they have faith; then when trial comes they fall away.
The seed that falls in the briars stands for those who, when they 14
have heard the word, go off and allow themselves to be stifled
by the anxieties, the riches, and the pleasures of life; they never
reach maturity.
Finally, the seed that falls on the good soil stands for those who 15
hear the word and let it take root in a noble and good heart; after
patient trial they yield a rich harvest.

That I may walk before God, in the light of life

No one lights a lamp and puts it away under a vessel or a bed; 16
he puts it on a stand, so that all who enter may see the light.
There is nothing hidden that will not be revealed, nothing 17
covered up that will not be disclosed and come to light.

18 Be careful, therefore, how you listen.
So long as a man has something to start with, he will be given more; if he has nothing, even what he thinks he has will be taken from him."

To the place where God was homeless
And all men are at home

19 His mother and brothers came to visit him, but could not reach
20 him because of the crowd. So a message was brought to him "Your mother and your brothers are waiting outside to see you.
21 And he replied, "My mother and my brothers—who are they? They are those who hear my word and obey it."

Winds of the world give answer

22 One day, having got into a boat with his disciples, he said to them "Let us cross over to the other shore."
23 So they rowed away, and as they were sailing Jesus slept. Then a storm of wind came down on the lake and they were in danger
24 because the boat was filling. They came rushing to waken him "Master, Master, we're going down!"
And Jesus, awakened, commanded the wind and the raging waters; and all of a sudden they stopped, and a great calm came down.
25 He said to them, "Where is your faith?"
And they, in fear and wonder, asked themselves, "What kind of man is this, that he has power to command the winds and the waves and they obey him?"

Some wander the world and never find a home

26 They rowed over to the country of the Gerasenes, which lie opposite Galilee.
27 And as Jesus was landing from the boat, he was met by a man from the town who was possessed by demons, who for a long time had worn no clothes and lived in the tombs of the dead rather than in a house.
28 As soon as he saw Jesus he fell down before him with a cry, and

houted in a loud voice, "What do you want from me, Jesus, Son
f the Most-high God? Do not torment me!"

This was because Jesus was ordering the evil spirit to go out 29
rom the man. The spirit had had him in its clutches for many
years; although he used be bound hand and foot, to keep him
n check, he would break the fetters and be driven away out to
onely places.

What is your name?" Jesus asked him. 30
And he replied, "My name is Army."

'or there were many demons in possession of him; and they 31
egged Jesus not to command their return to hell.

A large herd of pigs was feeding there on the hill-side; so they 32
asked him to be allowed to enter the pigs. And Jesus allowed it.
They came out from the man and took possession of the pigs; 33
nd the whole herd rushed down the hill into the lake, and were
rowned.

'oo much reality can be a dazzle, a surfeit

Iaving seen all this, the herdsmen ran off to tell the news in the 34
own and the villages. And the people came out to see for them- 35
elves. They came to Jesus and found the man who had been
reed of the demons sitting at his feet, now clothed, and in his
ight mind. Great fear came upon them. And those who had 36
een what happened told them how the man had been saved
rom the demons.

All the people of the Gerasene country then asked him to go 37
way; for they were in the grip of a terrible fear.

So he got into the boat and turned for home. And the man from 38
vhom the demons had gone out wanted to stay with him. But
esus sent him away. "Go back home," he said, "and tell them 39
ll that God has done for you."

And the man went off, spreading news of what Jesus had done
or him all over the town.

An eagerness to understand more about sad men

On his return to the other side Jesus was welcomed by the 40
eople; for they had all been waiting for him.

And who should come but a man called Jairus, who was actually 41

223

a ruler of the synagogue. Falling at his feet, he begged Jesus to come to his house; **for he had an only daughter, twelve years old,**

42 and she was dying. So Jesus set out, with a large crowd pressing round him as he went along.

43 Among them was a woman who for twelve years had been suffer-
44 ing haemorrhages and had failed to get anyone to cure her. She stole up from behind and touched the fringe of his cloak; and immediately her bleeding stopped.

45 Jesus asked, "Who touched me?"
But no one around would admit to having touched him, so Peter said, "Look, Master, there are crowds of people pressing round and pushing you!"

46 But Jesus said, "I know that someone has touched me; I felt a force go out from me."

47 The woman, therefore, seeing that she had not got away un-noticed, came up and fell trembling at his feet; and she told him before all the crowd why she had touched him and how she had suddenly been healed.

48 And Jesus said to her, "Daughter, your faith has saved you. Go in peace."

49 No sooner had he said it than someone came to announce to the synagogue-ruler, "Your daughter is dead. No need to trouble the Master any further."

50 But Jesus, hearing it, turned to him and said, "Have no fear. Just have faith, and she will be saved."

51 On arriving at the house he would not allow anyone to go in with him, except Peter, John, and James, and the child's father and
52 mother. And all the people were weeping and mourning for the girl.

53 "Stop weeping," he said to them. "The child is not dead, but asleep."
And they only laughed at him, for they knew she had died.

54 Jesus however took hold of the girl's hand and called to her, "Wake up, child!"

55 Immediately life came back to her and she got up. And he told
56 them to give her something to eat. Her parents were utterly astounded; but he forbade them to tell anyone what had happened.

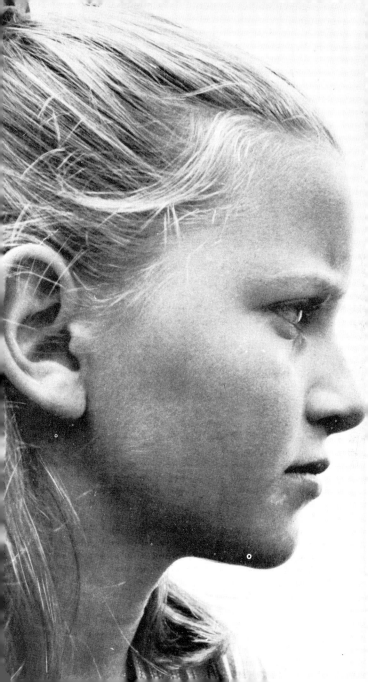

The perfected Work which is not ours

9, 1 He summoned the Twelve to him and gave them special power and authority to drive out demons and to heal the sick.

2 Then he sent them out to proclaim God's kingdom and to heal.

3 "Take nothing for the journey," he said to them. "No staff, no
4 bag, no food, no money—nor even a second coat. Once you take up residence in a house, remain in it until you move on from
5 there. But if the people do not give you a welcome, go out from that town and shake the dust from your feet, for evidence against them in judgement."

6 So they set out; they went through all the villages proclaiming the news of the gospel, and healing people everywhere.

Rulers who neither see, nor feel, nor know

7 Now Herod, the ruler of the country, came to hear of all this, but did not know what to make of it; some people told him that
8 John had risen from the dead, others that Elia had appeared, others again that one of the ancient prophets had risen.

9 Herod said, "John I beheaded myself, but who is this man about whom I hear all these things?"
   He was therefore anxious to meet him.

And the rich and the poor are no longer separate nations,—
They are brothers in night

10 On their return, the Apostles gave Jesus an account of what they had done. So he took them away privately and withdrew to a town called Bethsaida.

11 But the people got to know of it and went after him; and Jesus, giving them a welcome, spoke to them about the kingdom of God. If any needed healing, he healed them.

12 Meanwhile, it was getting late. The Twelve said to him, "Send the people away! Let them go to the neighbouring villages and farms to get lodging and food. We're out in a desert here."

13 "Let you give them food," Jesus said.
   "But we have only five loaves and two fish," they replied, "unless

you want us to go and buy provisions for all these people.''
(The men alone numbered about five thousand.)

He said to the disciples, "Get them all sitting down in groups 14
of about fifty.''
This they did, and got everyone sitting down. 15
Then, taking the five loaves and the two fish and raising his eyes 16
to heaven, he blessed them, and broke them, and passed them
to the disciples to distribute to the people.
All ate a full meal. And afterwards they gathered up the frag- 17
ments, twelve basketfuls.

Freely let me take of Thee
Spring Thou up within my heart

On one occasion the disciples were with him as he was praying 18
privately; and he asked them, "Who do people say that I am?''
They replied, "Some say John the Baptist, others Elia, and others 19
again that one of the ancient prophets has risen.''
"But who do you say that I am,'' he asked. 20
And Peter replied, "God's anointed Messiah.''
He warned them strictly not to tell this to anyone, saying to 21
them, "The Son of Man must go through great suffering and be
rejected by the elders of the people, the chief priests and the
doctors of the law; he will be put to death; and on the third day
he will rise again.''

In order to arrive at what you are not
You must go through the way in which you are not

He said to all his followers, "Any man who wants to be a disciple 23
of mine must renounce himself, take up his cross each day, and
come with me. The man who would save his own self shall lose it; 24
the man who is willing for my sake to lose his own self, shall save
it.
For even if one gains the whole world, what is the advantage, if 25
it's at the cost of losing one's true self?
Indeed, if anyone is ashamed of me and of my words, the Son 26
of Man will also be ashamed of him, when he comes in his glory

27 and that of his Father and the holy angels. And I tell you, there are some standing here who will not have died before they see the kingdom of God."

I saw through all the fleshly dress
Bright shades of everlastingness

28 About eight days after he had spoken these words, Jesus took Peter, John, and James with him and went up into the hills to pray.

29 As he was praying the appearance of his face was changed and
30 his garments shone with a brilliant whiteness. All of a sudden
31 they saw two men in conversation with him: Moses and Elia appearing in glory and talking about his forthcoming departure and all he was to fulfil in Jerusalem.

32 Peter and his companions were then overcome by sleep; and when they awoke they still saw his glory, and the two men
33 standing beside him. And as these began to draw away from him Peter said to Jesus—without really knowing what he was saying, "Master, **we find it so good to be here!** Let us make three tents, one for you, one for Moses, and one for Elia."

34 The words were still on his lips when a cloud came and overshadowed them; and as they entered the cloud they feared greatly.

35 And a voice spoke from it: "This is my Son, my chosen one. Listen to him."

36 As soon as the voice stopped they found Jesus alone with them again. The disciples kept it secret and told no one at the time of what they had seen.

Without me you can do nothing

37 The following day, when they had come down from the moun-
38 tain, they were met by a large crowd. And a man in the crowd called out to him, "Please, Master, look to my son—the only
39 one I have. Whenever the spirit seizes him it suddenly shouts out and throws him into a foaming fit; and it won't leave him,
40 except after a long, wearying struggle. I asked your disciples to drive it out, but they could not."

N SCHOOL OF ECONOMICS
POLITICAL SCIENCE
JOIN YOUR BOYCOTT
WE ARE NOT KIDDS TO BE CAINED! WE ARE RESPONSIBLE STUDENTS

And Jesus said, "O generation of unbelieving and misguided 41 people, how long shall I be with you? How long shall I bear with you? Bring your son to me."

And as the boy was coming up the demon threw him down, 42 bringing on a fit. But Jesus rebuked the spirit, and the boy was healed; he gave him back to his father.

And the people were all speechless at the extraordinary power 43 of God.

In the blood-red dawn, where two worlds strive

At this time, when all were wondering over his many deeds, Jesus said to his own disciples, "Listen carefully, and take my 44 words to heart: The Son of Man will be surrendered to men."

But they did not see the significance of what he said; it was all 45 so obscure to them that they failed to grasp it, and they were afraid to ask him about it.

Give me, made lowly wise,
The spirit of self-sacrifice

An argument arose among them as to **which of them ranked the** 46 **highest.**

And Jesus, knowing what was in their minds, took a little child, 47 placed him beside him, and said to them, "Anyone who receives 48 this child in my name, receives me; and whoever receives me, receives him who sent me.

Whoever is the least of all among you is the one who is great."

Say yes instead of no

John said to him, "Master, we saw someone driving out demons 49 in your name and we stopped him, because he was not one of ours."

But Jesus replied, "You should not stop him. Anyone who is 50 not against you is on your side."

As the time approached when God was to take him, he set his 51 mind with determination on the journey to Jerusalem and sent

52 messengers ahead of him. As they went their way they entered
53 a village of the Samaritans to prepare lodging for him, but the
people here refused to receive him, in view of the fact that he
was heading for Jerusalem.
54 The disciples James and John, when they saw this, said to him,
"Lord, do you want us to call down fire from heaven to consume
them?"
55 But Jesus gave them a sharp telling-off; and they moved on to
another village.

In order to possess what you do not possess
You must go by the way of dispossession

57 As they were travelling the road someone said to him, "I will
follow you wherever you go."
58 And Jesus replied, "The foxes have dens and the birds of the
sky have nests, but the Son of Man has nowhere to rest his head."

59 Another he invited to become his disciple; but the man replied,
"Allow me first to go home and bury my father."
60 And Jesus said, "Let the dead bury their dead. Go you, and
preach the kingdom of God."

61 Another said to him, "I will join you, Lord, but first allow me to
say good-bye to my family."
62 And Jesus replied, "No man who puts his hand to the plough
and looks behind is of the right mettle for the kingdom of God."

By winning words to conquer willing hearts

10, 1 Afterwards the Lord appointed seventy-two others and sent
them ahead in pairs to every town he was going to visit.
2 "The harvest to be reaped is vast," he said to them, "but the
workers are scarce. Pray the Lord of the harvest to send workers
to reap his crop.
3 Go then. I am sending you as sheep among wolves. Take no
5 purse, no bag, no shoes, and salute no one on the road. On
entering a house let your first words be, 'Peace to this house!'

If the man there is a peaceful man, your peace will rest upon 6
him; but if not, it will return to you.

Remain in the same house, eating and drinking what they give 7
you; for a working man deserves his pay. Do not move from
house to house.

When you come to a town and are welcomed, take the food that is 8
offered you and heal the sick¬whom you find there. Say to its 9
people, 'The kingdom of God is upon you.'

Till truth were freed, and equity restored

But if you come to a town and you are not welcomed, pass 10
through its streets and say to its people, 'The very dust of your 11
town that begrimes our feet, we shake it off against you. But
this you must know: the kingdom of God has drawn near.'

I tell you, the people of Sodom will get off more lightly on the 12
day of judgement than the people of that city.

Woe to you Chorazin! Woe to you Bethsaida! If the miracles 13
worked among you had been worked in Tyre and Sidon, these
cities would have long ago mourned for their sins and been
converted.

But Tyre and Sidon will get off more lightly in judgement than 14
you.

And you, Capharnaum, will you be exalted to heaven? You shall 15
be brought down to hell!

Anyone who hears you, hears me; anyone who rejects you, 16
rejects me; and whoever rejects me, rejects him who sent me."

Blessed by that Wholly Other Life

The seventy-two disciples returned full of enthusiasm and said 17
to him, "Lord, even the demons submit to us in your name."

He replied, "I have seen Satan fall like a lightning-flash from 18
the sky. Yes, I have given you power to trample every evil under 19
foot, to counter all the might of the enemy; nothing whatever
shall harm you.

But if you have reason to rejoice, it's not that the demons submit 20
to you but that your names are written in heaven."

233

So near is God to man

21 At that moment Jesus thrilled with joy in the fulness of the Holy
Spirit and said, "I thank you, Father, Lord of heaven and earth.
You have hidden these things from the wise and the learned, and
22 have revealed them to little ones. Yes, Father, such has been
your pleasure. All things have been committed to me by my
Father. Who the Son is, no one knows but the Father; who the
Father is, no one knows but the Son, and those to whom the Son
chooses to reveal him."

23 Turning to his disciples he said to them personally, "Happy the
24 eyes that see what you see! I tell you, many prophets and kings
have wished to see what you see, but have not seen it, and to
hear what you hear, but have not heard it."

To love or not; in this we stand or fall

25 A doctor of the law once stood up and asked him a leading question: "Master, what must I do to obtain eternal life?"
26 And Jesus said, "What is written in the law? Can you quote it?"
27 He replied, "You shall love the Lord, your God, with all your
heart, and all your soul, and all your strength, and all your mind
and you shall love your neighbour as you love yourself."
28 "Your answer is correct," Jesus said to him. "Keep this rule
and you will have life."
29 But the other, not to be outdone, said to him, **"Who is my
neighbour?"**

Any man's death diminishes me, because I am involved in mankind

30 Taking up his question Jesus told the following story:
"There was this man who was travelling from Jerusalem down
to Jericho and had the bad luck to come upon robbers. They
stripped him naked, gave him a cruel beating, and went off
leaving him half dead.
31 Now a priest happened to be travelling down that way; and he
saw the man, but passed by on the other side.
32 And a temple servant came by, who also gave a look and passed
by on the other side.

33 But a Samaritan was travelling down that road, and came upon
34 him; and the moment he saw him, his heart went out to him.
He went over to him, treated his wounds with oil and wine, and
bandaged them up; he mounted him on his own animal, brought
35 him to an inn, and looked after him. And the next day he pulled
out some money and gave it to the inn-keeper. 'Take care of him,'
he said. 'If you have any extra expenses I will pay you on my
return.'
36 Now which of those three do you think showed himself a neighbour to the man who was attacked by the robbers?"
37 And the other answered, "The one who had pity on him."
"Go then," said Jesus to him, "and follow the same example."

Elected silence, sing to me

38 When he came to a certain village in the course of their journey
39 a woman called Martha received him in her home. She had a
sister called Mary; and Mary sat at the Lord's feet listening to
40 his words, whereas Martha had her hands full with all the work
of the house. Eventually she came to him and said, "Lord, how
can you sit there and let my sister leave me to get the supper on
my own? Tell her give me a hand!"
41 And the Lord replied to her, "Martha, Martha, you are worried
42 and fussed about so many things. And there is so little required
—in fact one thing only. Mary has chosen the best part; it shall
not be taken from her."

Nearer to the fount of life

11, 1 On one occasion Jesus was praying at a certain place. When he
had finished, one of his disciples said to him, "Lord, teach us to
pray; for John also taught his disciples how to pray."
2 And he said to them, "When you pray, let it be like this:
Father,
May your holy name be known,
and your kingdom come.
3 Give us each day the bread that we need,
4 and forgive us our sins,
for we too forgive everyone who has wronged us;
and keep us safe from trial."

Begin betimes, and teach your little son
To serve and fear God also

He said to them, "Suppose one of you has a friend, and you go 5
to him in the middle of the night and say, 'Friend, lend me three
loaves. A friend of mine is breaking his journey with me and I 6
have nothing to offer him.'
Suppose this man shouts out to you, 'Don't be bothering me! 7
I've the door locked and the children here with me in bed. I just
can't get up and give you bread!'
Now even if he will not get up and give you what you need, on 8
the ground that you are a friend, let me tell you this: if you beg
shamelessly, then he will get up and look after your request.

To the depth of our desire

So too, I say to you, 9
Ask and you will receive,
seek and you will find,
knock and the door will be opened to you.
Everyone who asks receives; everyone who seeks finds; everyone 10
who knocks has the door opened to him.
If a son asks for a fish, will any father among you give him a 11
serpent?
If he asks for an egg, will you give him poison? 12

Or come we of an Automaton
Unconscious of our pains?

You people are by no means saints, but you know how to give 13
good things to your children. How much more will the Father
in heaven give a holy Spirit to those who ask him?"

Cease denying, begin knowing

One day he was driving out a spirit from a dumb man. And 14
when the spirit had gone out, the man was able to speak, and
the people were astonished.
Some of them however said, "His power is from Beelzebul, the 15
chief of demons. That's how he drives out demons."

16 Others wanted him to procure a sign from heaven, as a proof.
17 But Jesus, knowing their minds, said to them, "If a kingdom is divided, it loses its power; and if a house is divided, it falls to
18 pieces. What then if Satan has become divided? Can his kingdom survive?
19 Now you say that I get my power over demons from the ruler of demons; but if that is where I get mine from, from whom do your people get theirs?
Therefore they shall be your judges.
20 On the other hand, if I drive out demons by the finger of God, it is a sign that God's kingdom has come upon you.

21 So long as a strong man is armed and keeps guard on his house,
22 his property will be secure. But if a stronger one attacks and overcomes him, he takes away the arms on which he relied, and can then divide the spoils.

23 The man who is not with me is against me; the man who does not gather with me scatters.

Winning the war and losing the peace

24 When an unclean spirit goes out from a person, it scours the waterless desert looking for a place of rest. When it does not find
25 it, it says, 'I will go back to the house I left.' So it goes back and
26 finds the house all swept and tidied up. Then it sets out again, and picks up seven other spirits worse than itself; and they enter the house and take possession of it.
At the end, therefore, that man's plight is worse than it was at the start."

Happy he with such a mother

27 While he was saying these things, a woman in the crowd raised her voice and exclaimed, "Blessed the mother who bore you in her womb, and fed you at her breast!"
28 And he replied, **"Blessed, rather, those who hear God's word and keep it!"**

Precious the penitential tear
And precious is the sigh sincere

As the crowds were thronging to him, Jesus said, "The present 29 age is evil. It wants a sign, and no sign will be given it, except the sign of Jona. As Jona was a sign for the people of Niniveh, so 30 too the Son of Man will be a sign for the men of the present age.
The queen of the South will rise in judgement with the people 31 of the present age and will condemn them; for she came from the ends of the earth to hear the wisdom of Solomon.
And look! Here stands a greater than Solomon.
The men of Niniveh will rise in judgement with the people of 32 the present age and will condemn them; for they repented at the call of Jona.
And look! Here stands a greater than Jona.

Light shines out of darkness

Nobody lights a lamp and hides it in a cellar, or under a vessel; 33 it is set on a stand so that all who enter may enjoy its light.

If once we lose this light

The lamp of your body is the eye. If your eye is unclouded, your 34 whole body is lighted; but if your eye is evil then your body is dark.
Watch therefore **lest the light within you be covered in darkness.** 35 When your body is bright all over, and has no dark shadows in 36 it, it will be altogether bright, as if the beam of a lamp were shining on you."

No inner vileness that we dread?

When he had finished speaking he was asked to dinner by a 37 Pharisee; Jesus therefore went to his house and took a place at table. And the Pharisee was shocked to see that he did not wash 38 himself before the meal.
So the Lord said to him, "Now you Pharisees make clean the 39

40 outside of cup and dish, while your own hearts are filled with greed and wickedness. How senseless! Did not the same Creator
41 who made the outside also make the inside? Give instead to the poor the contents of cup and dish, and then all is clean for you.

42 But woe to you, Pharisees! You pay tithes of every garden herb and vegetable, while you disregard justice and the love of God. These it was your duty to observe, while not omitting the rest.

43 Woe to you, Pharisees! You like to have the top seats in the synagogue, and special honours in the streets.

44 Woe to you! You are like graves with weathered slabs; people walk on them without knowing it."

There are men whose minds the Dead have ravished

45 One of the doctors of the law said to him in reply, "Master, by these words you are also insulting us."

46 And Jesus said to him, "Woe to you as well—you doctors of the law! You load men down with unbearable loads, and will not touch them yourselves with a finger.

47 Woe to you! You build the monuments of the prophets—when
48 it was your own fathers who murdered them. You attest your approval of their deeds; they killed them, and you build the monuments!

49 That is why the Wisdom of God has said, 'I will send them prophets and apostles and some of these they will persecute and
50 kill.' Therefore the present age will answer for the blood of all
51 the prophets shed since the beginning of the world; from the blood of Abel to the blood of Zachary, who was killed between the altar and the temple—yes, I tell you, the present age will answer for it all!

52 Woe to you, doctors of the law! For you have taken away the key of knowledge. You yourselves did not go in; and the people who were on the way in you stopped."

53 Jesus then went away.
And the teachers of the law and the Pharisees became extremely hostile, hanging on every word he said, and laying traps in the hope of snaring him through his own words.

*To grow straight in the strength of thy spirit, and live out thy life
   as the light*

Meanwhile, when so many thousands of people had come 12, 1
together that they were walking on one another, Jesus first began
to warn his own disciples: "Be on your guard against the in-
fluence of the Pharisees—I mean hypocrisy. For nothing is 2
covered up that will not come to light; nothing is hidden that
will not be disclosed. Whatever you have whispered in the dark 3
will be heard in the light of day; whatever you have spoken in
secret will be proclaimed from the house-tops.

*The place where, in the end,
We shall find our happiness, or not at all*

To you my friends I say: have no fear of those who may kill the 4
body, but afterwards can do no more. Let me tell you whom to 5
fear. Fear the One who, after the killing, has power to hurl into
hell. Yes, I tell you, he is the One to fear!

Are not five sparrows sold for a couple of pence? And yet, not 6
one of them is forgotten before God. Not only that—even the 7
hairs of your head are all numbered. Have no fear therefore. God
lays more store on you than on all the birds.

The everlasting yea—or nay

I tell you this: if anyone declares for me before men, the Son 8
of Man will also declare for him before the angels of God; if 9
anyone disowns me before men, he will be disowned before the
angels of God.

Tell me what you mean by a sense of sin

Whoever speaks a word against the Son of Man, can still be 10
forgiven; but whoever slanders the Holy Spirit, will never be
forgiven.

Set a watch O Lord before my mouth, keep the door of my lips

Whenever you are brought before court-assembles and state- 11
authorities, do not worry about what you are to say in your

12 defence. When the actual moment comes, the Holy Spirit will tell you whatever needs to be said."

A chronicle of wasted time

13 Someone from the crowd said to him, "Master, please make my brother share the inheritance with me."

14 And Jesus replied, "Friend, who has appointed me to be judge or arbitrator over you?"

15 Then he said to them, "Be on your guard against avarice in any form. **A man's life does not depend on his possessions,** not even when he is rich."

16 And he told them the following story:

"There was once a rich man whose lands produced heavy crops.

17 'What am I to do,' he asked himself, 'since I've nowhere to store

18 my crops?' Then he decided, 'I know what I'll do! I'll pull down my barns and build bigger ones, where I can store away

19 my wheat and all my goods. And then I'll be able to sit back and say to myself: Listen, man, you've put away enough good things to last for many years! Take things easy. Eat, drink, and have a good time.'

20 God, however, said to him, 'You fool! This very night your life will be taken from you. All that you have stored away here—who is it for?'

21 That is the way with the man who gathers riches for himself, and is not rich towards God."

Wherefore tonight so full of care?

22 "I tell you therefore," he said to the disciples, "do not worry over the needs of life or of body—what to eat, or where to find

23 clothing; for life counts more than nourishment, and the body more than clothing.

24 Learn from the crows: they neither sow nor reap, they have neither stores nor barns, but still God looks after them.

And you, are you not much more important than the birds?

25 Can any of you by worrying add to the span of his life? And if even that much is not in your power, why are you anxious about the rest?

Look at the lilies: they neither spin nor make themselves clothes. 27
And yet, I tell you, not even Solomon in all his splendour was
dressed like one of them.

If that is how God clothes the grass of the field, which blooms 28
today and tomorrow is thrown in the fire, how much more will
he look after you, for all your want of faith! So you too should 29
not be anxious about what you are to eat or drink. Do not
worry about them. People of the world go running after these 30
things, but you have a Father who knows that you need them.
Let your care be for God's kingdom, and the rest will be looked 31
after by God.

So small the flock, so rich the promise!

Have no fear, little flock. It has pleased your Father to give you 32
the kingdom.

—Take all thou art, and give it to the poor

Sell your property and give all away in charity. Make yourselves 33
purses that will not wear out. Store up an imperishable treasure
with God, where no thief breaks in, or moth destroys.
Wherever your treasure is, there your heart will be. 34

Duly and daily serving him

Be ready for action and have your lamps lighted, like men 35
awaiting their master's return from the feast; the moment he 36
arrives and knocks at the door, they are ready to receive him.
Happy indeed the servants whom the master finds awake at his 37
return! Believe me, he will sit them at his table, and put on his
apron, and come himself and wait upon them.
And if he comes late in the night, or early in the morning, and 38
still finds them ready, happy those servants!
At least you know that if the master of the house knew the hour 39
when the thief was coming, he would take care not to have his
house broken into.
Therefore you too must be ready; for the Son of Man will come 40
at a moment when you least expect him."

Tears of years unharvested

41 Peter asked him, "Do you mean this parable only for us, or is it for everyone?"

42 And the Lord replied, "Who do you think is a reliable and careful steward? Whom does the master put in charge of his servants, to distribute rations when they are due?

43 Happy the servant whom the master finds doing his duty when
44 he comes. I assure you, he will put him in charge of his whole business.

45 Suppose, however, that that servant says to himself, 'My master won't be back for a long time yet!' Suppose he starts bullying the men and women in his care, or goes in for orgies of eating
46 and drinking—what then? His master will come on a day when he is not expected, at an hour that he does not know, and will give him a trouncing; he will put him down with the good-for-nothings.

47 When a servant knows his master's wishes but does not follow
48 them up or carry them out, he will be severely punished. But when a servant does not know his master's wishes—even if he does wrong and deserves a beating—he will be less severely punished.

If much has been given to a man, much will be expected of him; **and the more has been entrusted to him, the more will be demanded of him.**

Far into the country of Sorrow

49 I have come to set fire to the world. And how I wish the flames were already kindled!

50 But first I have to pass through a baptism of suffering, and great is my anguish until it be over.

51 Do you think that I have come to bring peace to the world? No,
52 I tell you, not peace but division. From now on, even within a household of five people, there will be division. Three will be
53 divided from two, or two from three: a father from his son, or a son from his father; a mother from her daughter, or a daughter from her mother; a mother-in-law from her daughter-in-law, or a daughter-in-law from her mother-in-law."

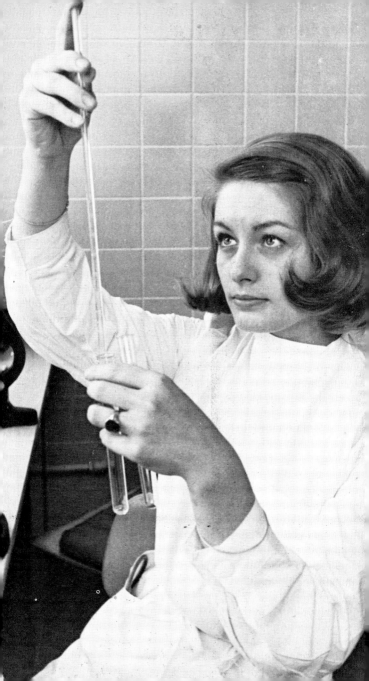

The proper darkness of humanity

He said to the people, "Whenever you see clouds rising in the 54
west, you know that rain is on the way; and the rain comes.
Whenever a south-wind blows, you know that heat is on the way; 55
and the heat-wave comes.
Hypocrites! You know how to discern the signs of earth and sky. 56
How is it that you cannot discern the signs of the present age? 57
Or why can you not judge for yourselves what is right?

Can two walk together except they be agreed?

If you are going to law with an opponent, you will do well to 58
make peace with him on the way to court. For there is a danger
that he may land you before the judge, that the judge may hand
you over to the police, and the police may throw you in jail.
I tell you, **not until you have paid the last penny** will you get out." 59

In this world
It is inexplicable, the resolution is in another

On that occasion people came with news of the Galileans whose 13, 1
blood Pilate had shed along with that of their victims of sacrifice.
Jesus replied, "Do you think that, because they suffered all this, 2
these Galileans were proved to be sinners more than the others? 3
That is not so. I assure you, unless you are converted, you will
all perish as they did.
Or do you think that the eighteen people who were killed when 4
the tower collapsed on them at Siloam were more guilty than
all the other residents of Jerusalem? That is not so. Unless you 5
are converted, you will all perish as they did."

Only love hath no decay

He told them this parable: "A certain man had a fig-tree growing 6
in his vineyard and came to it looking for fruit, but found none.
So he said to his gardener, 'For three years now I have been 7
coming to this tree looking for fruit and have found none. Cut
it down! Why let it take the good out of the soil?'
But the gardener replied, 'Sir, let it stand for another year. I'll 8

251

9 dig round it and manure it. Who knows? It may yet produce fruit. If it doesn't, then you can cut it down.' "

Honour has come back, as a King, to the earth

10 One sabbath-day Jesus was teaching in one of their synagogues.
11 And there was a woman present with a terrible affliction which she had borne for all of eighteen years; she was completely doubled up, and could not straighten herself.
12 On seeing her, Jesus called her over and said, as he laid his hands on her, **"Your bondage is at an end."**
13 And she immediately straightened up and began to pour out thanks to God.
14 But the master of the synagogue was very angry, because Jesus healed her on the sabbath. He announced to the people, "There are six working-days on which to work. Come to be healed on one of these—and not on the sabbath."
15 And the Lord replied to him, "Hypocrites! Is there any one of you who will not untie his ox or ass from the stable on the sabbath
16 and lead it out to water? Here is a daughter of Abraham whom Satan has tied up for eighteen years; should she not have been freed of her handicap, even on the sabbath?"
17 His opponents were all put to shame by his words; and the people were all filled with joy over his wonderful deeds.

What in itself it is, and would become

18 He once said, "What is God's kingdom like? Or how shall I
19 describe it? It is like a grain of mustard-seed which a man planted in his garden; it grew up to become a tree, and the birds of the sky made their home in its branches."

20 Again he asked, "How shall I describe God's kingdom?
21 It is like a pinch of ferment which a woman worked into a large quantity of flour, until the whole was fermented."

We are closed in, and the key is turned
On our uncertainty

22 As he journeyed towards Jerusalem he visited towns and villages

23 and taught in them. Someone asked him, "Sir, is it true that only few are saved?"

24 And Jesus replied, "Strive to enter by the narrow gate. I tell you, many will want to enter, and will not be able.

25 Once the man of the house has got up and closed the door you may come along and stand knocking outside, and say to him, 'Please, Lord, please open to us!'
He will reply, 'You are no friends of mine. Where are you from?'

26 At that you may well protest, 'But we ate and drank with you.

27 You taught us in our streets,' and still he will say to you: 'You are unknown to me. Get away from me, all you evil-doers!'

28 There, I tell you, will be the wailing and anguish of remorse—when you see Abraham and Isaac and Jacob and all the prophets in God's kingdom, and you yourselves thrown out!

While the rejected and condemned become
Agents of the divine

29 From the east and the west, from the north and the south, they will come and sit at table in God's kingdom.

30 For that is the way: people are now last who will be first, and people first who will be last."

And I am not in danger : only near to death

31 At that time some Pharisees came to him and said, "You had better leave this place and go away. Herod plans to kill you."

32 Jesus said to them, "Go and tell that fox: today and tomorrow I drive out demons and work cures; the third day I shall reach

33 my goal. Nevertheless today and tomorrow, and the day after, I must pursue my journey; for it is not possible that a prophet should die outside Jerusalem.

He who wept for Jerusalem
Now sees his prophecy extend
Across the greatest cities of the world

34 Jerusalem, Jerusalem, the city that kills the prophets and stones the men whom God sends to you, how often I have wanted to

gather your children, as a hen gathers her brood under her wings, but you were not willing. The word of the prophet will 35 come true: 'your home will be lost to you.'

I tell you this: you shall not see me again until the time comes when you will say, 'God's blessing on him who comes in the name of the Lord.' "

All that I would like to be is human

One sabbath-day, when he came to dinner at the house of a 14, 1 leader of the Pharisees, they were all watching him closely.
Directly in front of him there was a man who suffered from swell- 2 ing of the limbs.
And Jesus asked the doctors of the law and the Pharisees, "Is it 3 permitted to heal on the sabbath or not?"
But they said nothing. 4
So he laid his hands on the man, healed him, and sent him away.
Then he turned to them and said, "If one of you has a child or 5 an ox that falls into a pit, will you not immediately pull it out, even on the sabbath?"
And they had no answer to this. 6

Friend, go up higher

He noticed how the guests were trying to get places of honour 7 at the table, so he told them this parable: "Whenever you are 8 invited to a wedding-feast, be sure not to go to the place of honour. For it could happen that someone more important than you has been invited, and the host may have to come to you and 9 say, 'Give this man your place.' Then you will have to swallow your pride and go down to the last place.

Whenever you are invited you should go instead to the last place, 10 so that when the host comes along, he will say to you, 'Friend, go up higher.' And you will be distinguished before all your fellow-guests.

The man who exalts himself will be humbled; the man who 11 humbles himself will be exalted."

255

But all mankind's concern is charity

12 He said to his host, "Whenever you give a dinner or a party, take care not to invite your friends or brothers or relatives or rich neighbours; for there is a danger that they may return your
13 invitation and you will be repaid. When giving a banquet you should rather invite the poor, the crippled, the lame, the blind;
14 and it will be all to your good that these cannot pay you back, for you will be rewarded on the day that the saints rise from the dead."

For God's invincible spring our love is made afraid

15 One of the guests who was listening exclaimed, "Happy the man who will feast in God's kingdom!"
16 And Jesus told him the following story:
17 "A man once gave a great banquet and invited many guests. At the time for the dinner he sent his servant to tell the invited guests, 'Come along, everything is ready.'
18 And from the very start they all began to make excuses. One said to him, 'I have bought a farm and I have to go and look it over. My apologies!'
19 Another, 'I have bought five yoke of oxen and am going to try them. My apologies!'
20 And another, 'I have just married, so I cannot come.'

They told me there, that He was lately gone
About some land, which He had dearly bought

21 The servant came and reported all this to his master. And the man of the house was very angry, so he said to his servant, 'Go out quickly to the city-squares and streets and bring the poor people in here, and the crippled, the blind, and the lame.'
22 The servant reported, 'Sir, your orders have been carried out, but there is still room.'
23 And the master said to his servant, 'Go out along the roads and the hedge-rows and compel them to come in, so that my house
24 may be filled. For I tell you, none of those who were invited shall enjoy my banquet.'"

*It is one thing to be asked to leave sin and evil, quite another to
leave the good, the great, the beautiful*

Large crowds of people were travelling the road with him. And 25
Jesus turned round and said to them, "If anyone comes to me 26
without setting aside his father, mother, wife, children, brothers,
sisters—yes, even his own life—he cannot be my disciple.
Whoever is not prepared to carry his cross and come after me, 27
cannot be my disciple.

Now comes the pain of truth, to whom 'tis pain

Suppose one of you is thinking of putting up a building. Will he 28
not first sit down and count the cost, to see if he has enough to
finish it? Otherwise, when he has laid the foundations and cannot 29
complete the work, his neighbours will start making fun of him: 30
'Look at the fellow who started to build, and couldn't finish!'

Or suppose a king is making war on another king. Will he not 31
first sit down and seek advice before setting out, to see whether
with an army of ten divisions he is strong enough to take on an
enemy attacking with twenty? If not, he will send delegates to 32
sue for peace while the enemy is still a long way off.
So too, if anyone among you is not prepared to give up all belong- 33
ing to him he cannot be my disciple.

The mortal sickness of a mind

Salt is useful. But if salt becomes insipid, is there any way of 34
restoring its taste? It is no longer fit for either soil or dung-heap. 35
It is just thrown out.
Whoever has ears to hear with, let him listen."

*The wretched plead against us; multitudes
Countless and vehement, the Sons of God*

All the tax-collectors and the social outcasts were also approach- 15, 1
ing Jesus to listen to him.
But the Pharisees and the doctors of the law murmured dis- 2
approval. "Why," they said, "this man receives sinners and
dines with them!"

The heart half broken in ashes and in lies
But sustained by the immensity of the divine

3 Jesus replied with the following story: "Suppose one of you has a hundred sheep and loses one of them. Will he not leave the ninety-nine others wander on the moor and go looking for the

5 one that was lost, until he finds it? And how glad he will be to

6 find it! He will carry it on his shoulders, and go home and invite his friends and neighbours and say to them, 'Come and rejoice with me; I have found the sheep that I lost!'

7 So too, I tell you, there will be more joy in heaven over one sinner who repents than over ninety-nine good people who don't have to repent.

8 Or suppose a woman has ten silver coins and loses one of them. Will she not light a lamp and sweep the house and search everywhere until she finds it?

9 And as soon as she finds it she calls in her friends and neighbours and says to them, 'Rejoice with me! I have found the silver that I lost.'

10 So too, I tell you, there is joy among God's angels over a single sinner who repents."

I fled him down the nights and down the days
I fled him down the arches of the years

11 Then he told another story:

12 "A man once had two sons. And the younger one said to his father, 'Father, let me have my share of the property.'
So the father shared his property between them.

13 Some days later, the younger son gathered up his belongings **and left home for a country far away,** where he soon squandered his money, living recklessly.

14 Then, when he had spent everything, a terrible famine came to

15 that country, and he began to suffer need. So he went and got a job from a citizen, who sent him to look after pigs on his farm;

16 and he would have liked to fill his belly with the swill fed to the pigs, but no one gave him a thing.

17 Finally he came to his senses and began to reflect, 'To think of

all the servants employed by my father and the plenty they have to eat, while I'm here dying of hunger!

18 I will get ready and go back to my father. I will say to him,
19 Father, I have sinned against God and against you. I'm no longer fit to be called your son. Treat me as one of your paid servants.'

20 So he got ready and went back to his father. And his father saw him coming when he was still a long way from home; he felt sorry for him and, running out to meet him, hugged him and kissed him.

21 And the son said to him, 'Father, I have sinned against God and against you; I am no longer fit to be called your son.'

22 But the father said to his servants, 'Go quickly there! Get a good Sunday suit and dress him! Put a ring on his finger and shoes
23 on his feet, and bring in that stall-fed calf and kill it. We're going
24 to celebrate with a dinner. For this son of mine was dead and has come to life; he was lost, and has been found.'

So they began to celebrate.

Victim to his heart's invisible furies

25 Now the elder son was still out on the farm. And as he got near the house on his way home, he could hear the sound of music
26 and dancing. He called one of the servants and asked what it
27 was all about. And he was told, 'Your brother has come back and your father has killed the stall-fed calf out of joy that he has received him safe and well.'

28 This made him so angry that he would not go into the house; and his father came out and tried to calm him down.

29 'Look!' he answered back to his father, 'I have slaved hard for you during all these years and I have never disobeyed your orders. And yet, you never gave me so much as a kid-goat, to
30 let me celebrate with my friends. But when this son of yours comes back, having spent all your money on prostitutes, you go and kill for him the stall-fed calf!'

31 'My boy,' replied his father, 'you have always been with me; everything I have is yours. But the least we could do was to have
32 a dinner and celebrate. Your brother here was dead and has come to life; he was lost and has been found.' "

What buried worm of guilt,
Or what malignant doubt?

He said to his disciples: 16, 1
"A rich man once had a manager who was reported to him for
mismanaging his property.
So he summoned him and said, 'What is this I hear about you? 2
I want a report of what you have been doing. You can't continue
to be manager.'

And all arrogance of earthen riches

So the manager began to think it over: 'What am I to do? My 3
employer is dismissing me from my job. Digging is beyond me,
and I'd rather die than start begging.
But of course! Now that I'm losing my job as manager, the thing 4
to do is to make friends who will give me hospitality.'
So he called in his master's debtors, one at a time.   5
He asked the first, 'How much do you owe my master?'
And he replied: 'A hundred casks of olive-oil.'   6
'Quick!' said the manager, 'take your account-book, sit down and
write fifty.'
He asked the second, 'How much do you owe my master?'   7
And he replied, 'A hundred bushels of wheat.'
'Take your account-book and write eighty,' said the manager."

And the Lord commended the dishonest manager for the fore- 8
sight he showed. He added, "The men of this world, in their
dealings with their own people, show greater foresight than the
children of light.

Who love their fellows even to the death
Who feel the giant agony of the world

I say to you then, use that evil money to make yourselves friends; 9
when the money ceases to count, you will be received into the
eternal home.

Heaven is our heritage
Earth but a player's stage

The man who is faithful in the little things is faithful also in the 10 great; the man who is dishonest in the little things is dishonest also in the great.

11 **If you have not been faithful in your use of evil money, who will**
12 **trust you with real wealth?** If you have not been faithful in what belongs to another, who will give you what is your own?

Life's business—a terrible choice

13 A servant cannot serve two masters. Either he will hate the one and love the other; or he will take to the one and despise the other. You cannot at the same time serve God and money."

I have seen the righteous forsaken

14 Now the Pharisees were fond of money; so when they heard all this they expressed their scorn.
15 And Jesus said to them, "You Pharisees think yourselves righteous before men, but the verdict is your own. God sees through you; for what men count as distinction God regards as an abomination.

O Christ who holds the open gate

16 The law and the prophets had their day until John. Since then God's kingdom is being preached, and all are storming into it.
17 Heaven and earth will pass away sooner than the smallest detail of the law will lose its force.

Till death us do part

18 Any man who divorces his wife and marries another commits adultery; and any man who marries a wife divorced from her husband commits adultery.

Oh teach me to see Death and not to fear

19 There was once a rich man who used dress in clothes of the finest material and enjoy himself in a big way day after day.
20 And there was a poor man called Lazarus who lay, covered with
21 sores, outside the rich man's door, asking only to be fed with

262

scraps from his table. Even the dogs used come and lick his sores.

22 Now one day the poor man died and was carried away by the angels to recline at the feast with Abraham.

And the rich man also died and was buried.

23 From his torment in the world of the dead he looked up and saw Abraham in the far distance, and Lazarus in happiness with him.

24 So he called to him, 'Father Abraham, have pity on me! Allow Lazarus to come and dip the tip of his finger in water and cool my tongue; for I suffer agony in this flame.'

25 And Abraham replied, 'Son, remember that during your life you received the good things and Lazarus the bad. So he is now being comforted here, whereas you suffer pain.

26 Besides, there is a great gulf set between us; those who wish to cross from our place to yours cannot do so, nor can your people come over to us.'

27 And the rich man said, 'Then I beg you, Father Abraham, to
28 send him to my father's house; for I still have five brothers. If only he could warn them, lest they, too, come to this place of torment.'

29 'They have Moses and the Prophets,' said Abraham, 'let them listen to them.'

30 And the rich man said, 'No, they won't, Father Abraham; but if someone from the dead visits them, then they will change their ways.'

31 And Abraham replied, 'If they won't listen to Moses and the Prophets, neither will they be impressed if someone rises from the dead.' "

The worst sin towards our fellow-creatures

17, 1 He said to his disciples, "It is impossible that scandal and corruption should ever have an end; but woe to any man who causes scandal!

2 It would be better for him to be hurled into the sea with a mill-stone hung about his neck, than to cause one of these little ones to fall away. So be careful.

Corroding silence is the worst

3 If a fellow-Christian wrongs you, admonish him; and if he is

264

sorry for it, forgive him. Even if he wrongs you seven times a 4
day, and comes back seven times saying 'I'm sorry!', you must
still forgive him."

That Light whose smile kindles the universe

The Apostles said to the Lord, "Increase our faith". And the 5
Lord replied, "If you had faith no greater than a mustard-seed,
you could say to this mulberry-tree, 'Be uprooted and planted
in the sea' and it would obey you.

To give and not to count the cost

Suppose one of you employs a ploughman or a shepherd. 7
Will you say to him, when he comes in from the fields, 'Sit down
here and eat'?
Won't you rather say, 'Get me my dinner! Put on your apron and 8
serve me, while I eat and drink; afterwards you can eat yourself.'?
Is the servant to be thanked for doing what he was told? 9
The same with you. When you have done all you have been told 10
to do, your comment should be: 'We're just ordinary servants;
we have only done our duty.'"

Beggar that I am, I am even poor in thanks

On his way up to Jerusalem he was going through Samaria and 11
Galilee. And as he was entering a certain village ten lepers were 12
there to meet him. They stood well out of the way and raised 13
their voices to say, "Jesus, Master, have pity on us!"
Seeing them Jesus said, "Go and show yourselves to the priests." 14
And while they were on their way they were cured.
Then one of them, when he found himself cured, returned to 15
Jesus, praising God at the top of his voice. He threw himself at 16
his feet to thank him. And the same man was a Samaritan.
Jesus said, "Were there not ten lepers cured? Where, then, are 17
the other nine? Was none of them prepared to come back and give 18
thanks to God except this foreigner?"
And he said to him, "Go your way; your faith has saved you." 19

Divine providence has a noiseless course

20 Asked by the Pharisees when the kingdom of God was going to
come, Jesus replied, "God's kingdom does not come in a way
21 that can be observed. It will be impossible to say, 'Look, it is
here' or 'Look, it is there'. For the kingdom of God is already
among you."

Though often named He is unknown
To the dark kingdom at his feet

22 Turning to his disciples he said, "A time will come when you
will desire to see one of the days of the Son of Man, but will not
see it.
23 People will say to you, 'Look there!' or 'Look here!' But stay
where you are, and do not go running after it.
24 For as lightning flashes its light from one end of the sky to the
other, so the Son of Man will be on the day of his coming.
25 But he must first go through great suffering and be rejected by
the men of this generation.

Luxury and riot, feast and dance

26 As things were in the days of Noah, so they will be in the days
of the Son of Man.
27 **People were eating and drinking,** marrying and being married,
until the day when Noah entered the ark. And then the flood
came and destroyed them all.
28 So too in the days of Lot; people were eating and drinking,
29 buying and selling, planting and building, until the day that Lot
came out from Sodom, when fire and sulphur rained down from
heaven and destroyed them all.
30 And that too is how it will be on the day that the Son of Man is
revealed.

Everlasting farewells

31 On that day, if a man should happen to be on the roof of his
house and his goods are all downstairs, let him not go down to

fetch them; if he is outside on his farm, let him not turn back.
Remember what happened to Lot's wife! 32
Whoever tries to preserve his life will lose it; whoever is pre- 33
pared to lose it, will preserve it.
On that night, I tell you, two men will be in the same bed; one 35
will be taken and the other left. Two women will be grinding
flour at the same mill; one will be taken and the other left."
"Where, Lord?" the disciples asked. 37
And he replied, "Where the carcass lies, there the vultures
gather."

We are not alone in our loneliness

To show how unfailingly one must pray, without ever giving 18, 1
up, Jesus told this story:
"In a certain town there was a judge, who neither feared God 2
nor bowed to men.
And in the same town there was a widow, who was for ever com- 3
ing to him with the same story: 'Defend me against my accuser.'
For a long time the judge refused; but in the end he said to 4
himself, 'I'm not one to fear God or bow to men, but this widow 5
is getting on my nerves. I will defend her. If I wait any longer
she'll drive me crazy.'

Now, listen to that decision by a godless judge!" said the Lord. 6
"And will not God see that justice is done for his chosen ones, 7
who call to him day and night? Or will he leave them waiting?
I tell you, he will come to their help quickly. 8
But when the Son of Man does come, **will he find faith on earth?"**

One to brag, the other to pray

There were some people who were full of confidence in them- 9
selves and in their own piety, while they despised others. To
these Jesus told this story:
"Two men went up to the temple to pray; one was a Pharisee, 10
the other a tax-collector.
The Pharisee stood upright and prayed like this: 'I thank you, 11
God, that I am not like other men—the thieves, the crooks, the

12 adulterers—or like this tax-collector here! I fast twice a week; I pay tithes of my whole income.'

13 But the tax-collector stood well behind and would not even raise his eyes to heaven; he struck his breast and said, 'O God, have mercy on me a sinner.'

14 I tell you, he was the one who went home acquitted by God— not the other.
    The man who exalts himself will be humbled; the man who humbles himself will be exalted."

Here a little child I stand

15 Women even brought their babies to him, to have him touch them; and when the disciples saw it, they scolded them.

16 But Jesus called for the children and said to his disciples, **"Let the children come to me**, **and do not stop them;** for God's kingdom belongs to their kind.

17 Believe me, anyone who does not receive God's kingdom as a child shall not enter it."

Yet was I sore afraid,
Lest having him I must have nought beside

18 A leading Councillor of the Jews said to him, "Good Master, what must I do to enter eternal life?"

19 And Jesus said to him, "Why do you call me good? No one is good except the one God. You know the commandments:

20 'Do not commit adultery, do not kill, do not steal, do not give false witness, honour your father and your mother.' "

21 "But I have kept all these ever since I was a boy," said the man.

22 And to this Jesus replied, "Only one thing is wanting to you. Sell your property and give the money to the poor—your wealth will be in heaven—and then come and follow me."

23 And the man became very saddened at this reply, because he was extremely rich.

Dust are our frames; and gilded dust our pride

24 Seeing how he reacted Jesus said, "How hard it will be for the
25 rich to enter God's kingdom. It is easier for a camel to pass

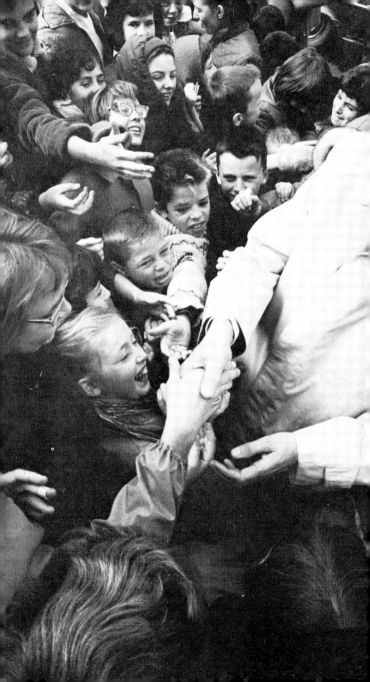

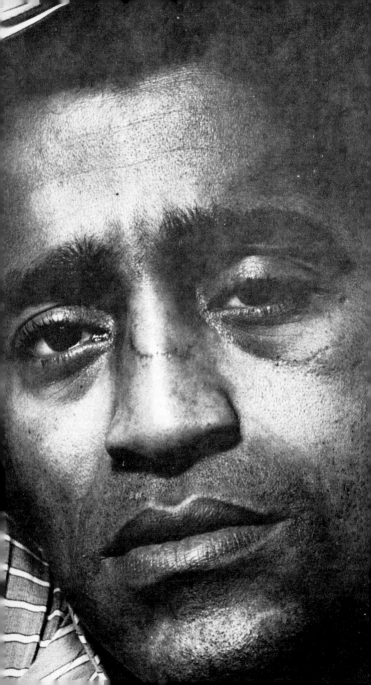

through the eye of a needle than for a rich man to enter God's kingdom."

"Who then can be saved?" his hearers said.   26

And he replied, "What is impossible for men is possible for 27 God."

How serenely they walk, not as I!

"Look, now," said Peter, "we have given up all belonging to us 28 and have followed you!"

And Jesus said to them, "Believe me, no man gives up home, 29 wife, brothers, parents, or children, for the sake of God's kingdom, who will not get a rich reward—even in the present 30 age. And in the world to come he will have eternal life."

*May we
Be mindful of this road to Calvary*

He took the Twelve aside and said to them, "We are now going 31 up to Jerusalem, and all the prophecies of Scripture are to be fulfilled in the Son of Man. He will be handed over to the pagans; 32 they will mock him, insult him, spit upon him; they will beat 33 him cruelly and put him to death; and on the third day he will rise again."

But the disciples did not grasp this at all; his words remained 34 for them a complete mystery which they did not understand.

Light to shine upon the road

As he was approaching Jericho a blind man sat begging by the 35 roadside. Hearing the noise of the passing crowd, he asked what 36 it was all about; and they told him that Jesus of Nazareth was 37 coming. He called out, "Jesus, Son of David, have pity on me!" 38 And the people up in front warned him to hold his tongue. 39 But he shouted all the more, "Son of David, have pity on me!" So Jesus stopped and asked them to bring the man to him. "What 40 do you want of me?" he asked him, as soon as he came near. And the blind man answered, **"Lord, that I may see again."** Jesus said, "Receive your sight; your faith has saved you." 42

43 Immediately he got his sight back, and began to follow him, giving thanks to God.
   And all the people who saw it gave praise to God.

We are too much alone

19, 1 Jesus entered Jericho and was passing through the town. Now there was this man called Zacchaeus who was a chief tax-collector and very wealthy; he wanted to see what kind of man
3 Jesus was, but could not do so **because the crowd was very big,**
4 **and he himself was a small man.** So he ran ahead and climbed a sycamore-tree, to get a view of Jesus as he was passing by.

He was a man who used to notice such things

5 When Jesus came to the spot he looked up and said to him, "Zacchaeus, come down quickly! Today I must stay in your house."
6 Zacchaeus therefore hurried down and was very glad to receive him.
7 And on seeing it they all began to murmur disapproval. "Why," they said, "this man has entered the house of a sinner to be his guest!"
8 But Zacchaeus stood a moment and said to the Lord, "Lord, I am prepared to give half my goods to the poor; and if I have wronged any man, I will repay him four times over."
9 And Jesus said, "Salvation has come to this house today. For
10 this man too is a son of Abraham; and the Son of Man has come to seek and to save what was lost."

But all the rest is nothing,
When you have tired your thoughts on earthly things

11 The people who heard these things began to think, now that he was nearing Jerusalem, that the kingdom of God would be
12 revealed at once. Jesus therefore told them another parable: "A nobleman once went to a distant country to receive a kingdom, intending to return.
13 So he summoned ten of his servants and gave to each a large sum of silver. 'Trade with it,' he said, 'until I return.'

14 But his fellow-citizens hated this man and sent a delegation after him to say, 'We refuse to have you as our ruler.'

My task accomplished and the long day done

15 In due course he returned after being invested as king and summoned the servants to whom he had given the silver, to see how each had got on.

16 The first came to him and said, 'Sir, your sum of silver has increased ten times.'

17 And the king replied, 'Well done! You're an excellent servant. Since you've proved yourself in this small matter, you shall have charge of ten cities.'

18 The second servant came and said, 'Sir, your sum of silver has increased five times.'

19 And the king said to him, 'You shall have charge of five cities.'

The past unsighed for and the future sure?

20 Then the other servant came and said, 'Here, sir, is your sum
21 of silver. I have kept it hidden away in a napkin. I was afraid of you, because you're a hard man; you collect what you didn't put away, and you reap what you didn't sow.'

22 And the king replied to him, 'My verdict on you has come from your own lips, you lazy fellow! You knew that I'm a hard man, that I collect what I didn't put away, and reap what I didn't
23 sow. Was there any reason then for not investing my money in the banks, so that on my return I should have got it back with interest?'

24 He said to the attendants, 'Take that silver from him and give it to the man who made the big profit.'

25 And they said to him, 'Sir, that man already has a fortune.'

26 'I tell you,' he said, 'when a man has something to start with, he will be given more; but whoever has nothing in reserve will forfeit even what he has.

27 As for my enemies, who would not have me as their king, bring them here and kill them before my eyes.' "

28 Having said this Jesus continued his journey, heading towards Jerusalem.

O Christ the Patron of the Poor

When he got to Bethphage and Bethany on the Mount of Olives, 29
he sent ahead two of his disciples and said to them, "Go into 30
the village facing you, and as you enter it you will find a donkey
tethered on which no man has yet ridden. Untie it and bring
it to me. If anyone asks you, 'Why are you untying the donkey?' 31
say to him, 'The Lord has need of it.' "
The messengers went off and found everything as he had said. 32
As they were untying the donkey, the owners asked them what 33
they were doing, and they replied, "The Lord has need of it." 34
They brought the donkey to Jesus, flung their coats on its back, 35
and mounted him on it. And as he rode off, others spread their 36
coats on the road.

and everywhere
The ceremony of innocence is drowned

Soon he approached the descent on the other side of the Mount 37
of Olives. And the whole crowd of disciples burst out in joyful 38
praise to God for all the mighty works they had seen. They
shouted aloud:
"Hail to the king,
who comes in the name of the Lord.
Peace in heaven,
And glory to God on high!"

Some of the Pharisees among the crowd said to him, "Master, 39
tell your disciples to be quiet."
But Jesus replied, "If they keep quiet, the very stones will cry 40
out."

Since Thou didst weep, as many tears
Have flowed like hour-glass sand

As he came nearer, Jesus had a view of the whole city. He wept 41
over it and said, "If only you knew at this moment the way to your 42
peace. But no, it is hidden from your eyes. A time will come upon 43
you, when your enemies will barricade you all around and hem
you in on every side; when they will raze you to the ground— 44

277

you and your people within you—**and will not leave a stone standing upon a stone,** because you did not open your eyes to the time of God's gracious coming."

The nerve for action, the spark of indignation

45 Then he entered the temple and began to drive out the people
46 who were trading there. He said, "It is written in Scripture: 'My house shall be a house of prayer'; but you have made it a hide-out for thieves."

Deceit that loves the night and fears the day

47 Every day he was teaching in the temple. And the chief priests, doctors of the law, and leading citizens of the people were most
48 anxious to do away with him; but they were at a loss what action to take, for the people were all enthralled by his words.

Soon hot, soon cold,
There is no stability

20, 1 One day he was in the temple, teaching and proclaiming the gospel to the people, when a delegation of chief priests, doctors
2 of the law, and elders accosted him and said, "We would like to know by what authority you do these things. Who gave you this authority?"
3 Jesus replied, "I too have a question for you, if you will be so
4 good as to answer me. What authority had John for his baptism? Was it from God or from men?"
5 Having talked it over among themselves, they concluded, "If we say from God, he will ask us why we didn't put faith in John;
6 if we say from men, the people will all stone us, for they are convinced that John was a prophet."
7 So they replied that they did not know.
8 And Jesus said, "Neither will I tell you by what authority I do these things."

But let not all that wealth of love be wasted

9 He went on to tell the people this story:
"A man once planted a vineyard and let it out to tenants, while he himself went abroad for a long time.

10 In due course he sent a servant to the tenants to collect his share of the wine-harvest; but the tenants beat up the servant and sent him back empty-handed.

11 He sent a second servant; and they beat him up too, treated him outrageously, and sent him back empty-handed.

12 He sent a third servant; but they wounded this one too, and threw him out.

13 So the owner of the vineyard said to himself, 'What can I do now—except to send my own son who is dear to me? Perhaps they will respect him.'

14 And as soon as the tenants saw who it was, they decided on their plan: 'This is the son and heir. Let's kill him, and the property will be ours.'

15 So they threw out the son from the vineyard and killed him.

Now what do you think the owner of the vineyard will do to these men?

16 He will come and destroy these tenants and give the vineyard to others."

Moving towards the unfathomable dark

"God forbid!" they replied.

17 But Jesus, fixing his eyes on them, said, "What then does this saying of Scripture mean:
'The stone rejected by the builders has itself become the foundation-stone'?

18 Anyone who falls on this stone will be broken; and anyone on whom it falls will be crushed."

19 The doctors of the law and the chief priests would have given anything to arrest him then and there, for they knew that this parable was against themselves; but they feared the people.

Two spirits of a diverse love
Contend for loving masterdom

20 So they kept an eye out. They had as their agents men who pretended to be pious folk, whom they sent to him, hoping to catch him in his words, and to hand him over to the authority and jurisdiction of the governor.

These questioned him as follows: "Master, we know that you 21 are a man of integrity, that you teach the way of God in all truth and are not swayed by public opinion.

What do you think? Is it right for us to pay tax to Caesar or 22 not?"

But Jesus, knowing what was behind it, said to them, "Show me 23 the coin of the tax. This image I see here, and this inscription— to whom do they belong?"

They replied, "To Caesar."

And he said to them, "Give then to Caesar what is Caesar's, and 25 to God what is God's."

So they failed to catch him out in anything he said to the people. 26 After this last reply they were stunned to silence.

Only those who have flown home to God have flown at all

Some of the Sadducee party, the people who deny the resurrec- 27 tion, approached him and asked the following question: "Master, 28 Moses prescribed for us that if ever a man dies and leaves a wife but no children, his brother should marry the wife and raise up a family to the dead man.

Now there were once seven brothers. The first took a wife and 29 died without children; and the second and third, and all the rest 30 of the seven, took her as wife, and died, all of them, without leaving children. Then the wife herself died. 32

Now which of these will have her as wife on the day of resurrec- 33 tion? For all seven had married her."

Look for me in the nurseries of heaven

Jesus replied, "In this world men and women marry. But those 34 who are judged worthy to participate in that other world and in the resurrection of the dead neither marry nor are married. For 36 they are no longer subject to death, but are like angels; having been privileged to rise, they are children of God.

As for the resurrection of the dead, Moses gave the answer in 37 the passage about the burning bush. He speaks of the Lord as 38 the 'God of Abraham, God of Isaac, God of Jacob.' Thus he is not a God of the dead, but of the living; for all are alive to him."

39 And at this even some doctors of the law spoke up and said, "Well answered, Master!"

40 In fact no one dared to ask him any more questions.

In me past, present, future, meet

41 But he put this question to them: "How can the Messiah be
42 called David's Son? For David himself says in the book of
43 Psalms, 'The Lord said to my lord, Sit at my right hand, until I lay your enemies under your feet.'
44 If David calls him 'Lord', how can the Messiah be David's Son?"

He waited after no pomp and reverence

45 He said to his disciples, in the hearing of the whole crowd, "Do not be led by the doctors of the law. What they like is to parade around in long robes, and to be saluted respectfully in the streets;
47 they look for reserved seats in the synagogues and top places at banquets; they swallow up the property of widows, and yet they make pretence of praying long prayers.
For them, judgement will be all the more severe."

The will of the giver is more than the gift

21, 1 Jesus happened to notice the rich throwing their offerings into
2 the temple treasury; and he also saw a poor widow throwing in a couple of small coins.
3 "Believe me," he said, "this poor widow has given more than
4 all of them. All these others have given what they could well afford; she was needy, and yet she gave the last penny she had for a living."

When the world despairs

5 Some of them were discussing the temple and the fine appearance
6 of its splendid stone-work and votive offerings. Jesus said to them, "A time will come when not a single stone of what you see there will be left intact. All will be torn asunder."

And they asked him, "Master, when will this be? And what will 7
be the sign that this is to happen?"

He replied, "Take care that you are not led astray. Many will 8
come claiming my authority and saying, 'I am the one', or 'The
time has come', but do not follow them. And when you hear of 9
war and rebellions, do not be alarmed; for these must inevitably
come. The end is not yet."

He also told them, "Nation will rise against nation, kingdom 10
against kingdom. There will be mighty earthquakes, and in some 11
places famines and plagues; frightening portents will occur, and
great signs from heaven.

Carried in the hand of God

But prior to all this they will arrest and persecute you, and 12
hand you over to assemblies, and put you in prison, and bring you
before kings and rulers because of my name. Here then will be 13
your chance to give witness to me. Be assured therefore that 14
you must not worry beforehand about your defence. For I will 15
inspire you with such eloquence and wisdom that none of your
enemies will be able to oppose you or refute you.

You will be given up even by parents and brothers, by relatives 16
and friends. Some of you will be put to death; and you will be 17
hated by all men because of my name. Nevertheless, not a hair 18
of your heads will perish; so long as you hold out patiently, 19
your lives will be safe.

Till the Spinner of the Years
Said "Now!"

When you see Jerusalem surrounded by armies, then you may 20
know that the hour of its destruction has come. Let whose who
are in Judaea make for the mountains; let those who are in the
city get out; let those who are in the country stay away. For 22
these will be the days of punishment, to bring about everything
foretold in the Scriptures.

Alas for women with child, or with infants at the breast when 23
those days come! There will be great distress in the land, and
punishment for this people. They will fall by the edge of the 24

sword, and will be led away captive among all the nations. Jerusalem will be trampled on by the gentile nations, until these too have had their day.

25 Portents will appear in the sun, the moon, and the stars; on earth there will be dismay among the peoples, confusion over the roar
26 of the surging sea. Men will die from fear, from dread of what is to come upon the world; for the mighty powers of heaven will be shaken.
27 And after that the Son of Man will be seen coming in a cloud with great power and splendour.
28 When all this begins to happen, then you can stand and raise your heads; for the hour of your salvation is at hand."

The price of freedom—vigilance

29 And he gave them a parable: "Look at the fig-tree or any other
30 tree. Once they begin to sprout, you know at a glance that summer is near.
31 In the same way, when you see all this happen, you can know for sure that God's kingdom is near.
32 Believe me, this generation will not have passed away before all these things happen.
33 Heaven and earth will pass away; my words will not pass away.

Act—in the living present
Heart within and God o'erhead

34 Watch yourselves! **Do not let your minds become clouded** by dissipation, or drunkenness, or the cares of the world, lest that
35 day come upon you suddenly like the shutting of a trap; for that day will surely come—upon all the inhabitants of the whole world.
36 Stay awake, therefore! Pray unceasingly, so as to be able to escape these coming trials and to stand in the presence of the Son of Man."

37 During the day Jesus used teach in the temple; late in the evening
38 he used go out to spend the night on the Mount of Olives. And first thing in the morning the people used come to the temple to hear him.

Only a friend can betray

22, 1 The feast of the unleavened bread or the Pasch was drawing
2 near And the chief priests and doctors of the law were still at a
loss how they would do away with him, for they feared the
people.

3 Then Satan entered the heart of Judas, the man called Iscariot,
4 who belonged to the group of the Twelve. He went off and discussed with the chief priests and the temple-officers his plan for
5 betraying Jesus to them. They were very pleased and agreed to
6 pay him money. Judas gave them his word, and from then on
began to look out for a suitable occasion; he would betray him
to them when the people were not around.

A large room, prepared

7 Then came the day of the unleavened bread, when the paschal
8 lamb had to be sacrificed. Jesus sent off Peter and John, saying
to them, "Go and prepare the pasch for us."
9 "Where do you wish us to prepare?" they said to him.
10 And he replied, "As you go into the city you will be met by a
man carrying a jar of water. Follow him to the house he will
11 enter and say to the owner, 'The Master wishes to know where
is the dining-room in which I am to eat the pasch with my
12 disciples.' He will show you a large room upstairs, laid out in
readiness. And there you can prepare."
13 They went away, found everything as he had told them, and
prepared the pasch.

He is in agony till the world ends

14 The time having come, Jesus sat down to supper along with the
15 Apostles. He said to them, "I have very much desired to eat this
16 pasch with you before my death; I tell you, never again shall I
eat the pasch until it has been fulfilled in God's kingdom."
17 Having taken a cup of wine, he gave thanks and said, "Take this
18 and share it among you; for I tell you, never again shall I drink
this wine of the grape until the kingdom of God has come."

Then he took bread and gave thanks; and as he broke it and gave 19
it to them, he said, "This is my body which is sacrificed for you.
Do this in remembrance of me."

So too, after the supper, he passed the cup to them, saying, "This 20
cup seals the new covenant in my blood, which is to be shed for
you.

And we are onlookers at the crime

Mark my word, the man who will betray me has his hand with 21
me on this table!

The Son of Man must go the way determined for him. Neverthe- 22
less, woe to the man by whom he is betrayed!"

And they began to ask one another who among them could 23
possibly do this deed.

Freely we serve because we freely love

They also began to squabble as to which of them ranked the 24
highest.

So Jesus said to them, "The rulers of the foreign nations rule 25
them with a high hand, and the men in authority call themselves
benefactors.

But with you it shall be different. The highest among you shall 26
be as the youngest; and the leader among you as the servant.

For who is the greater, the one who sits at table or the one who 27
serves? Surely the one who sits at table. And yet I am with you
as the one who serves.

And you are the men who have stood loyal to me during my 28
trials. I therefore assign the kingdom to you, as the Father has 29
assigned the kingdom to me. You shall eat and drink at my table 30
in my kingdom; you shall sit on thrones as judges over the twelve
tribes of Israel.

Let us void out this nonsense and be healed

Simon, Simon, listen to me. Satan has asked for you all, to sift 31
you like wheat. But for you I have prayed that your faith may 32
not fail. Let you, then, when you have come back, be a support
to your brothers."

33 Peter replied, "Lord, I am ready to go with you to prison and to death."

34 And Jesus said, "I tell you, Peter, the cock will not crow tonight before you have disowned me three times."

Unless the battle has preceded there cannot be victory

35 He said to them, "When I sent you on your mission without bag, or purse, or shoes, did you find yourselves in need?"
"No," they replied.

36 "Well now it is different," he said. "Whoever has a purse, let him take it, and also a bag. And if anyone is without a sword, let him

37 sell his coat and buy one. For I tell you, the saying of Scripture, 'he was numbered among criminals', must come to pass in me; all prophecies about me are now to be fulfilled."

38 The disciples said to him, "Lord, there are two swords here." And he replied, "It is enough."

See where the victor-victim bleeds

39 He left the room and proceeded as was his custom to the Mount
40 of Olives, accompanied by his disciples. When he arrived at the place he said to them, "Pray that you escape trial."

41 He himself withdrew from them about a stone's throw; and he
42 fell on his knees and began to pray. "Father," he said, "if it is your will, spare me this cup of suffering. Nevertheless, let your will be done—not mine."

43 There appeared to him an angel from heaven, bringing him
44 strength. And as his anguish grew greater, he prayed more intensely, and his sweat ran to the ground like drops of blood.

45 On rising from prayer he went to his disciples and found them
46 asleep; for they were weighed down with sorrow. He said to them, "Why are you sleeping? Rise, and pray that you escape trial."

The coward does it with a kiss

47 No sooner had he spoken than a large crowd suddenly appeared, and at their head the man called Judas, one of the Twelve. He came up to Jesus to kiss him.

And Jesus said to him, "Judas, do you betray the Son of Man 48 with a kiss?"

When his companions realized what was happening, they asked, 49 "Lord, shall we strike with the sword?"

One of them struck the high priest's servant and cut off his right 50 ear.

But Jesus, turning to him, said, "Stop! That will do." And 51 he touched the man's ear and healed it.

But our hearts we lost—how long ago

Jesus addressed the chief priests, temple-officers, and elders who 52 had come to arrest him, "So you have come with swords and clubs, as if I were a common criminal? Day after day I was with 53 you in the temple, and you did not touch me; but now the hour is yours—and the power of darkness."

And did not thee deny?

They seized him, led him away, and took him to the house of 54 the high priest.

Peter followed behind at a distance and took a seat along with 55 others who were sitting round a fire which had been lit in the courtyard.

As he was sitting by the fire, a young servant-girl saw him and 56 looked closely at him. "This man too was a companion of Jesus," she said.

But Peter denied it. "The man is unknown to me, woman," he 57 said.

Shortly afterwards someone else saw him and said, "You too are 58 one of these people."

But Peter answered back, "No, I'm not."

And about an hour later another was emphatic about it: "This 59 man was certainly in his company; he's a Galilean!"

Peter replied, "Listen, I don't know what you are talking about." 60
And as he spoke the cock crowed. 61

The Lord turned round and looked at Peter. And Peter remembered his words: "Before the cock crows to-night you will disown me three times."

He went outside and wept bitter tears. 62

10

Derided and defied

63 The men who had custody of Jesus mocked him and beat him.
64 Having blindfolded him they would call out, "Prophesy who it
was that struck you."
65 **And they did many other insulting things.**

Thou forsaken—even thou!

66 At day-break the elders of the people, chief priests, and doctors
of the law, met for a session of the supreme Council, and brought
him before them.
67 "Are you the Messiah?" they asked. "Tell us!"
68 Jesus replied, "If I tell you, you will not believe, and if I question
69 you, you will not answer. But from now on the Son of Man will
be seated at the right hand of Almighty God."
70 "So you are the Son of God?" they all said.
And Jesus replied, "You yourselves say what I am."
71 Then they said, "What more evidence do we need? We have had
a confession from his own lips."

May we draw near
Considering in our hearts what man is here

23, 1 The whole assembly then arose, and brought Jesus before
2 Pilate. And they stated their case against him in these words:
"We found this man misleading our people, forbidding tax to
be paid to the emperor, and making himself out to be Messiah
and king."
3 Pilate asked him, "Are you the king of the Jews?"
And Jesus replied, "The words are yours."
4 Pilate then told the chief priests and the people, "I can find no
case against this man."
5 But they insisted, "He is stirring up the people, preaching his
doctrine all over Judaea, from Galilee right down to here."
6 Hearing mention of the word Galilee, Pilate asked if this was
7 where the man was from. And when he learned that he belonged
to Herod's jurisdiction, he sent him over to Herod, who happened
to be in Jerusalem at the time.
8 Now Herod was delighted to see Jesus. Having heard about him

he had been wanting for a long time to meet him, and was hoping to see a miracle worked by him.

9 He therefore questioned him at length, but Jesus gave no reply.
10 And the chief priests and doctors of the law stood by, accusing
11 him vehemently. Herod and his soldiers treated him with shameful contempt and ridicule. Then they draped him in a gorgeous robe and sent him back to Pilate.
12 And from that day friendship was restored between Herod and Pilate; previously they had been enemies.

A plea to obscure the show of evil

13 Pilate summoned the chief priests, councillors, and people, and
14 said to them, "You have brought this man to me on a charge of misleading the people. The fact is that I have examined him in your presence and can find no evidence to support the charge
15 you bring against him. And neither could Herod, seeing that he sent him back here. Obviously, therefore, he is not guilty of any
16 crime deserving of death. I will have him flogged and let him go."

Behold the Man: he is Man's Son

18 But they shouted with one voice, "Away with this man! Give us Barabbas!"
19 (Barabbas had been thrown in prison for a revolt in the city and for murder.)
20 Again Pilate reasoned with them, desiring to release Jesus.
21 But they kept shouting, "Crucify him! Crucify him!"
22 And for a third time Pilate protested, "What wrong has the man done? I have not found him guilty of any capital charge; so I will have him flogged and let him go."

Politicians neither love nor hate

23 But they kept insisting with shouts and threats, demanding that he be crucified.
24 And their shouts prevailed. In the end Pilate decided to let them
25 have their way; he released the man they were asking for, the

one who was in prison for rebellion and murder, and surrendered Jesus to their will.

In his Master's steps he trod

They led him away to be crucified. And they laid hold of a man 26 from Cyrene called Simon, who was on his way from the country, and put the cross on his shoulders to have him carry it behind Jesus.

Mountains and hills, come, come, and fall on me
And hide me from the heavy wrath of God

A large number of people were in the procession behind, and 27 many women who gave loud vent to their grief.
Turning to these Jesus said, "Women of Jerusalem, do not weep 28 for me, but for yourselves and for your children. For the days 29 are coming when people will say, 'Happy the women without child, the wombs that have never borne, and the breasts that have never nursed'; when they will call to the mountains, 'Fall 30 upon us', and to the hills, 'Cover us up'. For if this is what they 31 do to the green wood, what will happen the dry?"

Christ on the Cross! Thorns on his brow

Two criminals were also led out to be crucified with him. And 32 on reaching the place called 'The Skull', they crucified him— and also the criminals, the one on his right, the other on his left.

And dying bless the hand that gave the blow

And Jesus said, "Father, forgive them; for they do not know 34 what they are doing."

The soldiers divided his garments by drawing lots, while the 35 people stood looking on.
And the rulers jeered at him, "The man who saved others! If this is God's Messiah, God's chosen One, let him save himself." Even the soldiers mocked him, as they ran up to the cross and 36 offered him vinegar. "Save yourself," they said, "if you are the 37 King of the Jews."

And his pure soul unto his captain Christ

38 Over his head there was an inscription: 'This is the king of the Jews.'

39 And one of the two criminals who hung beside him jeered at him, "Aren't you the Messiah? Then save yourself—and us!"

40 But the other answered back and rebuked him, "Have you no
41 fear of God—and you suffering the same punishment? Our fate is just; for we are getting what our crimes deserve. But this man has done no wrong."

42 And turning to him he said, "Jesus, remember me when you come into your kingdom."

43 Jesus replied, "I promise you, today you will be with me in paradise."

In dim eclipse

44 It was now about midday; and from then until three o'clock
45 darkness came over the whole earth, with the disappearance of the sun.

And the curtain of the temple was torn in two.

Into thy hands

46 Then Jesus called in a loud voice, "Father, I commit myself to you."

And with these words he died.

Both woe and fury speak

47 The officer in charge, having seen it all, gave praise to God: "Indeed," he said, "this was an innocent man."

48 And all the people present at the scene, having witnessed everything, returned to their homes beating their breasts.

49 His own friends too were all standing there at a distance; and the women who had followed him from Galilee were also watching.

These too have their part in me
As I too in these

50 Now there was a man called Joseph from the Jewish town of

294

Arimathaea, himself a councillor, but a decent, upright man who 51
did not go along with the vote and action of his fellows; in fact
he was awaiting the kingdom of God.

Having approached Pilate, Joseph asked for the body of Jesus; 52
and taking it down from the cross he wrapped it in a linen shroud 53
and laid it in a rock-tomb, where nobody had yet been buried.

It was the 'preparation-day' or eve of the sabbath, and the 54
sabbath was about to commence.

And the women who had accompanied Jesus from Galilee went 55
along with Joseph; they saw the tomb and the place where the
body was laid, and then returned home to prepare aromatic 56
herbs and perfumes.

On the sabbath itself they rested, as the law prescribed.

Is it he? Is it surely he?

But very early on the first day of the week they went to the tomb, 24, 1
bringing the perfumes they had prepared. They found the stone 2
rolled back from the tomb, but on going inside they did not find 3
the body of the Lord Jesus. And then, as they were wondering 4
about this, whom should they see standing beside them but two
men, dressed in shining garments. Seized with dismay, they 5
bowed themselves to the ground.

And the men said to them, "Why are you looking for the living
among the dead? Remember what he told you while he was still 6
in Galilee, 'The Son of Man must be surrendered to sinful men 7
and crucified; but on the third day he will rise again.'"

And they recalled his words. 8

Then they returned from the tomb and brought the news to the 9
eleven and the others.

These women were Mary the Magdalene, and Johanna, and 10
Mary the mother of James. And the other women who accompanied them confirmed all this to the Apostles.

And doubt is brother-devil to despair

The Apostles, however, thought the whole story to be nonsense; 11
they would not believe them.

But on the same day two of them were travelling to a village 13

295

14 called Emmaus, some seven and a half miles from Jerusalem, and were chatting about all these events.

15 As they were deep in conversation, Jesus himself came up and
16 joined them; but their eyes were prevented from recognizing him.
17 He said to them, "This is a lively conversation of yours, as you walk along. What has happened?"

And they stood still, a sad look in their eyes.

18 One of them called Cleopas remarked, "You must be the only stranger in Jerusalem who has not heard of the events there during these last days!"

"What events?" he asked.

19 And they replied, "All about Jesus of Nazareth, this man who showed himself a prophet, mighty in deed and in word, in the
20 sight of God and of all the people; how our chief priests and councillors gave him over, and had him sentenced to death and
21 crucified. We were hoping that he was the coming Saviour of Israel; but now, to top it all, this is the third day since these
22 things took place, and some of our women have completely astounded us. Having gone to the tomb at a very early hour and
23 not found his body, they came with a story that they had even seen a vision of angels, who say that he is alive.
24 Finally some of our own companions went to the tomb; and they found that the women's report was true, but himself they did not see."

To be ignorant of the scriptures is to be ignorant of Christ

25 He said to them, "How dull and sluggish are your minds, that you will not believe in all that has been foretold by the prophets!
26 Was it not necessary for the Messiah to suffer these things, in order to enter his glory?"
27 He then began with Moses and the Prophets and expounded to them all that stood written in the Scriptures about himself.

28 By this time they had almost arrived at the village to which they were travelling, and their companion made out that he was
29 going further. But they would not hear of it: "Stay with us," they said. "It is now evening and the day is almost over."

So he went in along with them to stay.

The holy bread, the food unpriced

They sat down together to supper. And when he had taken 30
bread in his hands and said the blessing, he broke it and gave it
to them.

Then their eyes were opened and they recognized him; and he 31
vanished from their sight.

Thinking it over they realized, "Weren't our hearts on fire within 32
us, as he talked to us during the journey and expounded the
Scriptures?" So they got up without delay and returned to 33
Jerusalem; and they found the eleven and their companions
already assembled.

They were told, "The Lord has risen indeed and has appeared 34
to Simon."

Then they gave their own account of what had happened on 35
the journey, and how they had recognized him in the breaking
of bread.

Thy everlasting mercy, Christ

As they were still talking about all this, Jesus himself came and 36
stood among them. But they, in panic and great fear, thought 37
they were seeing a ghost.

And he said to them, "Why this anxiety? And why these thoughts 38
in your minds? Look at my hands and feet. It is I! Touch me 39
and see. A ghost does not have flesh and blood as you see in me."

But it was too good to be true, and they were still slow to believe, 41
and still wondering.

"Have you anything here to eat?" he asked them.

And when they gave him some fried fish he took it and ate it in 42
their presence.

I know that Christ had given me birth
To brother all the souls on earth

He said to them, "These things bring to fulfilment the words 44
that I spoke while I was with you, that everything written about
me in the law of Moses, in the Prophets, and the Psalms, had to
come true."

297

45 Then he opened their minds to an understanding of the Scrip-
46 ture. He showed them how all this had been written: that the
Messiah had to suffer death and rise from the dead on the third
47 day; that in his name all the nations had to be called to repentance
for the forgiveness of sins. "You must begin from Jerusalem,"
48 he said. "For you are the witnesses of these things. I am sending
49 you very soon what my Father has promised; therefore remain
here in the city until you are equipped with power from on
high."

Lifting their hearts to heaven, they turned back home

50 Jesus brought them out as far as Bethany, and raising his hands,
51 he blessed them and as he blessed them he was taken from them.
52 They returned to Jerusalem in great joy and spent all their time
in the temple giving thanks to God.

JOHN'S
ACCOUNT

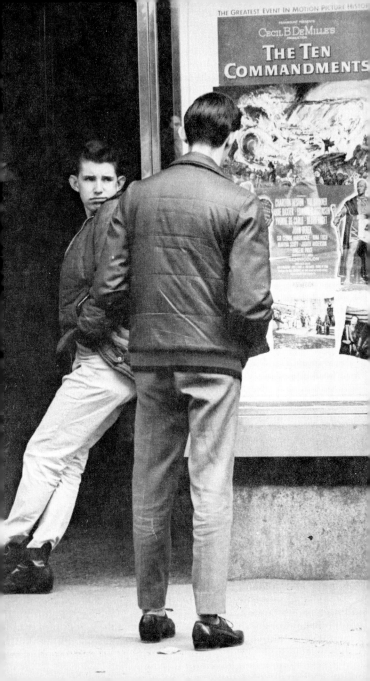

That light is present and that distant time
Is always here, continually redeemed

In the beginning the Word already was,   1, 1
The Word was with God;
the Word was himself God.
From eternity the Word was with God.   2
Through him all things came to be;   3
without him nothing whatever came to be.
All that exists had life in him,   4
and the life was the light of men.
The light shines in the darkness,   5
and the darkness did not overcome it.

An echo and a light unto eternity

There came a man, sent by God, whose name was John. He 6
came as a witness, to give testimony to the light, so that through
him all men should have faith.
He himself was not the light; he was sent as a witness to the light. 8

From fields of uncreated light

There is one who enlightens every man born into the world; he 9
was the true light.
He was in the world, and through him the world came to be; 10
yet the world did not recognize him.
He came to his own realm: yet his own did not accept him.   11
But to those who accepted him, who gave him their faith, he 12

13 gave the right to become children of God, who were born not
by a natural birth, nor by human desire, nor by the will of man,
but as children of God.

And solves the riddle of the universe

14 And the Word became flesh **and lived among us;** we saw his
glory, the glory of the only Son from the Father, full of grace
and truth.

O world unknowable we know thee

15 John cried out in testimony to him, "This is he, the one of whom
I said, 'After me comes one who is greater than I, because he
already existed before me.'"
16 For we have all received of his riches, and grace upon grace.
17 The law was given through Moses; grace and truth came with
18 Jesus Christ. No man has ever seen God; God's only Son, who
lives in the intimacy of his Father, has alone made him known..

O world invisible we view thee

19 Here now is the testimony of John, when the Jews sent priests
and temple-servants from Jerusalem to ask him who he was.
20 He told them straight, without any reservation, "I am not the
Messiah."
21 "Who are you, then?" they asked. "Are you Elia?"
"No."
"Are you the promised prophet?"
"No."
22 "Well who are you? We must give an answer to those who sent
us? Who do you claim to be?"
23 And John replied, quoting the prophet Isaia, "I am the voice
of him who cries in the wilderness, 'Make ready the way of the
Lord.'"
24 Now the messengers from Jerusalem had a brief from the
25 Pharisees. "Why then do you baptize," they wanted to know,
"if you are not the Messiah, nor Elia, nor the prophet?"
26 And he answered, "I baptize you with water. But there stands

among you a man whom you do not know, who comes after me, and I am not worthy to unfasten the straps of his shoes."

28 All this took place at Bethany, on the other side of the Jordan, where John was baptizing.

29 Next day John was looking on as Jesus approached him and he
30 said, "Here is the lamb of God who takes away the sin of the
31 world. This is the one of whom I said, 'After me comes one who is greater than I, because he already existed before me.' I too did not know him; and yet the reason I came baptizing with water was that he might be revealed to the people of Israel."
32 And John testified, "I have seen the Spirit descending from
33 heaven like a dove and resting upon him. Even I did not know him; but he who sent me to baptize with water said to me, 'The man upon whom you see the Spirit come down to rest—he is the one who baptizes with the Holy Spirit.'
34 I have seen it with my own eyes; I therefore testify that this is the Son of God."

Rise, clasp my hand and come

35 Next day John was again standing with two of his disciples as
36 Jesus was walking by. He looked towards him and said, "There is the lamb of God!"
37 The two disciples heard what he said and followed Jesus.
38 Jesus looked round and saw them following him. "What are you looking for?" he asked.
And they replied, "Master, where are you staying?"
39 "Come and see," he said.
So they went, and saw where he was staying, and spent the remainder of the day with him; it was about the tenth hour.

40 Andrew, the brother of Simon Peter, was one of the two who had been listening to John and had followed Jesus.
41 And the first thing Andrew did was to look for his brother Simon and tell him, "We have found the Messiah (that is, the Christ)."
42 He brought him to Jesus. And Jesus, looking at him, said, "You are Simon, the son of John; you shall be called Kephas" (that is, Peter, 'the Rock').

Beholders of the promised dawn of truth

Next day Jesus decided to go to Galilee. He met Philip and said 43
to him, "Follow me." Philip was from Bethsaida, the same town
as Andrew and Peter.
Philip found Nathanael and told him, "We have found the man 45
foretold by the scriptures of Moses and the Prophets; he is
Jesus, the son of Joseph, from Nazareth."
"From Nazareth!" said Nathanael. "Do you mean to say there's 46
something good from Nazareth?"
And Philip replied, "Come and see."

As Jesus saw Nathanael coming towards him, he said of him, 47
"Here is a true Israelite, a man in whom there is no deceit."
"How do you know me?" Nathanael said to him. 48
And Jesus replied, "Before Philip called you, I saw you under
the fig-tree."
Nathanael answered, "Master, you are the Son of God; you are 49
the King of Israel!"
And to this Jesus replied, "So you have faith, now that I have 50
told you how I saw you under the fig-tree? You will see greater
than this." And he added, "Believe me you will see heaven 51
opened and the angels of God ascending and descending upon
the Son of Man."

God is in the bits and pieces of Everyday

On the third day there was a wedding-feast at Cana in Galilee. 2, 1
The mother of Jesus was at it, and Jesus and his disciples were 2
also invited.
The wine ran out, and his mother said to Jesus, "They are short 3
of wine."
He replied, "Mother, why ask me about it? My time has not 4
come yet."
And his mother said to the servants, "Do whatever he tells you." 5

Now the Jews have customs of ritual purification; so there were 6
six stone jars there, each of them holding some twenty or thirty
gallons of water.

7 Jesus said to the servants, "Fill the jars with water." And they filled them to the brim.

8 "Draw a sample now," he said, "and bring it to the steward of the feast."

9 They did this. And when the steward tasted the water made into wine, having no idea himself where it came from—although the servants knew—he called over the bridegroom and said to him,

10 "The normal practice is to serve the good wine first and the less good later on, when the guests are drunk; but you have kept the good wine till now."

11 That was how Jesus inaugurated his miracles, at Cana in Galilee; he revealed his divine glory and his disciples believed in him.

I have loved the beauty of thy House

12 Subsequently he went down to Capharnaum along with his mother, his brothers, and his disciples, but stayed only a few days.

13 The Jewish pasch was approaching and he went up to Jerusalem.

14 He found in the temple sellers of cattle, sheep and pigeons, and

15 also money-changers at their desks. Jesus made a whip of cords and drove them out from the temple—sheep, cattle and all. He overturned the money-changers' desks and scattered their coins.

16 And he said to the pigeon-sellers, "Take away all these! You must not turn my Father's house into a market."

17 And his disciples recalled the words of Scripture: 'Zeal for your house shall consume me.'

18 The Jews therefore said to him, "What sign can you show us, to justify this action of yours?"

19 And he replied, "Destroy this temple, and in three days I will raise it again."

20 The Jews replied, "Forty-six years it took to build this temple. Are you going to raise it in three days?"

21 But the temple Jesus had in mind was that of his body.

22 Later on, when he had been raised from the dead, his disciples recalled these words; they believed in the Scripture and in the words he had spoken.

Lord, thou hast searched me

While he was in Jerusalem for the paschal feast many came to 23
have faith in him, when they saw the miracles he worked.
But Jesus did not trust himself to them; he saw through all men, 24
and had no need to be informed about any man. 25
He himself knew what was to be known about the human heart.

To dream of new dimensions

There was a man called Nicodemus who belonged to the 3, 1
Pharisee party and was a member of the supreme Council. He 2
came to him under cover of night and said, "Master, we know
that you must be a teacher from God; no one but a man of God
could work these miracles that you work."
And Jesus replied, "Believe me, no man can see the kingdom of 3
God unless he is born again."
"But how?" said Nicodemus. "How can a grown man be born 4
again? Surely he cannot return to his mother's womb and be
born a second time?"
And Jesus replied, "I tell you, no man can enter the kingdom 5
of God unless he is reborn of water and the Spirit.
Man's life is born of man; the life of the Spirit is born of Spirit. 6
You need not wonder at my saying, 'You must all be born again'. 7
The wind, for instance, comes and goes at will, and you can hear 8
its sound; but you do not know where it comes from or where
it goes. And that is the way with everyone who is born of the
Spirit."
"But how can this be?" asked Nicodemus. 9
And Jesus replied, "You are a teacher in Israel. Surely you must 10
know this? Believe me, we speak what we know, and we testify 11
to what we have seen, but you do not accept our testimony. If 12
your faith falls short when I tell of the things of earth, how can
you have faith when I tell of the things of heaven? And no man 13
ascends to heaven, except the one who came down from heaven,
the Son of Man.
The Son of Man must be lifted up, as Moses lifted up the serpent 14
in the desert, so that everyone who has faith in him may have 15
eternal life.

And at this moment I believe
In love, and scout at death

16 For God so loved the world that he sacrificed his only Son, so that everyone who has faith may not die but have eternal life.

17 God, indeed, did not send his Son into the world to judge the world, but to save the world.

18 When a man has faith in him, he is not judged; but the man who refuses him faith is already judged, because he has refused faith in God's only Son.

Weep for the lives your wishes never led

19 And the judgement is this, that the light has come into the world **and men have preferred the dark to the light,** because their deeds

20 were evil. For all those who do evil hate the light and shun it,

21 lest their deeds be shown up. But whoever follows truth comes into the light, so that his deeds may be revealed as having been done in God."

You are so great, and I so small,
I am nothing, you are all

22 Having afterwards moved with his disciples to the country of Judaea Jesus went about with them there and was baptizing.

23 And John too was baptizing at Aenon, near Salim, because there

24 was plenty of water in the area. People were coming to him and being baptized; for John had not yet been put in prison.

25 Then there was an argument about purification between some

26 of John's disciples and a Jew. And they came to John and told him, "Master, that man who was with you beyond the Jordan, for whom you have testified, is now baptizing himself and all the people are flocking to him."

27 John answered, "A man cannot receive a grace unless it be given

28 him by God. You yourselves are witnesses to what I said: 'I am not the Messiah; I have been sent to prepare for him.'

29 Only the bridegroom can claim the bride; but the bridegroom's friend stands by, and hears him, and is gladdened by his voice.

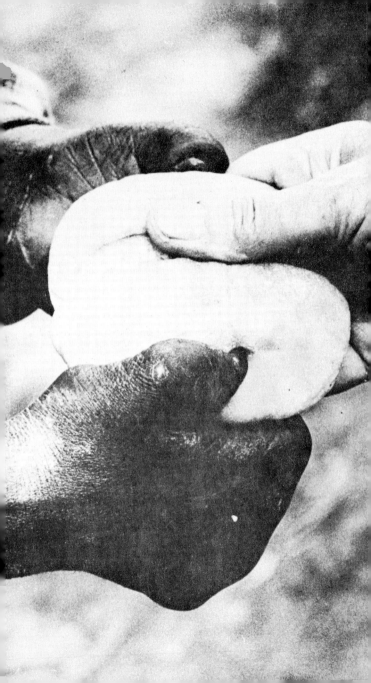

My hour of joy has therefore come; he must increase more and more, and I must grow less. The man who comes from above stands above all; but the man of the earth belongs to the earth, and his words do not exceed the earth. He who comes from heaven stands above all, and testifies to what he has seen and heard; and no one accepts his testimony. To accept his testimony is to endorse that God is true. For the man whom God has sent speaks the words of God, since God does not give the Spirit by measure; the Father loves the Son and has entrusted all things to him.

Any man who has faith in the Son already possesses eternal life; but whoever refuses faith in the Son will not see life. God's anger rests upon him."

His weakness, my triumph

Now the Pharisees had heard that Jesus was receiving and baptizing more disciples than John, although it was not Jesus himself who baptized but his disciples. So when the Lord got to know this he left Judaea and returned to Galilee. To get there he had to travel through Samaria; and he came to a Samaritan town called Sychar, close to the piece of ground which Jacob had given to his son Joseph.

Jacob's well was there. And Jesus, being tired after the journey, sat down by the well; it was about midday.

His disciples had gone into the town to buy food. So when a woman of Samaria came to draw water Jesus said to her, "Give me a drink."

Now the Jews and the Samaritans do not get on together; the woman therefore said to him, "How can you ask a drink of me, since you are a Jew and I am a woman of Samaria?"

As the hart panteth after the water brooks

Jesus replied, **"If only you knew the gift of God,** or the one who is asking you for a drink, you would have asked him and he would have given you living water."

"Sir," she said, "you have no bucket, and this well is deep; where do you get the living water? Are you greater than our father, Jacob, who gave us this well and used it for himself and his children and flocks?"

13 Jesus replied, **"Everyone who drinks of this water will be thirsty**
14 **again;** but the person who drinks of the water that I shall give him will never be thirsty. The water that I shall give him will become a spring of water welling up to eternal life within him."
15 The woman said to him, "Sir, give me this water! Then I shall not be thirsty again, or have to come here to draw."

When the whirl of circumstance is past

16 "Go home," he said to her. "Call your husband and come back here."
17 "I have no husband," the woman replied.
18 And Jesus said, "How true indeed that you have no husband! You have had five husbands, and the man you now live with is not your husband. What you have said is true."
19 The woman answered him, "Sir, I see that you are a prophet.
20 Our fathers worshipped God on this mountain; but you Jews say that Jerusalem is the place where God must be worshipped."

The Lord is in his holy temple, the Lord's throne is in heaven

21 Jesus said to her, "Woman, believe me, the day is coming when you will worship the Father neither on this mountain nor in
22 Jerusalem. You worship in ignorance, we worship in knowledge;
23 for salvation belongs to the Jewish people. But the hour is coming —is already here—when those who are true worshippers will worship the Father in spirit and in truth. For that is how the
24 Father wants men to worship him. God is spirit; those who worship him must worship in spirit and in truth."
25 The woman replied to him, "I know that the Messiah (or the Christ) is coming. He will tell us all things."
26 And Jesus said to her, "I am he, who am speaking to you."

What if this friend happens to be—God?

27 At this point his disciples arrived. They were surprised to find him talking with a woman; but none of them asked what he was looking for or talking about.

So the woman left her water-jar behind and went back to the 28
town.

She said to the people, "Come and see a man who has revealed 29
to me my whole past. Do you think he could be the Messiah?"
And they came out to him from the town. 30

The seed ye sow another reaps

Meanwhile his disciples were urging him, "Master, take some 31
food."

But he said, **"I have food to eat of which you know nothing."** 32
"Has someone brought him food?" they began to wonder. 33
And Jesus replied, "My food is to do the will of him who sent 34
me, to complete his work. You say, do you not, 'No harvest 35
without waiting for it'? But look, I tell you, lift up your eyes
and look on the fields around; they are already golden, ready
for the harvest.

Already the reaper is being rewarded and gathering in harvest 36
for eternal life, so that sower and reaper can both rejoice together.
In this respect the proverb is true, that one sows and another 37
reaps. I have sent you to reap where you have not laboured; 38
others have laboured, and you have come in for the fruit of their
labour."

Move then with new desires

Many of the Samaritans in the town began to have faith in him, 39
on the word of the woman's testimony that he had revealed her
whole past; so when they came to him, they asked him to stay. 40

He stayed for two days. And many others put faith in him because 41
of his own word. They said to the woman, "Our faith no longer 42
rests on what you say; we have heard him ourselves and we know
that this man is indeed the Saviour of the world."

Yet nothing is impossible, nothing
To men of faith and conviction

After the two days he set out from there for Galilee; for Jesus 43 himself had testified that a prophet is unhonoured in his own country.

45 So when he arrived in Galilee the people gave him a reception; for they too had gone up to the festival and had seen all that he had done in Jerusalem.

46 He came again to Cana in Galilee, where he had made the water
47 into wine. And a certain royal officer had a son who lay ill at Capharnaum. When he heard that Jesus had arrived from Judaea, he went to him and asked him to go down and heal his son, who was dying.

48 Jesus said to him, "Unless you see signs and portents you will not have faith."

49 But the officer said, "Sir, please go down before my boy dies."

50 And Jesus replied, "Go home. Your son will live."
The man believed what Jesus had said and set out for home.

51 And while he was on his way his servants came to meet him,
52 with news that his son was going to live. He asked what time he had got better and was told that the fever had left him at one
53 o'clock on the previous day. And the father knew that this was the moment when Jesus had said to him, "Your son will live." So he and all his household had faith.

54 This second miracle Jesus worked on his return from Judaea to Galilee.

Even though I walk through the valley of the shadow of death

5, 1 After this there was a Jewish feast and Jesus went up to
2 Jerusalem. There is a pool with five porticoes near the sheep-gate
3 in Jerusalem, which is called Bethzatha in Hebrew; in the porticoes there used lie a large number of suffering people:
5 blind, lame, paralysed. Among them was a man who had been
6 ill for thirty-eight years. Jesus saw him lying there and knew that he had been ill for a long time. "Would you like to be made well?" he asked him.

7 And the sick man replied, "Sir, **I have no one** to let me down into the pool whenever the water is stirred; while I am on my way someone else gets there before me."

8 Jesus said to him, "Stand up! Take your bed and walk."

316

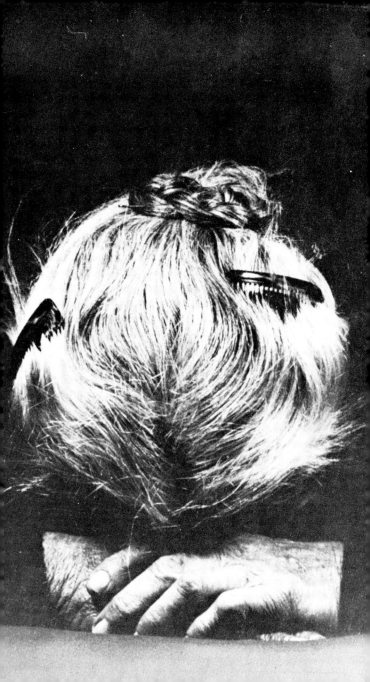

9 The man immediately became strong and well; he picked up his bed and walked away.

I need the living heart, the holy knowledge

Now this day happened to be a sabbath.

10 The Jews therefore said to the man who had been healed, "It's the sabbath. You are not allowed to carry your bed."

11 "But I was told to," he replied. "The man who cured me said, 'Take your bed and walk.' "

12 And they asked him, "Who is this man who told you to take your bed and walk?"

13 But the cured man did not know. There was a crowd in the place and Jesus had slipped away.

14 Later Jesus found him in the temple and said to him, "Now that you have been made well, take care not to sin again, lest something worse should happen you."

15 Then the man went off and told the Jews that it was Jesus who had cured him.

Full of tumultuous life and great repose

16 The Jews therefore began to persecute Jesus because he did these works on the sabbath.

17 He replied, "Even at this moment my Father is working, and I also work."

18 But their desire to kill him was only whetted. Not only did he break the sabbath; he also called God his Father, and so made himself equal to God.

The chain of God's silence
Held in his hand

19 Jesus therefore said to them in reply, "The Son, I tell you, can do nothing on his own account; he does only what he sees the

20 Father doing. Whatever the Father does, the Son also does. For the Father loves the Son and shows him all his works; and he will show him even greater works than these, so as to make you

wonder. Just as the Father raises the dead and makes them live, 21
so too the Son gives life as he wills, and to whom he wills.

Nor does the Father judge anyone; he has given all right of 22
judgement to the Son, that all may honour the Son as they 23
honour the Father. Whoever refuses honour to the Son refuses
honour to the Father who sent him.

I tell you, the man who hears my word and believes in him who 24
sent me has eternal life; he does not come to judgement, but has
already passed from death to life.

Indeed, the hour is coming—it is already here—when the dead 25
will hear the voice of the Son of Man, and all who hear it will live.

As the Father has life in himself, so too the Son has life in him- 26
self by the Father's gift. And he has given him the right to 27
execute judgement, because he is the Son of Man.

You should not wonder at this. For a day will come when all 28
who are in their graves will hear his voice, when those who have 29
done good will come out to a resurrection of life, and those who
have done evil to a resurrection of judgement.

In that last while, eternity's confine
I came to love, I came into my own

I can never act on my own; as I hear, so I judge. And my judge- 30
ment is just, because I do not seek my own interest but that of
him who sent me.

If I were to testify on my own behalf, my testimony would not 31
be true. But there is another who testifies to me, and I know that 32
his testimony is true.

You yourselves sent delegates to John; and John has given his 33
testimony to the truth. Not that human testimony is adequate 34
in my case, but I say this that you may be saved.

John was a lamp, burning for all to see; and for a while you were 35
glad to rejoice in his light.

But I have a testimony greater than that of John: the very works 36
that the Father gave me to achieve, the very works that I do,
these are my testimony that the Father has sent me. And the 37
Father who sent me has also borne testimony to me. But you
have neither heard his voice nor seen his face; and you do not 38

have his word rooted in your hearts, since you do not believe in the one whom he sent.

39 **You study the Scriptures,** in the view that they are for you a means to eternal life; in effect, they bear testimony to me, and

40 yet you are not willing to come to me that you may have life.

41 I do not look to men for glory; but apart from that I know you— that you have no love in you for God.

43 I have come on the authority of my Father and you do not accept me; but if another comes on his own authority him you will accept.

44 How can you have faith in me, since you look to one another for

45 glory and do not look for the glory that is from God alone? You need not think therefore that I shall be your accuser before the Father; your accuser will be Moses, the one in whom you have

46 placed your hope. For if you had faith in Moses, you would also

47 have faith in me, since I am the one he wrote about. But if you do not believe his writings, how are you to believe my words?"

I am Hunger

6, 1 Afterwards Jesus crossed to the other side of the lake of Galilee, or Tiberias.

2 A large crowd of people followed him, for they had seen the miracles he worked for the sick.

3 So he went up the hill-side and sat there with his disciples; and the Jewish festival of the pasch was drawing near.

He shall feed his flock like a shepherd

5 On looking around and seeing how large was the multitude flocking towards him, Jesus said to Philip, "Where can we buy bread to feed these people?"

6 Now he really said this to test him; for he knew himself what he was going to do.

7 Philip replied, "A day's wages for two hundred men would not be enough to supply each with a little."

8 Then one of his disciples, Andrew the brother of Simon Peter,

9 said to him, "There is a boy here who has five barley loaves and two fish; but what is that for a crowd like this?"

10 Jesus said, "Get the people to sit down."

There was plenty of grass in the area; so the men sat down—some five thousand in number.

Jesus took the loaves in his hands and gave thanks. He passed 11 them to the people as they were sitting on the ground; and the same again with the fish, as much as they wanted.

Then, when all had eaten their fill, he said to his disciples, 12 "Gather up what is left over, so that nothing is lost."

This they did, and filled twelve baskets with the fragments of 13 barley loaves left uneaten by the people.

The haunted labyrinth of the heart

When the people realized what a miracle he had worked they 14 exclaimed, "Surely this is the prophet who was to come into the world!"

But Jesus knew that they would come to seize him and make 15 him king; he therefore withdrew alone into the hills.

The race is not to the swift
Nor the battle to the strong

Late in the evening his disciples went down to the lake, embarked 16 in the boat, and began to head for Capharnaum on the other side. Darkness had already come down and Jesus had not yet come to them.

A strong wind was blowing and the lake was getting rough. And 18 when they had rowed some three or four miles they saw Jesus walking on the lake, approaching the boat. They were terrified. But he called out to them, **"It is I. Do not be afraid."** 20 And when they set about taking him into the boat, the boat landed at the place they were heading for. 21

The eye is not satisfied with seeing
Nor the ear filled with hearing

Next day the people stood on the opposite shore of the lake. They 22 saw that only one boat had been on the other side, and that Jesus had not embarked in it with his disciples, that these had gone away without him. Meanwhile other boats had come from 23

Tiberias to the vicinity where they had eaten, on the occasion
24 when the Lord gave thanks. And when the people found that
Jesus was not there, nor his disciples, they got into these boats
25 and made the crossing to Capharnaum, looking for him. Finding
him now on the other side, they asked, "Master, when did you
get here?"
26 Jesus replied, "The truth is, I tell you, that you look for me not
because you have seen signs but because you have eaten your fill
27 of bread. **Your work should not be for the bread that perishes,**
but for that which remains to eternal life, which the Son of Man
will give you; for it is upon him that the Father has set his seal."
28 They asked, "What must we do if we are to work the works of
God?"
29 And Jesus replied, "To do the work of God you must have faith
in the one whom he sent."

Without expression, waiting for a sign

30 "What do you do, then, as a sign?" they said to him. "What are
you going to accomplish? Let's see it, if we are to believe in you!
31 Our fathers ate manna in the desert; we read in Scripture that
'he gave them bread from heaven to eat.' "
32 Jesus replied, "Believe me, Moses did not give you bread from
heaven; it is my Father who gives you the true bread from
33 heaven. The bread of God is he who comes down from heaven
and gives life to the world."
34 And they said to him, "Sir, give us this bread at all times."
35 "I am the bread of life," Jesus replied. "Whoever comes to me
will never go hungry; whoever believes in me will never suffer
36 thirst. But as I have told you, while your eyes have seen, nevertheless you do not have faith.

He who Joy of Life would store
Heart of his be widely open

37 Everyone whom the Father gives me will come to me; and the
38 one who comes to me I will not reject. For I have not come down
from heaven to do my own will, but the will of him who sent me.
39 And the will of the Father who sent me is this, that of all whom

he has given me I should not lose any, but should raise them up on the last day.

40 The will of my Father is this, that everyone who looks to the Son and has faith in him shall have eternal life; and I will raise him up on the last day."

And, seeing, know; and, knowing, be at ease

41 The Jews began to protest over his saying to them, 'I am the
42 bread which came down from heaven.' "Surely this is Jesus, the son of Joseph?" they said. "Don't we know his father and mother? What's this talk about coming down from heaven?"

43 And Jesus replied, "Stop this murmuring! No man can come to me, unless he is drawn by the Father who sent me; and I will raise him up on the last day.

45 It is written in the prophets, 'They shall all be taught by God.' Therefore everyone who has listened to the Father, and learned from him, comes to me.

46 Not that anyone has ever seen the Father—apart from the one who is from God; he alone has seen the Father.

47 Believe me, whoever has faith already has eternal life.

Taste and see that the Lord is sweet

48 I am the bread of life. Your fathers ate manna in the desert, but
50 nevertheless they died; this is the bread which comes down from heaven, so that those who eat it may not die.

51 I am the living bread which has come down from heaven; any man who eats this bread shall live for ever. And the bread which I will give is my own flesh—for the life of the world."

The Body of our Lord—take and eat this

52 The Jews then began to debate furiously among themselves, "How can this man give us his flesh to eat?"

53 And Jesus replied, "I tell you the truth, unless you eat the flesh of the Son of Man and drink his blood, you have no life in you.

54 The one who eats my flesh and drinks my blood has eternal life, and I will raise him up on the last day.

My flesh is real food; my blood is real drink. He who eats my 55
flesh and drinks my blood lives in me, and I live in him.
As the living Father has sent me, and I live by the Father, so 57
too any man who eats me will live by me. This is the bread which 58
has come down from heaven—not like that which your fathers
ate, for they died; the man who eats this bread will live for ever."

This was the doctrine taught by Jesus in the synagogue at 59
Capharnaum.

To the last point of vision and beyond

Having heard it many of his disciples said, "This teaching is 60
unreasonable. Who can accept it?"
But Jesus, knowing in his own mind that his disciples were 61
muttering about it, said to them, "Does my teaching give you
offence? Suppose then you were to see the Son of Man ascending 62
to where he was before? The spirit alone gives life—not the 63
flesh, which can do nothing. The words that I have spoken to
you are both spirit and life.
But there are some among you who do not have faith." 64
For Jesus knew all along who were the ones who did not have 65
faith, and who was going to betray him. "This is why I said to
you," he added, "that no one can come to me unless the grace is
given him by the Father."
Following on this many of his disciples withdrew from him and 66
refused to go with him any more.

Whither thou goest, I will go

Jesus therefore said to the Twelve, "Do you also want to go?" 67
And Simon Peter answered, "Lord, to whom shall we go? You 68
have the words of eternal life; we have faith and have therefore 69
come to know that you are the Holy One of God."

For know, there are two worlds of life and death

Jesus replied, "Have I not chosen you Twelve? Yet one of you 70
is a devil."
He meant Judas, the son of Simon Iscariot. 71
He it was, one of the Twelve, who would later betray him.

A time to every purpose under heaven

7, 1 Afterwards Jesus went about in Galilee, not wanting to show himself in Judaea since the Jews were bent on killing him.

2 But as the Jewish feast of the Tabernacles drew near, his brothers said to him, "Leave this country and go up to Judaea;

4 let your disciples there see these works of yours. No man does things in secret, if he wants to be in the public eye. So if you do works like these, show yourself to the world."

5 For not even his brothers had faith in him.

6 Jesus said to them, "My time has not come yet, but your time

7 is always ready. The world cannot hate you, but it hates me, because I testify against it and the evil of its works.

8 Go up you to the feast. I am not going up to this one, because my time has not come for me yet."

9 And having given this answer he stayed behind in Galilee.

10 However, when his brothers had gone up to the feast, then he went up himself—not openly, but in secret.

11 The Jews were looking for him at the feast. "Where is this man?"

12 they were asking. And among the crowd many different opinions were being whispered about him. Some said, "He is a good man." Others, "No, he is leading the people astray."

13 But no one spoke openly about him, for fear of the Jews.

Only love can redeem

14 On the fourth day of the festival week Jesus went up to the temple and began teaching there.

15 At this the Jews began to wonder. "This man has never been a student of the law," they said. "How does he know the Scriptures?"

16 He replied, "The teaching I give does not come from me but

17 from him who sent me. Anyone who is prepared to do his will will know whether my teaching comes from God or whether I

18 speak on my own account. Whoever speaks on his own account is out for his own glory. But the man who seeks glory for the one who sent him is true; there is no falsehood in him.

Did not Moses give you the law? And yet none of you obeys it. 19
Why are you trying to kill me?"

The people answered, "You are mad! Who is trying to kill 20
you?"

Jesus replied, "One work I have done on the sabbath and you 21
are all wondering. But because Moses gave you circumcision— 22
although it really came from the patriarchs and not from Moses—
you therefore circumcise a man even on the sabbath. If circum- 23
cision is carried out on the sabbath, lest the law of Moses be
broken, are you angry with me for giving health to a whole man
on the sabbath?

Let your judgement be just—not superficial!" 24

But if you want me, if you need me,
Who waits at the terrible door but I?

Some of the people were saying, "Isn't this the one they want 25
to kill? Yet here he is speaking openly and no one says a word 26
to him. Can it be that even the rulers have decided that this is
in fact the Messiah?

But we know well where this man is from, whereas the origin 27
of the Messiah when he comes is completely unknown."

Jesus therefore raised his voice as he was teaching in the temple 28
and said, "So you know me! And you know where I am from!
But I have not come on my own account, I have been sent by
one who is true, whom you do not know. I know him, because 29
I am from him; he sent me."

They wanted therefore to arrest him; but no one laid hands on 30
him because his hour had not yet come. Nevertheless, there were 31
many among the people who put faith in him. "When the Messiah
comes," they said, "will he work more miracles than this man?"

Now the Pharisees heard these mutterings about him among 32
the people. So the chief priests and the Pharisees sent agents
to arrest him.

Jesus therefore said, "For yet a short while I am with you, and 33
then I go to him who sent me. You will look for me, but you will 34
not find me; and where I am, you cannot come."

The Jews therefore said to one another, "Where can he be going 35
that we shall not be able to find him? Does he intend to go to

36 the exiles of the Greek world and teach the Greeks? Or what does he mean by saying, 'You will look for me, but you will not find me' and 'Where I am, you cannot come'?"

There is a river whose streams make glad the city of God

37 On the last and most important day of the festival Jesus stood up and cried aloud, "If anyone is thirsty let him come to me and
38 drink; from the one who believes in me, as the Scripture says, **streams of living water will flow."**
39 He was speaking of the Spirit later to be received by those who had faith in him; as yet the Spirit had not been given, because Jesus had not yet been glorified.

Where there is no vision the people perish

40 There were many among the crowd who, when they heard these words, began to say, "This is indeed the Prophet," or again, "He is the Messiah."
41 But others replied, "Can it be that the Messiah comes from
42 Galilee? Hasn't Scripture made it clear that the Messiah comes of the family of David and from Bethlehem, the town where David lived?"
43 The people, therefore, were divided in their views about him.
44 Many would have liked to arrest him.
But no one laid hands on him.
45 When the agents returned to the chief priests and the Pharisees they were asked, "Why have you not brought him?"
46 And they replied, "Never has a man spoken as this man speaks."
47 The Pharisees said, "Have you too been taken in? Has any of
49 the rulers or the Pharisees believed in this man? As for this people, they are blighted by their ignorance of the law!"
50 But one of their party, Nicodemus, who had formerly had a
51 meeting with Jesus, asked them, "Does our law judge a man without first giving him a hearing and finding out what he has done?"
52 And they replied, "Are you too from Galilee? Search the Scriptures and see for yourself that no prophet comes from Galilee!"

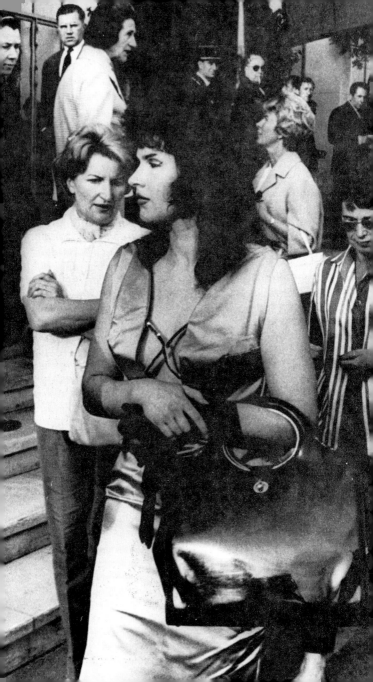

Thou, O Christ, art all I want
Raise the fallen, cheer the faint

[They all went away to their homes, and Jesus went out to the 8, 1
Mount of Olives. At daybreak he came again to the temple, and 2
the people flocked to him. He had seated himself and was teach- 3
ing them when the doctors of the law and the Pharisees brought
him a woman who had been caught in adultery. They led her out 4
in front of everybody, and said to him, "Master, this woman has
been caught committing adultery. Now Moses laid it down in the 5
law that such women should be stoned. What do you think?"
They said this to test him, so as to be able to accuse him. 6
Jesus however leant forward, and began writing with his finger
on the ground.
And as they kept pressing with their question, he straightened 7
up and said, **"Whichever of you is without sin let him cast the
first stone."**
Then he leant forward again and continued writing on the 8
ground.
And one after another his audience began to leave, starting from 9
the eldest.
At the end Jesus alone remained, with the woman standing be- 10
fore him. So he straightened up once more and said to her,
"Woman, where are they? Has none of them condemned you?"
She replied, "No one, sir." 11
And Jesus said, "Neither will I condemn you. Go home and sin
no more."]

The light we sought is shining still

Jesus, therefore, spoke to them again and said, "I am the light 12
of the world. Any person who follows me will never walk in
darkness but will have the light of life."

But if once we lose this light

The Pharisees said to him, "Since you are a witness in your own 13
cause, your testimony is not valid."
Jesus replied, "Granted that I am a witness in my own cause, 14

333

my testimony is nonetheless valid; for I know where I have come from and where I am going, whereas you do not know.

15 You judge by human standards, but I judge no man. And if I do judge, my judgement is true; for it is not I alone who judge but I and he who sent me.

17 It stands written in your law that when two witnesses are in agreement their testimony is true.

18 I am a witness for myself; and the Father who sent me is another witness for me."

19 "Where is your Father?" they asked.
And Jesus replied, "You know neither me nor my Father; if you knew me, you would also know my Father."

20 These words he spoke as he taught in the temple, near the treasury.
But no one arrested him, because his hour had not yet come.

'Tis with us perpetual night

21 He said to them again, "I am going away. You will look for me, but you will die in your sin; for where I go, you cannot come."

22 The Jews therefore asked, "Is he going to kill himself? Is this what he means by saying, 'Where I go you cannot come'?"

23 Jesus said to them, "You are from below; I am from above. You
24 are of this world; I am not of this world. That is why I told you that you will die in your sins; for if you will not believe that I am he, you will die in your sins."

25 "Who are you?" they asked him.

26 And he replied: "Why do I speak to you at all? There are many things I have to say about you—and in judgement. But he who sent me is true; and what I speak to the world is what I have heard from him."

27 They did not understand that he was speaking of the Father.

28 And Jesus said, "When you have lifted up the Son of Man, then you will know that I am he and that I do nothing on my own
29 account but speak only what the Father has told me. He who sent me is with me and has not left me alone; I do always what pleases him."

30 And as he said this, many came to have faith in him.

For truth only is living
Truth only is whole

To the Jews who had faith in him, Jesus said, "Take my word 31
to heart and you are truly disciples of mine; you will know the 32
truth and the truth will make you free."
They answered, "We are descended from Abraham and have 33
never been slaves to any man; what do you mean by saying,
'You will be free'?"
Jesus replied, "Believe me, anyone who commits sin is a slave 34
of sin, and no slave can claim to belong for ever to the house. 35
Only the son of the house belongs to it for ever; therefore if the 36
Son gives you freedom, you will really be free.

And query, what does this vaingloriousness down here?

I know that you are descended from Abraham. Nevertheless you 37
are bent on killing me, because my word does not go home to
you. What I have seen in my Father's presence, that is what I 38
speak; what you have learned from your father, that is what you
do."
They replied, "Abraham is our father." 39
And Jesus said, "If you are children of Abraham, follow the
example of Abraham.
As it is, you are bent on killing me, a man who have told you 40
the truth I have heard from God. This is not what Abraham did.
The example you follow is that of your own father." 41
"We are not children born of infidelity," they said to him. "God
is our father—and God alone."
And Jesus replied, "If God were your father, you would love 42
me, for I am here because I have come from God. I have not
come on my own account; it was he who sent me.
Why do you not understand my teaching? Because your minds 43
are closed to my word.
You belong to your father, the devil, and the desires of your 44
father you choose to carry out. From the beginning he was a
destroyer of men; he has not stood in the truth, because there is
no truth in him. When he speaks a lie, he speaks in character;
for he is a liar, and the father of lies.

Before Abraham was—I am

45 But I speak the truth, and therefore you refuse to believe me.

46 Can any of you prove wrong against me? And if I speak the truth, why do you refuse to believe?

47 Anyone who has God for father accepts the words of God; and if you do not accept them, it is because you do not have God as your father."

48 The Jews answered him, "Are we not right in saying that you are a foreign heretic and possessed by a demon?"

49 Jesus replied, "On the contrary—far from being possessed—I

50 honour my Father, whereas you dishonour me. I am not seeking glory for myself; there is another who seeks it—and judges.

51 Believe me, anyone who is faithful to my word shall never see death."

52 The Jews therefore said to him, "Now we know for sure that you are possessed. Abraham and the prophets are all dead; but you say, 'Anyone who is faithful to my word shall never taste

53 death.' Are you greater than our father Abraham, who died? Or the prophets, who also died? Who do you think you are?"

54 Jesus answered, "If self-glory were my ambition, my glory would be worthless. But it is my Father who glorifies me. While you

55 claim that he is your God, you have never known him. But I know him. And if I were to say I did not know him, I should be a liar like you.

I know him, and I am faithful to his word.

From eternity to eternity—I am

56 Your father Abraham rejoiced that he should see my day; he saw it, and was glad."

57 The Jews answered, "You are not yet fifty! Have you seen Abraham?"

58 And he replied, "Believe me, before Abraham was born, I am."

59 They picked up stones to stone him.

But Jesus was hidden from them and left the temple.

And see, no longer blinded by our eyes

9, 1 As he was walking along, he saw a man who had been born

blind. And his disciples asked him, "Master, why was this man 2
born blind? Was it he himself who sinned, or was it his parents?"
Jesus answered them, "There was no sin, either on his part or 3
that of his parents; he is blind because the works of God were
to be revealed in him. So long as it is day we must do the work 4
of him who sent me; the night is coming, when no man can work.
While I am in the world, I am the light of the world." 5
Having said this, he spat on the ground and made a paste of the 6
spittle. He put the paste on the man's eyes and said to him, "Go 7
and wash in the pool of Siloam." (The word is interpreted
'Sent'.)
And the man went off and washed and came back with his sight
restored.

His lone might 'gainst all darkness opposing

His neighbours and those who had known him before as a beggar 8
began to wonder, "Isn't this the one who used to sit begging?"
Some said, "Yes, it is." Others thought, "No, it's someone like 9
him."
But he himself said, "I am the man."
"How did you get your sight back?" they asked. 10
And he replied, "The man called Jesus made a paste, smeared 11
it on my eyes and said to me, 'Go to Siloam and wash.' So I went,
and washed, and now I can see."
They asked him, "Where is this man?" 12
And he replied, "I don't know."
So they brought the man who had been blind to the Pharisees; 13
the day on which Jesus made the clay paste and restored the 14
man's sight was a sabbath.
The Pharisees, therefore, asked him again how he had got his 15
sight back.
And the man replied, 'He put clay on my eyes; then I washed,
and now I see."
Some of them said, "Surely this man can't be from God, since 16
he doesn't keep the sabbath!"
"But how can miracles like these be the work of a sinner?"
others asked. So they were divided.
They turned therefore to the blind man and said to him, 17

"What do you think, seeing that it was your eyes he opened?"
He replied, "He is a prophet."

18 The Jews therefore refused to believe he had been blind and had
19 got back his sight, until they summoned his parents and asked
them, "Is this your son? Do you say that he was born blind?
And how is it that he can now see?"

20 The man's parents replied, "Yes, he's our son all right, and we
21 know that he was born blind. But how he got his sight back or
who opened his eyes we have no idea. Ask himself! He's of age;
let him speak for himself."

22 The parents gave this answer because they were afraid of the
Jews. For the Jews had already agreed that anyone who
acknowledged Jesus as the Messiah should be banned from the
synagogue.

23 That was why his parents said, "He is of age; ask himself."

What place shall open to Him? Shall the day,
Shall darkness, to His urgency give heed?

24 For a second time therefore they called the man who had been
blind and said to him, "Tell the truth before God! We know
that this fellow is a sinner."

25 He answered, "Whether he is a sinner or not, I don't know. But
I know one thing: I was blind and now I can see."

26 "What did he do to you?" they asked. "How did he restore your
sight?"

27 And he replied, "I have told you already and you wouldn't listen.
Why do you want it repeated? Are you thinking of becoming his
disciples?"

28 At this they abused him roundly and said to him, "Disciples of
29 his? You may be one! We are disciples of Moses. We know that
God's revelation was to Moses; but who this fellow is, or where
he is from, we do not know."

30 The man answered them, "Now this is strange indeed! Here's
a man who opened my eyes, and you don't know where he's
31 from! We all know that God does not listen to sinners; he listens
32 to the one who respects and obeys him. Who ever heard of a
33 man opening the eyes of a person born blind? If this man were
not from God, he could do nothing."

338

And they replied, "You were bred and born in sin; how dare you 34
teach us!"
And they threw him out.

Jesus heard that he had been thrown out; when he found him 35
he said to him, "Do you believe in the Son of Man?"
"Who is he, sir," the man asked, "that I may believe in him?" 36
And Jesus answered, "You have seen him; it is he who speaks 37
to you."
The man flung himself at his feet, and confessed, "I believe, 38
Lord."
And Jesus said, "For judgement have I come into the world: 39
that those who are blind should see, and that those who see
should become blind."

Some Pharisees in the company heard these words, and asked, 40
"Are we too blind."
And Jesus replied, "If you were really blind you would have no 41
sin; now that you say 'we see', your sin remains."

The Lord is my shepherd

"Believe me, any man who does not enter the sheep-fold by 10, 1
the door but climbs in somewhere else is a thief and a robber;
he who enters by the door is the shepherd of the sheep. To him 2
the door-keeper opens; he is the one whose voice the sheep obey,
as he calls his own by name and leads them out. And when he 4
has brought them all out, he goes ahead of them; and his sheep
follow him, because they know his voice.
They will not follow a stranger, but will run away from him, 5
because they do not recognize the voice of strangers."
Jesus told them this parable; but they did not understand what 6
he meant by it.

The Lord shall preserve thy going out and thy coming in

Jesus therefore said to them again, "Believe me, I am the door 7
of the sheep. All who came before me were thieves and robbers, 8
but the sheep would not listen to them. I am the door; any man 9

who enters by me will be saved. **He will go in, and go out, and**
10 **will find pasture.** The thief comes only to steal and kill and
destroy; I have come that they may have life in all its fulness.

Except for love's sake only

11 I am the good shepherd; the good shepherd gives his life for his
sheep.
12 The hired man, or any other stranger to whom the sheep do not
belong, abandons the sheep and runs away as soon as he sees the
13 wolf coming, allowing the wolf to seize and scatter them. Since
he only works for pay, he has no real interest in the sheep.
14 I am the good shepherd; I know my own and my own know me,
15 as the Father knows me and I know the Father. And I lay down
my life for the sheep.
16 And I have other sheep that do not belong to this fold; these too
I must lead. They will obey my voice; and there will be one
flock and one shepherd.

By your death I have lived

17 If the Father loves me it is because I lay down my life, so as to
18 take it up again. No one takes it from me; I lay it down of myself.
I have the right to lay it down, and the right to take it up again,
having received this commandment from my Father."

19 Once again his words caused division among the Jews.
20 Many said, "He is mad—possessed by a demon. Why listen to
him?"
21 Others replied, "These are not the words of a man with a demon.
Can a demon open the eyes of the blind?"

22 The feast of the temple dedication was being held at the time in
23 Jerusalem. It was winter. Jesus was in the temple, walking back
and forth in Solomon's cloister.
24 The Jews therefore gathered round him and asked, "How long
more are you going to keep us in suspense? Tell us straight, if
you are the Messiah."

Can I outleap the sea—
The edge of all land, the final sea?

25 Jesus answered, "I have told you, but you do not believe. The works that I do in my Father's name, these are my testimony;
26 but you do not believe, because you are not sheep of my flock.
27 My sheep listen to my voice. I know them, and they follow me;
28 and I give them eternal life. They shall never perish, and no one shall snatch them from my hand.
29 My Father who gave them to me is greater than all; and no one can snatch them from the hand of the Father.
30 The Father and I are one."

Faith's transcendent dower

31 Once again the Jews picked up stones to stone him.
32 And Jesus said to them, "Many are the works that I have shown you from the Father, and all of them good; for which of these would you stone me?"
33 They answered, "It's not for any good work that we would stone you, but for blasphemy; because you, a mere man, make yourself God."
34 Jesus replied, "Does it not stand written in your law, 'I said,
35 You are gods'? If the people to whom God's word was spoken can be called 'gods' and the Scripture cannot be set aside, how
36 can you accuse me of blasphemy when I assert—I whom the Father consecrated and sent into the world—that 'I am the Son of God'?
37 If the works that I do are not those of my Father, do not believe
38 in me; but if they are, at least believe in the works, even if you do not believe in me. Then you will know indeed that the Father is in me and I am in the Father."
39 And again they wanted to seize him.
But he escaped them.

Struggling towards God

40 He departed once more to the other side of the Jordan, where John had formerly been baptizing; here he stayed and many

came to him. "John worked no miracle," they said, "but every- 41
thing John said about this man was true."

And many came to believe in him there. 42

And death shall have no dominion

A man called Lazarus fell ill; he was from Bethany, the village 11, 1
where Mary lived, with her sister Martha. Mary was the one 2
who anointed the Lord with an expensive perfume and wiped
his feet with her hair; the one who had fallen ill was her brother
Lazarus.

The sisters sent a message to him: "Please, Lord, your friend is 3
ill."

And on hearing it Jesus said, "This illness is not going to end 4
in death but is for the glory of God; through it the Son of God
will be glorified."

Therefore, although Jesus was a dear friend of Martha and her 5
sister and Lazarus, when he got news of the illness he stayed 6
where he was for another two days.

Only then did he say to his disciples, "Let us go back to Judaea." 7

"Master," they replied, "recently the Jews wanted to stone you. 8
Are you going back already?"

He answered, "Are there not twelve hours of daylight? When a 9
man walks in day-time he does not stumble, because he sees the
light of this world; but he stumbles if he walks in the night 10
because he has no light in him."

Having said this he added, "Lazarus our friend has fallen asleep; 11
but I will go and wake him."

The disciples said, "Lord, if he has fallen asleep he will be all 12
right."

But Jesus was speaking of his death. They thought he meant 13
ordinary sleep.

Then he said openly, "Lazarus is dead. I am glad on your account 14
that I was not there, so that you may have faith. Let us go to
him."

Thomas, the one called the "Twin", said to his fellow-disciples, 16
"Let us all go that we may die with him."

343

In the faith that looks through death

17 On arrival, Jesus found that Lazarus had been four days in the
18 grave. Bethany was near Jerusalem, only about two miles away,
19 and many of the Jews had come out to Martha and Mary to
console them over their brother's death.
20 Therefore as soon as she heard that Jesus was coming, Martha
went out to meet him, while Mary stayed at home.
21 And Martha said to Jesus, "If you had been here, Lord, my
22 brother would not have died. But I know that even now God will
give you anything you ask."
23 Jesus said to her, "Your brother will rise again."
24 "Yes, I know." Martha replied, "He will rise in the resurrection
of the last day."
25 And Jesus said, **"I am the resurrection and the life.** Any person
26 who has faith in me will live, even though he die; and no living
person who has faith in me will ever die. Do you believe this?"
27 "Yes, Lord," Martha replied, "I believe that you are the Messiah,
the Son of God, who was to come into the world."

Bid me to live, and I will live

28 Having said this Martha went home and quietly called for her
sister Mary. "The Master is here," she said. "He wants you."
29 So Mary on hearing it got ready in a hurry and went out to him.
30 For Jesus had not yet come into the village but was still at the
place where Martha had met him.
31 The Jews in the house with her, who were consoling her, when
they saw Mary get ready and hurry out, went out after her,
thinking that she was going to the grave to mourn there.
32 And Mary, when she came to where Jesus was, fell at his feet on
seeing him and said, "Lord, if you had been here, my brother
would not have died."
33 Jesus noticed her weeping, and the Jews who were with her
weeping. A feeling of anger came upon him and he was troubled.
34 "Where have you buried him,?" he asked.
And they replied, "Lord, come and see."
35 Jesus wept.
36 And the Jews exclaimed, "How dearly he must have loved him!"

37 But some remarked, "He restored sight to the blind man, didn't he? Could he not have prevented this other from dying?"

38 And Jesus again felt anger, as he arrived at the tomb. It was a cave and a stone lay against it.

39 He told them to remove the stone. But the dead man's sister, Martha, said to him, "Lord, by now the body is decaying; this is the fourth day."

40 Jesus replied, "Did I not tell you that if you had faith you would see the glory of God?"

41 Then they took away the stone.
Jesus raised his eyes and said, "Father, I thank you for hearing

42 me. I know that you always hear me; but I say this on account of the people present here, that they may believe you have sent me."

43 Having said this, he called in a loud voice, "Lazarus, come out!"

44 And the dead man came out, his hands and feet bound in linen bands, and his face covered with a cloth.
Jesus said to the people, "Release him and let him go home."

Cursed be the social lies that warp us from the living truth

45 Many of the Jews who had come to Mary, and had seen the miracle that Jesus worked, now believed in him.

46 But some of them went to the Pharisees and reported his action.

47 So the chief priests and the Pharisees assembled the Council and said to them, "Where are we getting? This man goes on working

48 miracles. If we let him continue, everyone will believe in him. Then the Romans will come and take away our temple and our nation."

49 But one of them, Caiphas, who was the high priest for that year,

50 said to them, "You people have no sense! You don't use your heads. Your own interest demands that one man should die for the people, rather than that the whole nation should perish."

51 Now Caiphas did not say this of himself; he was the high priest for that year, and therefore his words were a prophecy that Jesus

52 was to die for the nation, and not only to die for the nation but also to gather into one all the scattered people of God.

All this in the house of my friends

53 From that day on they were resolved to kill him.

Jesus, therefore, no longer went about openly among the Jews; 54
he retired to a town called Ephraim on the edge of the desert and
remained there with his disciples.

The Jewish pasch was approaching. Many people had gone up 55
to Jerusalem from the country, in time to purify themselves for
the feast. All were looking for Jesus, asking one another, as they 56
stood in the temple, "What do you think? Is he not coming to
the feast?" The chief priests and the Pharisees had issued orders 57
that anyone who knew where he was should let them know, so
that they could arrest him.

And, in her face, the whole earth's anguish prays

Six days before the pasch Jesus came to Bethany, where Lazarus 12, 1
lived whom he had raised from the dead.

They gave a dinner for him; Martha did the serving and Lazarus 2
was one of the guests.

And Mary, taking a full pound of genuine and very costly per- 3
fume, anointed the feet of Jesus and wiped them dry with her
hair. The whole house was filled with the scent of the perfume.

One of his disciples, Judas Iscariot, the man who was to betray 4
him, remarked, "This perfume was worth a lot of money. Why 5
wasn't it sold, and the money given to the poor?"

He said this not because he was interested in the poor but because 6
he was a thief; for Judas was the bearer of the common purse
and used pilfer the money put into it.

Jesus therefore said, "Leave her alone! Let her keep it for my 7
burial-day. You will always have the poor with you, but you will 8
not always have me."

Cruelty has a human heart

A large number of the Jews who had learned that he was at 9
Bethany came out there, not only to see Jesus but also to see
Lazarus, whom he had raised from the dead.

And since, because of him, many Jews were being converted to 10
faith in Jesus, the chief priests decided to destroy Lazarus as
well.

Those holy fields
Over whose acres walked those blessed feet

12 Next day it came to the ears of the multitude who had come for
13 the feast that Jesus was about to enter Jerusalem. So they got themselves palm-branches and went out to meet him. And they shouted:

"Praise to God! Blessings on him who comes in the name of the Lord, the King of Israel!"

14 Jesus had found a donkey and was riding it, for so it had been written in Scripture:

15 'Fear not, daughter of Sion.
See! Your king is coming, riding a donkey-colt.'

16 At first his disciples did not see the meaning of this; but when Jesus had been exalted to glory, then they recalled that this had been done to him.

17 The people who had been with Jesus when he called Lazarus
18 from the tomb and raised him to life were telling of it. And that was why the crowd went out to meet him; they had learned of this great miracle which he had worked.

19 The Pharisees could only say to one another, "You see! There is nothing you can do! The whole world has gone after him."

There rises an unspeakable desire

20 Among the people who had come up to worship at the feast were
21 some Greeks. These approached Philip, who was from Bethsaida in Galilee, and said to him, "Sir, we would like to see Jesus."

22 Philip then went and told Andrew, and the two of them went to tell Jesus.

To act for life's sake

23 And Jesus replied, "The hour has come for the Son of Man to
24 be glorified. Believe me, if the grain of wheat does not fall into the earth, it remains a single grain; but if it dies it yields a rich harvest.

25 The man who loves his life will lose it; the man who hates his life in this world will keep it for life eternal.

Anyone who wishes to be my servant must follow me; and 26
wherever I am, there too my servant will be. The one who serves
me will be honoured by my Father.

Now my heart is sorely troubled, and what am I to say? 27
'Father, save me from this hour'?

But no! For why else have I come to this hour? 28
So then, 'Father, glorify your name.' "

But here is the finger of God

At that a voice echoed from heaven, "I have glorified it; and I
will glorify it again."

The people who were standing around heard it. Some thought 29
it to be thunder; others said, "An angel has spoken to him."

But Jesus replied, "This voice was for you, not for me. 30

An answer for seekers of Jesus

Now has come the judgement of this world; the ruler of this 31
world is now to be driven out. And I, if I am lifted up from the 32
earth, will draw all men to myself."

This he said in prediction of how he was going to die. 33

How my light is spent

The people replied, "We have been taught in the law that the 34
Messiah is to remain for ever. What do you mean by saying that
the Son of Man must be lifted up? Who is this Son of Man?"

Jesus said to them, "For yet a little while the light is with you. 35
Walk while you have the light, lest the dark come upon you.
When a man walks in the dark, he does not know where he is
going. While you have the light, believe in it, so that you may 36
be children of light."

And it was I who did it all
  Who did it all

When he had said these things Jesus went away and was hidden 37
from them. He had done so many signs for them to see, yet they
would not have faith in him.

38 Thus the words of the prophet Isaia were to be fulfilled:
'Lord, who has believed our report?
To whom has the power of the Lord been revealed?'

39 And the reason why they could not believe was also given by
Isaia:

40 'He has blinded their eyes,
and closed their minds,
lest they should see with their eyes,
and perceive with their minds,
and be converted,
and I should heal them.'

41 These things Isaia said because he saw his glory and spoke about
him.

Without fear and without reproach?

42 Nevertheless, even among the rulers there were many who had
faith in him; but because of the Pharisees they would not confess

43 to it, lest they should be banned from the synagogue. They
valued the respect of men more than the glory of God.

All death and all life, and all reigns and all ruins, drop through
me as sands

44 Jesus cried out and said, "The man who has faith in me, has
45 faith in him who sent me; the man who sees me, sees him who
sent me.

46 I have come into the world as a light; no one therefore who has
47 faith in me shall remain in darkness. And if one hears my words
but does not remain faithful, it is not I who judge him; for I have
48 not come to judge the world but to save the world. Any man who
rejects me or refuses to accept my words already stands under
a judge: the very word that I have spoken will speak his judgement on the last day.

49 I have not spoken on my own account; the Father who sent me
has himself given me commandment what to say and how to
50 say it. And I know that his commandment stands for eternal life.
What I say, therefore, is what the Father has told me to say."

Our voluntary service he requires

The feast of the pasch was at hand. Jesus knew that the hour 13, 1
had come for him to leave this world and to go to the Father.
He had loved his own who were in the world, and he would love
them to the end.

The devil had already entered the heart of Judas, the son of 2
Simon Iscariot, to betray him.

During supper, therefore, Jesus, knowing that the Father had 3
entrusted all things to him, and that he had come from God and
was about to return to God, got up from table, laid aside his 4
garments, and wrapped a towel round him. Having poured 5
water in a basin he began to wash the disciples' feet, and to wipe
them dry with the towel he had wrapped round him.

To bear new life or learn to live is an exacting joy

He came to Simon Peter. And Peter said to him, "Are you, Lord, 6
going to wash my feet?"

Jesus said, "What I am doing is not clear to you now, but you 7
will understand it later."

"You shall not wash my feet," said Peter. "Never!" 8
And Jesus replied, "Unless I wash you, your place is not with
me."

"In that case, Lord," said Simon Peter, "not only my feet but 9
my hands and my head."

Jesus said to him, "When one has fully bathed one needs no 10
further washing, but is altogether clean. And you are clean, but
not all of you."

He knew who was going to betray him; that was why he said, 11
'You are not all clean.'

The paradox and mode of all true loving

When he had washed their feet he put on his garments again and 12
resumed his place at table.

He said to them, "What I have just done for you, do you see 13
what it means? You call me 'Master' and 'Lord'—and rightly,
because I am. Therefore if I your Lord and Master have washed 14

15 your feet, you too must wash one another's feet. I have given you an example; what I have done for you, you also must do.

16 A servant, I tell you, is not greater than his master, an apostle is
17 not greater than the one who sent him. If you understand the lesson, act on it and you are blessed.

Judas arose and departed: night went out to the night

18 I am not speaking about all of you; I know whom I have chosen. But the Scripture must be fulfilled: 'One who shared meals with me has turned against me.'

19 I tell it to you now, before it happens, so that when it does happen you may believe that I am he.

20 Believe me, the man who receives an apostle of mine, receives me; and receiving me, he receives him who sent me."

21 Having said this Jesus—in deep anguish of spirit—spoke out his mind, "In God's name I tell you, one of you is going to betray me."

22 And the disciples began to look from one to another, wondering which of them he could have in mind.

23 Since one of them, the disciple whom he loved, lay beside Jesus
24 at table, Simon Peter beckoned to him with a sign, "Ask who it is he means."

25 So the disciple leant back against Jesus from where he lay, and asked, "Lord, who is it?"

26 Jesus replied, "I shall dip this bread in the dish and hand it to him; he is the one."
He then dipped the bread and gave it to Judas, the son of Simon Iscariot.

27 After the incident of the bread Satan entered Judas.
And Jesus said to him, "What you are doing, do it soon."

28 But none of the others at table knew exactly why he said this.

29 Since Judas held the purse several thought that Jesus was telling him to go and buy what was needed for the feast; others that he was telling him to give charity to the poor.

30 Judas took the bread and went straight out.
And it was night.

And then there comes the shutting of a door

After he had gone out Jesus said, "Now the Son of Man is 31
glorified; and in him God is glorified. If God is glorified in him, 32
God will also glorify him in himself, and will glorify him now.
My friends, I still have a short while with you. You will look for 33
me; and I say to you here, what I have said already to the Jews:
Where I go, you cannot come.

Be the ways of thy giving
  As mine were to thee

A new commandment I give to you—that you love one another. 34
As I have loved you, so must you love one another. In this way 35
all men will know that you are my disciples, that you love one
another."

Watchman, what of the night?

Simon Peter asked him, "Lord, where are you going?" 36
And Jesus replied, "You cannot follow me now to where I go,
but you will follow later."
Peter said, "Lord, why can't I follow you now? I will lay down 37
my life for you."
And Jesus answered, "So you will lay down your life for me? 38
Believe me, the cock will not have crowed before you deny me
three times."

Our souls have sight of that immortal sea

He said to them, "Do not be anxious. Have faith in God; have 14, 1
faith also in me. In my Father's house there are many dwelling- 2
places. Otherwise I should have told you; for the purpose of my
going is to prepare a place for you. And when I have gone and 3
prepared for you, then I will come again and take you to myself.
For where I am, there I want you to be.
And the way to where I go you already know." 4
Thomas said to him, "Lord, we don't know where you are going. 5
How can we know the way?"
Jesus replied, "**I am the way** and the truth and the life; no one 6
comes to the Father except by me.

I will lift up mine eyes to the hills

7 If you knew me you would also know my Father. But as from now you know him; you have seen him."

8 Philip said to him, "Lord, show us the Father and we'll be satisfied."

9 And Jesus replied, "Is it possible, Philip, that I have been so long with you and you still do not know me? When one sees me one sees the Father. How then can you say, 'Show us the Father'?

10 Do you not believe that I am in the Father and the Father is in me? The words that I speak to you I do not speak on my own account; it is the Father dwelling in me who does his works.

11 Believe me, I am in the Father, and the Father is in me; or at least believe because of what I do.

12 I assure you, the man who has faith in me will do the things that I do, and will do even greater than these. For I am going to the

13 Father, and will do for you anything you may ask in my name, that the Father may be glorified in the Son.

14 Anything you ask in my name, that I will do.

I am the breath of God. I am His liberty

15 If you love me you will keep my commandments. And I will ask the Father and he will give you another Advocate, the Spirit of

17 truth, to remain with you for ever. The world cannot receive him, because the world neither sees him nor knows him; but you know him, because he resides with you and will be in you.

18 **I will not leave you orphans;** I will come to you.

19 A little while now and the world sees me no more. But you will see me; for as I live, you too shall live.

*In thee I will overcome
The man who once against thee fought*

20 On that day you will know that I am in the Father—and you in

21 me, and I in you. The man who has my commandments and keeps them, he is the one who loves me. And loving me he will be loved by my Father; and I will love him and will reveal myself to him."

Then he was asked by the other Jude—not the Iscariot, "Lord, 22
how explain that you will reveal yourself to us and not to the
world?"

Jesus replied, "The one who loves me will be faithful to my word; 23
and my Father will love him, and we will come to him and will
stay with him.

Whoever does not love me is not faithful to my words. And the 24
word you hear is not mine; it is the word of the Father who sent
me.

Then dawns the Invisible : the Unseen its truth reveals

All this I have told you while I have been with you. 25
But the Advocate, the Holy Spirit whom the Father will send in 26
my name, will teach you all things and will bring to your minds
all that I have told you.

Grant us thy peace

Peace I leave to you, my own peace I give to you. **Not what** 27
the world gives do I give to you. Let no anxiety, no fear, trouble
your hearts. You have heard me say to you, 'I go away, and I 28
come to you again.' If you loved me, you would be glad that I
go to the Father; for the Father is greater than I.

I have told you now before the event, so that when it comes to 29
pass you may have faith.

I shall not say much more to you now; for the ruler of this world 30
is coming. Not that he has any power against me, but the world 31
must know that I love the Father, and that what I do is what the
Father has commanded me.

Rise, therefore. Let us go."

The life-tree am I

"I am the true vine; my Father is the vine-dresser. Any branch 15, 1
in me that fails to bear fruit, he cuts away; any branch that bears
fruit, he trims clean, to make it more fruitful still.

Already you have been cleansed by the word that I have spoken 3
to you.

359

4 Remain united with me, as I am with you. A branch cannot bear fruit of itself, unless it is united with the vine; so too you cannot bear fruit, unless you are united with me.

5 I am the vine; you are the branches.

So long as each of you is united with me, and I with him, you
6 will bear much fruit; for without me you can do nothing. But, like the branch, if one does not remain united with me one is thrown out and left to wither; and what is withered is gathered and thrown into the fire and burnt.

7 So long as you are united with me and my words find root in you, ask for anything you want and it will be given you.

8 And by this is my Father glorified, that you yield a rich harvest, being disciples of mine.

Be nothing first, and then be love

9 As the Father has loved me, I have loved you. Remain in my love.
10 If you keep my commandments you will remain in my love, as I have kept my Father's commandments and remain in his love.
11 I have told you this that my joy may be yours, and that your joy may be complete.
12 This is my commandment: Love one another, as I have loved
13 you. **The greatest love one can have is to give one's life for one's friends.**

Not as servant to lord, not as master to slave, shalt thou give thee to me

14 You are my friends, so long as you do what I command. Servants I do not call you, because a servant does not know what his master does; but I have called you friends, because I have made known to you all that I have learnt from my Father.
16 It was not you who chose me; it was I who chose you. I appointed you to go out and bear fruit, a fruit that will not pass away; so anything you ask in my name, the Father will give you.
17 And what I command you is this: Love one another.

Shall I go bound and you go free?

18 When the world hates you, bear in mind that it has hated me

360

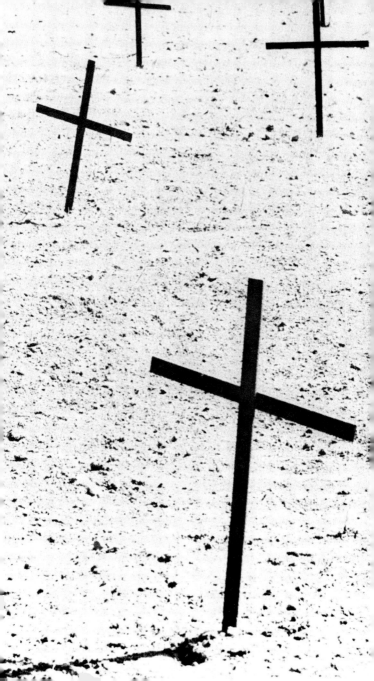

19 before you. If you were of the world, the world would love you as its own; but since you are not of the world, since I have chosen you out of the world, for this reason the world hates you.

20 Remember what I said: 'A servant is not greater than his master.' If they have persecuted me they will persecute you; if they have been faithful to my word they will also be faithful to

21 yours. Yes, all these things they will do to you because of me, because they have not known the one who sent me.

22 If I had not come and spoken to them, they would not be guilty of sin; but now they have no excuse for their sin.

23 Anyone who hates me hates my Father. If I had not done works among them that no one else has done, they would not be guilty of sin; as it is they have seen and hated both me and my Father.

25 But so it had to be; for so it stands written in their own law: 'They have hated me without cause.'

How in this absence thou dost steere
  Me from above

26 When the Advocate comes, whom I will send you from the Father, the Spirit of truth who comes from the Father, he will be my witness.

27 And you too are witnesses, because you have been with me from the beginning.

16, 1 I have told you these things to guard against your losing faith.

2 You will be shut out from the synagogues. Indeed, a time is coming when everyone who kills you will think he is offering

3 worship to God; and they will do these things because they have not known either the Father or me.

4 Therefore I have told you all this so that when their hour comes you may remember that I had warned you. I did not tell you from the beginning, because I was still with you.

5 And now that I am going to him who sent me, none of you asks me, 'Where are you going?'

6 But because I have told you these things sorrow has filled your hearts.

7 Nevertheless, I tell you the truth. It is for your own good that I

go away. If I do not go, the Advocate will not come; but if I go, I will send him to you.

Yea, Truth and Justice then
Will down return to men

And he, when he comes, will show up the world, in regard to sin, 8 and to justice, and to judgement.
In regard to sin, because they refused to believe in me. 9
In regard to justice, because I go to the Father, and therefore 10 you see me no more.
In regard to judgement, because the ruler of this world has 11 already been judged.

A master-light of all our seeing

I have much more to say to you, only you cannot bear it now. 12
But when he comes who is the Spirit of truth, he will guide you 13 to the whole truth. For he will not speak on his own account; he will speak what he hears, and will announce to you the things that are coming.
He will glorify me; for he will receive what is mine and will 14 announce it to you. All that the Father has is mine; that is 15 why I said: 'he receives what is mine and will announce it to you.'

Hereafter, in a better world than this

Soon you will see me no more; and soon again you will see me." 16
Some of his disciples began to ask one another, "What does he 17 mean by this 'Soon you will see me no more; and soon again you will see me'? And this 'going to the Father'?
What can he mean by this 'soon'? We don't understand." 18
Jesus knew that they wanted to question him and said, "You are 19 wondering why I said to you, 'Soon you will see me no more, and soon again you will see me'?

Infinite passion, and the pain
Of finite hearts that yearn

Believe me, you will weep and mourn, while the world will 20 rejoice; you will have sorrow, but your sorrow will turn to joy.

21 A woman has sorrow when she is about to give birth, because her hour has come; but when her child is born she no longer remembers her anguish, **for joy that a man has been born into the world.**

22 So too, you feel sorrow now. But I shall see you again; and then your hearts will rejoice, with a joy that no man can take from you.

23 And on that day you will have no more questions to ask me.

The costly doors flung open wide

Believe me, anything you ask of the Father he will give it to you in my name.

24 So far you have asked for nothing in my name; ask and you will receive, that your joy may be complete.

25 I have told you these things in figures of speech. A time will come when I shall no longer speak in figures, when I shall tell you of the Father in plain words.

26 On that day you will pray in my name; and I do not say to you

27 that I shall ask the Father on your behalf. For the Father loves you himself, because you have loved me and have believed that I have come from God.

The very throne of the eternal God

28 I came from the Father and have come into the world; now I leave the world and return to the Father."

29 His disciples replied, "Now you are speaking plainly! These are

30 no figures of speech! Now we are certain that you know all things, and do not have to be questioned; because of this we believe that you have come from God."

And a glory that shines upon our tears

31 Jesus replied, "Do you now believe?

32 Indeed the hour is coming—it has already come—when you will be scattered each to his own home and leave me alone. And yet I am not alone; for the Father is with me.

33 I have told you these things so that, united with me, you may have peace.

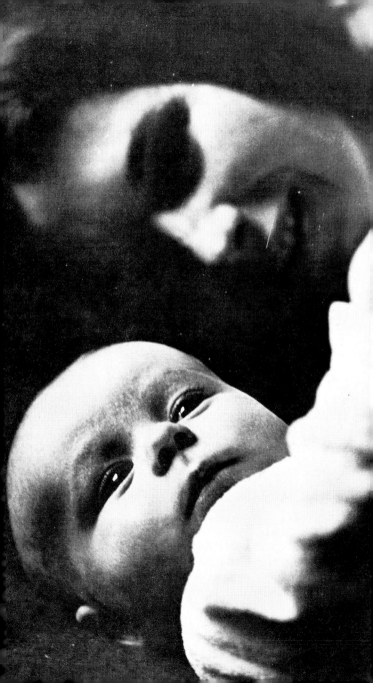

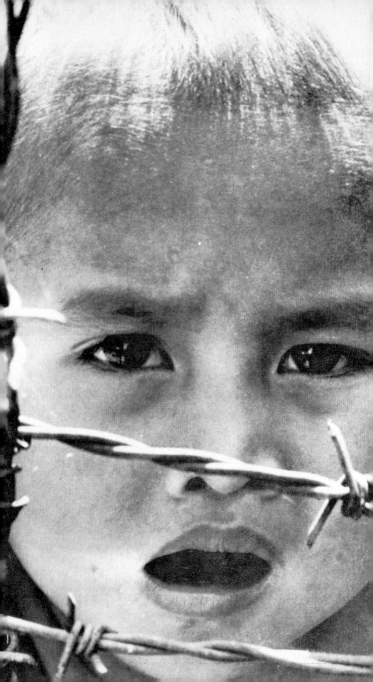

In the world you have suffering. **But courage! I have conquered the world."**

That which ever lives and moves

That was how Jesus spoke; and then he raised his eyes to heaven and said: 17, 1
"Father the hour has come. Glorify your Son, that your Son may glorify you.
For you have given him authority over all men, to give eternal 2 life to all whom you have given him.
And this is eternal life: that they know you, the only true God, 3 and Jesus Christ whom you have sent.
I have brought you glory on earth; I have completed the work 4 you gave me to do.

Behind the veil, behind the veil

And now, Father, bring me to glory with you, to the glory which 5 I had with you before the world began.

Behold I dream a dream of good

I have revealed your name to the men whom you gave me out 6 of the world. They were yours, and you gave them to me; they have been faithful to your word.
Now they know that everything I have has been given me by 7 you. For I have given to them the truth that you have given to 8 me. And they have received it, and have learned that I have really come from you; they have believed that you sent me.
I pray for them; not for the world do I pray, but for those whom 9 you have given me, since they are yours. All that is mine is yours, 10 all that is yours is mine; and by them I have been glorified.

And mingle all the world with thee

Now I am no longer in the world, because I am coming to you; 11 but they remain in the world. Holy Father, keep them in your name—the name which you have entrusted to me.
Let them be one, as we are one.

12 While I was with them I kept them in your name, and protected them. No one has been lost, except the man who was to be lost, because the Scripture had to be fulfilled.

13 But now I am coming to you; and I say this while I am still in the world, because I want their hearts to be filled with my joy.

14 I have delivered your word to them; and the world has hated them, because they do not belong to the world, as I do not belong to the world.

15 **I do not pray that you take them out of the world,** but that you keep them from evil.

16 They are not of the world, as I am not of the world.

17 Consecrate them in the truth—in your word which is truth.

18 As you· have sent me into the world, I have sent them into the world.

19 And for them I consecrate myself that they too may be consecrated in the truth.

He, They, One, All; within, without

20 I pray not only for these but for all others who through their
21 word shall have faith in me. Let them all become one; as you, Father, are in me and I am in you, let them be united in us, that the world may believe that you have sent me.

22 And I too have given to them the glory that you have given to
23 me. So let them be one, as we are one. As I am in them, and you are in me, so let them become perfectly one, that the world may know that you have sent me, and have loved them as you have loved me.

24 Father, I pray that all whom you have given me may be with me where I am; let them have vision of my glory—the glory you have given me because you loved me before the world began.

25 O righteous Father, the world does not know you; but I know you, and these know that you have sent me.

26 I have made your name known to them, and will make it known, so that the love you have had for me may also be in them, and I in them."

Poor, fleeting, fretful, little arrogant shapes

18, 1 After this prayer, Jesus went out with his disciples and crossed
the gorge of the Kedron river. Here there was a garden which
2 they entered. Judas the traitor also knew the place, because Jesus
3 and his disciples had often met in it; so Judas came there with a
company of soldiers and some agents of the chief priests and the
Pharisees, equipped with lanterns, torches and weapons.
4 Jesus knew all that was going to happen him.
He went out and said to them, "Who is it you want?"
5 And they replied, "Jesus of Nazareth."
He said, "I am he."
6 Judas the traitor stood among them; and as soon as Jesus said,
'I am he,' they drew back and fell to the ground.
7 Again he asked, "Who is it you want?"
And they replied, "Jesus of Nazareth."
8 He said, "I told you that I am he. Since I am the one you want,
let these others go away."
9 And so the word he had spoken would come to pass: 'I have lost
none of those whom you have given me.'

The brave man with a sword!

10 Simon Peter had a sword with him. He drew it and struck the
high priest's servant—his name was Malchus—and cut off his
right ear.
11 But Jesus said to Peter, "Put your sword back in its sheath.
Shall I not drink the cup of suffering that my Father has given
me?"

Dispersed in the night

12 The soldiers with their officer and the agents of the Jews then
13 seized Jesus and bound him. They brought him first to Annas;
for he was the father-in-law of Caiphas, the high priest for that
14 year and the one who had advised the Jews that in their own
interest one man should die for the people.
15 Jesus was followed by Simon Peter and another disciple. The
other disciple, being known to the high priest, was able to enter
with Jesus to the high priest's courtyard.

Peter was left standing at the door outside, until the other dis- 16
ciple who was known to the high priest came out; he spoke to the
girl at the door and brought Peter in.

But the girl said to Peter, "Aren't you one of this man's 17
disciples?"

And Peter replied, "No, I'm not."

It was cold. The servants and the agents had made a fire and 18
were standing round it warming themselves.

So Peter joined them too and stood there warming himself.

Have pity, master, this is a wicked land

Meanwhile the high priest interrogated Jesus about his disciples 19
and his teaching.

And Jesus replied, "I have spoken openly to the world. I have 20
never taught except where Jews come together, in synagogue or
temple, and have said nothing in secret. Why question me? Ask 21
the people who have heard what I said. They know my words."

When he had said this one of the agents who was standing by 22
struck him in the face and said, "Is that how you answer the high
priest?"

Jesus replied, "If what I have said is wrong, prove it; if I am 23
right, why strike me?"

Annas therefore sent him away bound to Caiphas the high priest. 24

And thus reveal my insufficiency
My lack, my weakness, my inferiority

Meanwhile Simon Peter stood warming himself. The others said 25
to him, "You're one of his disciples, aren't you?"

But he denied it flatly, "No, I'm not!"

And one of the high priest's servants, a relative of the man whose 26
ear Peter had cut off, said to him, "Did I not see you with him
in the garden?"

Peter denied it again. And at the same moment a cock crowed. 27

What are we in the hands of the great God?

They led Jesus from Caiphas to the headquarters of the Roman 28
governor. It was early in the morning. The Jews would not enter

371

the building; for they had yet to eat the paschal lamb and did not want to defile themselves.

29 Pilate therefore came out to them and asked, "What charge do you bring against this man?"

30 "He's a wrongdoer," they replied. "Why else do you think we have brought him to you?"

31 "Very well," said Pilate. "Take him yourselves and try him according to your own law."

32 "But we have no right to execute capital punishment," the Jews replied.

And so the prediction of Jesus about the manner of his death was to be fulfilled.

33 Pilate therefore again entered his residence and summoned Jesus. "Are you the King of the Jews?" he asked.

34 And Jesus replied, "Do you ask on your own account, or is this what others have said about me?"

35 "Am I a Jew?" replied Pilate. "Your own people and the chief priests have handed you over to me. What have you done?"

36 Jesus answered, "My kingdom is not of this world. If my kingdom were of this world my servants would have fought to prevent my arrest by the Jews; but my kingdom is not of this world."

37 "Nevertheless, you are a king?" said Pilate.

And Jesus answered, "What you say is true. I am a king. I was born and came into the world for this very purpose, to witness to the truth. Everyone who stands for the truth hears my voice."

38 "What is truth?" Pilate replied.

When honour's at the stake. How stand I then?

Having said these words he went out again to the Jews and told them, "I find no case against this man.

39 You have a custom however that I release a prisoner to you at the paschal season. Would you like me then to release to you the King of the Jews?"

40 And they all shouted out, "No, not him! We want Barabbas!" (Barabbas was a revolutionary.)

A little lower than the angels

19, 1 Pilate then had Jesus flogged. **And the soldiers plaited a crown of thorns** and fixed it on his head. Then they dressed him in a

3 scarlet robe and began to walk towards him and say, "Greeting to the King of the Jews!" And they struck him in the face.

'Twas I who made the blow to fall
On him who thought no guile

4 Once again Pilate came out and said to them, "I'm bringing him out to you to let you see that I find nothing against him."
5 And Jesus came out, wearing the crown of thorns and the scarlet robe.
"Just look at the man!" said Pilate.
6 And the moment they saw him the chief priests and the agents shouted out, "Crucify him! Crucify him!"
"Take him then yourselves and crucify him," Pilate said to them. "I find nothing against him."
7 And the Jews answered, "We have a law, and by that law he should die; he made himself out to be the Son of God."
8 When Pilate heard mention of this he was even more afraid;
9 he went in again to his residence and asked Jesus, "Where are you from?"
But Jesus gave him no answer.
10 "So you will not speak?" said Pilate. "Are you not aware that I have authority either to release you or to have you crucified?"
11 Jesus replied, "You would have no authority over me were it not given you from above; therefore those who betrayed me to you are guilty of the greater sin."

Why Caesar is their onely King, not I

12 After this Pilate was most anxious to release him.
But the Jews kept shouting, "If you release this man you are no friend of the emperor; anyone who claims to be king does so in defiance of Caesar."
13 On hearing this, Pilate ordered Jesus to be led out. And he took his seat on the bench, at the place called the "pavement" (in Hebrew *Gabbatha*).
14 It was about midday, on the day of preparation prior to the pasch.
And Pilate said to the Jews, "Just look at your king!"

They shouted back, "Take him away! Away! Away! Crucify 15
him!"

"Shall I crucify your king?" he asked.

And the chief priests replied, "We have no king but Caesar."

And I must take my Cross on me
For wronging him awhile

Pilate then handed him over to be crucified. 16

The soldiers took him in charge. And Jesus carried his own cross 17
and went out to the 'place of the skull,' as it was called (in
Hebrew *Golgotha*).

There they crucified him, along with two others—one on the 18
right and one on the left, with Jesus between them.

Pilate had a notice drawn up and fastened to the cross; it read, 19
JESUS OF NAZARETH, KING OF THE JEWS.

And many of the Jews read this notice, because the place where 20
Jesus was crucified was near the city; it was written in Hebrew,
Latin and Greek.

The chief priests and the Jews therefore protested to Pilate, 21
"King of the Jews is not what you should write, but that this man
claimed to be King of the Jews."

Pilate answered, "What I have written, I have written." 22

Having crucified Jesus the soldiers divided his clothes into four 23
parts, one for each soldier; there remained his inner tunic, which
was woven in a single piece and had no seam.

The soldiers therefore decided, "Instead of tearing it let us draw 24
lots to see who will get it."

And so the prophecy of Scripture would come true: 'They divided
my garments among them; they cast lots for my clothing.'*

For the soldiers did all these things.

Daughter of time and mother of eternity

Near the cross of Jesus stood his mother and her sister, Mary 25
the wife of Clopas, and Mary of Magdala.

When Jesus saw his mother standing nearby, with the disciple 26

375

whom he loved, he said to his mother, "Mother, there is your son."

27 To the disciple he said, "There is your mother."

And from that moment the disciple took her into his home.

His desiderate cry

28 Knowing that at this point everything had been brought to completion, Jesus said, to fulfil the scripture, "I am thirsty."

29 A jar of vinegar lay at hand; so they filled a sponge with the vinegar, put it on a stalk of hyssop, and held it to his lips.

I have trodden the winepress alone

30 And when he had taken the vinegar Jesus said, "All is brought to completion". He bowed his head and died.

Drink, Pilgrim, here

31 Since it was the day of preparation and the following day was a sabbath of special solemnity the Jews requested Pilate to have the legs broken and the victims removed, in order that the bodies should not remain hanging on the crosses on the sabbath.

32 So the soldiers came and broke the legs of the first, and then of the other of the two victims who had been crucified with him;

33 but when they came to Jesus they found that he was already

34 dead. Instead therefore of breaking his legs, one of the soldiers stabbed his side with a spear; immediately there flowed out blood and water.

35 The one who saw it can testify to it, and his testimony is true. And he too knows that he speaks the truth, so that you also may believe.

36 For all this took place to fulfil the Scripture, 'You shall not break

37 a bone in him'; and elsewhere the Scripture says, 'They will look on the one whom they pierced.'

There is no love without hope

38 Afterwards Joseph of Arimathaea, a disciple of Jesus—but in secret, out of fear of the Jews—asked Pilate for permission to remove the body of Jesus; and Pilate allowed it.

376

Joseph therefore came and took the body; he was joined by 39
Nicodemus, the man who had formerly come to him by night,
who came,with a mixture of myrrh and spices, weighing more
than a half a hundredweight.

They took the body of Jesus and wrapped it with the spices in 40
strips of cloth, according to the Jewish custom of burial.

Near the place where he was crucified there was a garden, and 41
in the garden a new grave in which no one had yet been buried.

Here therefore because it was the eve of the Jewish sabbath and 42
the tomb was so convenient they buried the body of Jesus.

No hope without love

Early on the Sunday morning, while it was still dark, Mary of 20, 1
Magdala came to the tomb and found the stone removed from
the entrance. She came running to Simon Peter and the other 2
disciple whom Jesus loved and told them, "They have taken the
Lord from the tomb and we don't know where they have laid
him." Peter, therefore, and the other disciple went off and came 3
to the tomb. Both set off together, running, but the other disciple 4
outran Peter and arrived at it first.

Bending forward he could see the linen strips lying inside, but he 5
did not go in.

Simon Peter then arrived, following him, and he went inside. 6
He saw the linen strips lying there, and also the cloth which had 7
covered his head, which was not with the strips but rolled up in
a corner by itself.

And then the other disciple went inside, the one who had arrived 8
first. He saw and believed; for they had hitherto not understood 9
from the Scriptures that he must rise from the dead.

The two disciples then returned home. 10

And neither hope nor love without faith

Meanwhile Mary stood outside near the tomb. She was weeping; 11
and as she wept she leant into the tomb and saw two angels in 12
white sitting there. One was at the head and the other at the feet
where the body had lain.

They said to her, "Woman, why are you weeping?" 13

377

And she said, "Because they have taken my Lord and I do not know where they have laid him."

14 As soon as she said it she turned round and saw Jesus standing behind, but did not recognize him.

15 "Woman, why are you weeping?" he said. "Who is it you are looking for?"

And Mary, thinking it was the gardener, said to him, "Sir, if you have removed him, please tell me where you have laid him, and I will take him away."

16 Jesus replied, "Mary!"

And she turned to him and said in Hebrew, "*Rabbuni*—My Master!"

The withered hand which time interred
Grasps in a moment the unseen

17 Jesus said, "Do not touch me! I have not yet ascended to the Father. But go and tell my brothers, I am ascending to my Father and yours, to my God and yours."

18 Mary of Magdala then went to the disciples to tell them that she had seen the Lord and had been given this message.

Joy the luminous cloud, Joy is the sweet voice

19 On the evening of the same Sunday, when the assembled disciples had the doors locked for fear of the Jews, Jesus came and stood among them.

20 "Peace to you," he said, and having said it he showed them his hands and side.

And the disciples rejoiced when they saw the Lord.

To lift the smothering weight from off my breast

21 He said to them again, "Peace to you.

22 As the Father has sent me, I also send you." Saying this he

23 breathed on them, and added, "Receive the Holy Spirit: those whose sins you forgive shall have them forgiven; if you reserve forgiveness, then it shall be withheld."

Believing where we cannot prove

One of the Twelve, Thomas the so-called 'Twin', was not in the 24
group when Jesus came. The other disciples therefore told him, 25
"We have seen the Lord." And he said, "Unless I see the mark
of the nails in his hands and can put my finger in their imprint,
and my hand into the wound in his side, I will not believe."

A week later when the disciples were again inside and Thomas 26
in the company, the doors being locked, Jesus came and stood
among them.
"Peace to you," he said.
Then he said to Thomas, "Put your finger here—and look at my 27
hands. Stretch out your hand and put it in this wound in my side.
Therefore, cease this unbelief and have faith."
And Thomas answered, "My Lord and my God!" 28
Jesus said to him, "So you have faith because you have seen me? 29
Happy those who come to the faith without having seen!"

Nothing is innocent now but to act for life's sake

Many other signs too Jesus did in the presence of his disciples, 30
which are not recorded in this book. This selection has been 31
written so that you may believe that Jesus is the Messiah, the
Son of God, and that through this faith you may have eternal
life in his name.

This abiding Fisherman

Afterwards Jesus again revealed himself to his disciples, by the 21, 1
lake of Tiberias. It happened in this way.
Simon Peter, Thomas the 'Twin', and Nathanael of Cana in 2
Galilee were along with the two sons of Zebedee and two other
disciples.
"I'm going fishing," Simon Peter said to them. 3
And they replied, "We'll come with you."
They went out and got into the boat, but caught nothing all that
night.

4 Early in the morning Jesus was standing on the shore, but the disciples did not know it was he.

5 He said to them, "Friends, have you caught anything?"
"No," they replied.

6 Then he said, "Let out your net to the right of the boat and you will make a catch."
They did so, and caught so many fish that they could not draw the net.

7 Then the disciple whom Jesus loved said to Peter, "It's the Lord!" And as soon as he learnt it was the Lord Simon Peter —not having been dressed—pulled on an overcoat and jumped

8 into the water. The other disciples came with the boat, dragging the net of fish; for they were only about a hundred yards from

9 the shore. When they landed they saw a fire with some fish on it, and bread beside it.

10 Jesus said to them, "Bring some of the fish you have caught."

11 Simon Peter then climbed into the boat and hauled the net to land. It was weighed down with one hundred and fifty-three big fish, but although the number was so large it was not torn.

12 Jesus said to them, "Come and have breakfast."
And none of the disciples had the courage to ask, "Who are you?" since they knew it was the Lord.

13 Jesus came, took the bread and gave it to them, and the fish as well.

14 And this was the third time that Jesus appeared to his disciples after his resurrection.

This unfailing guide

15 After breakfast he said to Simon Peter, "Simon, son of John, do you love me more than these do?"
"Yes, Lord," he replied, "you know that I love you."
And Jesus said, "Look after my little ones."

16 He asked him a second time, "Simon, son of John, do you love me?"
Peter answered, "Yes, Lord, you know that I love you."
And he said, "Shepherd my flock."

17 A third time he said to him, "Simon, son of John, do you love me?"

And Peter was hurt that he should ask him for a third time, 'Do you love me?' "Lord, you know all things," he said, "you well know that I love you."
And Jesus said to him, "Look after my flock."

And one that is stronger shall gird thee, and lead thee swiftly
Whither, O heart of Youth, thou wouldest not

"Believe me," he said to him, "when you were young, you 18 dressed yourself and were free to go where you liked; but when you grow old you will stretch out your hands for another to dress you and lead you where you won't like."
This he said in prediction of the death that Peter was to suffer 19 for the glory of God.
Then he added, "Follow me."

And they stretched forth their hands, and the wind of the spirit took
them

When Peter looked round he saw the disciple whom Jesus loved 20 following behind, the one who had leant back against him at the supper and asked, "Lord, who is going to betray you?"
Seeing him, Peter said to Jesus, "What will happen to him, 21 Lord?"
And Jesus answered, "If I want him to remain until I come, is 22 it any concern of yours? Let you follow me."

These words, therefore, went out among the Christians and were 23 taken to mean that this disciple would not die. But Jesus did not say that he would not die; all he said was, 'If I want him to remain until I come, is it any concern of yours?'

Now that I start my journey to the truth
Let me set down the burdens of my youth

This is the disciple who testifies to these things; he it was who 24 wrote them down. And we know that his testimony is true.
There are many other things that Jesus did. If all were recorded 25 in detail I doubt whether the world itself would hold the books that should be written.

ACKNOWLEDGEMENTS

Grateful acknowledgement is made to all modern poets (or their representatives) from whose writings lines have been used. Limited space does not allow the identification of titles and sources. The authors are as follows (reference being to page and place on the page):

A.E. (George W. Russell), 51[2] 236[2]; Conrad Aiken, 216[2] 287[3]; Martin Armstrong, 301[3]; W. H. Auden, 60[3] 62[2] 72[4] 82[1] 100[2] 152[1] 196[2] 212[1] 220[2,3] 226[1] 233[2] 260[2] 261[1] 308[2] 324[1]; George Barker, 81[3] 128[2] 174[1]; Laurence Binyon, 124[2] 152[4] 295[1] 320[1] 364[3]; Edmund Blunden, 262[2]; Robert Bly, 155[1]; Gordon Bottomley, 60[1]; Robert Bridges, 44[2] 126[1] 202[1] 215[2]; Rupert Brooke, 83[3] 171[2] 188[2] 205[2] 208[3] 210 252[1]; G. K. Chesterton, 94 214[3] 222[1] 289[1]; Padraic Colum, 115[3] 207[3] 273[2] 290[3] 360[3]; A. S. Cripps, 98[1]; H. Cust, 278[4]; C. Day Lewis, 64[2] 231[1] 236[4] 278[1] 315[2] 348[3] 351[3] 379[2]; Walter de la Mare, 62[1] 109[2] 290[2] 328[2]; Austin Dobson, 79[1] 108[3]; Ernest Dowson, 251[1]; T. S. Eliot, 10[1] 30[1] 43[2] 51[1] 55[2] 65[3] 72[2,3] 78[1] 93[1,2] 98[3] 115[1,2] 116[3] 125[3] 142[1] 162[1] 197 227[2] 232[1] 243[4] 251[3] 254[2] 306 315[3]; Norman Gale, 54[1] 131[1]; David Gascoyne, 179[2] 196[3] 198[1] 254[1,3] 277[3] 286[3] 287[1] 292[2] 371[2]; Edmund Gosse, 212[2]; Robert Graves, 30[2] 48[2] 51[3] 146[2] 307[2]; Thom Gunn, 126[3]; Thomas Hardy, 237[2] 274[2] 283[3] 335[2] 349[4] 374[1] 375[1]; Maurice Hewlett, 80[2] 277[1]; G. Manley Hopkins, 34[2] 66[2] 68[1] 116[4] 192[2] 236[1]; A. E. Housman, 257[3]; Ford Madox Hueffer, 302[1]; Randall Jarrell, 104[4] 105[1,2] 219[2] 340[1]; David Jones, 376[1]; Patrick Kavanagh, 58[3] 61[3] 166[1] 223[2] 269[1] 281[1] 305[2]; P. J. Kavanagh, 99[2]; Richard Kell, 214[2]; Brendan Kennelly, 28[3] 58[2] 156[2] 211[2] 219[3] 264[2] 280[1] 294[4]; Sidney Keyes, 192[1] 318[1] 371[1]; Rudyard Kipling, 73 222[1]; Robert Lowell 177[1] 371[3]; Louis MacNeice, 231[3] 255[1]; John Masefield, 61[1] 221[1] 263[2] 297[1,2,3]; Edgar Lee Masters, 56[3]; Herman Melville, 84[3]; George Meredith, 141[2]; Harold Monro 222[3] 266[2] 274[1] 329; John Montague, 126[2]; Thomas Moult, 171[3] 248[1]; Edwin Muir, 9[2] 43[3] 137[1] 308[3]; Henry Newbolt, 381[1,2]; Robert Nichols, 102[3] 352; Alfred Noyes, 25[3] 42[2] 55[1] 64[1] 66[1] 81[2] 108[1] 110 120[1,2] 151[1] 164 188[1] 195[3] 205[1] 237[1,2] 274[3] 298 323[1] 326[3] 347[1] 356[2]; Frank O'Connor, 273[1]; Arthur O'Shaughnessy, 8[2] 38[2] 39[1] 248[2]; Séamus O'Sullivan, 14[2] 127[4] 318[3]; Wilfred Owen, 84[4] 242 256[2]; Herbert Palmer, 163[2] 186[1]; Coventry Patmore, 318[2]; Ezra Pound, 104[3] 146[1] 155[2] 202[2] 261[2] 337; Arnold Price 311[1]; Kathleen Raine, 147[3] 375[2]; Herbert Read, 312[1]; Anne Ridler, 351[2]; Michael Roberts, 84[2]; Theodore Roethke, 14[1] 163[1] 192[3] 200[2] 223[1] 319 342[1]; Victoria Sackville-West, 308[1]; Siegfried Sassoon, 282[1]; Anne Sexton 96[2]; Edward Shanks, 370[2];

ACKNOWLEDGEMENTS

G. B. Shaw, 264[1]; Edith Sitwell, 226[3]; Stephen Spender, 160[1] 206[1] 211[1] 305[1] 355[1]; William Force Stead, 293[3]; James Stephens, 17[2] 18[1] 38[1] 83[1] 208[2] 247[2] 324[2] 326[1]; Wallace Stevens, 34[3] 127[1,2]; Jan Struther, 79[3]; Algernon C. Swinburne, 26[1] 169[1] 243[1] 294[5] 335[1] 350[2] 355[2] 359[3] 360[2]; Arthur Symons, 370[1]; Allen Tate, 61[2] 207[1]; Dylan Thomas, 69[2] 343; Francis Thompson, 95 187[2] 258[2] 270[2] 302[2,3] 304[1]; John Wain, 381[3]; Vernon Watkins, 40[2] 214[1] 301[1] 360[1] 378[1]; Lawrence Whistler, 198[2]; Walt Whitman, 72[1] 91[1] 106[1] 127[3] 159[2] 215[1]; Charles Williams, 131[2] 338; David Wright, 258[1]; William Butler Yeats, 14[3] 40[1] 65[4] 170[2] 211[3] 252[3] 277[2] 278[3].

*　　　　　*　　　　　*　　　　　*　　　　　*

For permission to use copyright material the editor is indebted to the authors (or their representatives) and the publishers: for lines from W. H. Auden, George Barker, T. S. Eliot, Randall Jarrell, David Jones, Robert Lowell, Louis MacNeice, Edwin Muir, Ezra Pound, Anne Ridler, Michael Roberts, Theodore Roethke, Herbert Read, Stephen Spender, Wallace Stevens, and Vernon Watkins, to Faber and Faber Ltd; for lines from Laurence Binyon, Walter de la Mare, A. E. Housman, John Masefield, and James Stephens, to the Society of Authors as the literary representatives of the estates of these authors; for lines from Edmund Gosse, Maurice Hewlett, Thomas Moult, and Arthur Symons, to William Heinemann Ltd.; for lines from *The Poetical Works of Robert Bridges,* to the Clarendon Press, Oxford; for lines from G. Manley Hopkins, Anne Sexton, Charles Williams, Conrad Aiken, and David Gascoyne, to the authors or their representatives and to Oxford University Press; for lines from *Collected Poems* by Thomas Hardy to the Trustees of the Hardy estate and to Macmillan and Co. Ltd.; for lines from *Collected Poems* by James Stephens, to Mrs. Iris Wise and Macmillan and Co. Ltd.; for lines from *The Collected Works* of Alfred Noyes, to John Murray; for lines from *Collected Poems* of Harold Monro, to Gerald Duckworth and Co. Ltd.; for lines from Patrick Kavanagh, to MacGibbon and Kee Ltd.; for lines from Brendan Kennelly, to the author and Allen Figgis Ltd.; for lines from G. K. Chesterton, to Miss D. Collins; for lines from Robert Graves, to the author; for lines from Rudyard Kipling, to Mrs. George Bambridge; for lines from Henry Newbolt, to Mr. Peter Newbolt; for lines from W. B. Yeats, to Mr. M. B. Yeats; for lines from Padraic Colum, to the author; for lines from John Wain to the author and Macmillan and Co. Ltd. If there are any omissions or mistakes the editor apologises and will have them corrected if there is a second edition.

PHOTOGRAPHS

Harry Arnold: 325

Associated Press: 366

Fergus Bourke: 45, 259, 354

Boever, Antwerp: 23

Camera Press: 11, 35, 122, 184, 199, 218, 230, 245, 246, 272, 275, 279, 285, 357

CIRIC, Geneva: 63, 213

Horst Deike: 225, 253

d'Haen: 229

Colman Doyle: 53, 70, 111, 130, 149, 175, 309

Willi François: 36

Inter Nationes: 16, 249, 314, 322

Irish Tourist Board: 268, 331

Keystone: 24, 27, 31, 41

Nasa: 190

National Film Board of Canada: 6, 15, 49, 50, 57, 117, 118, 139, 143, 153, 168, 263, 267, 271, 300, 303, 341, 373

Photographic P. R. Service, Dublin: 194

Louis Pieterse: 193

Quell-Verlag: 19, 20, 67, 97, 103, 114, 135, 144, 157, 167, 209, 235, 240, 291, 310, 317, 321, 332, 353, 358, 361, 369

F. Quigley: 76, 136

Refot, Stockholm: 129

Religious News Service: 107, 121

Thomas Ryan: 217

George Schofield: 75

Shelter: 32

Topix: 365

United Press Europix: 158, 203, 313

The present edition is substantially the same, with the exception several photographs, as that published earlier this year in Irelan by the Mercier Press Limited under the title *The Mercier New Testament*.